D1394104

DECEPTION and LIES

The Hidden History of the Arms Crisis 1970

DAVID BURKE

MERCIER PRESS

Dedication

To My Parents

MERCIER PRESS
Cork
www.mercierpress.ie

© David Burke, 2020

ISBN: 978 1 78117 787 7

A CIP record for this title is available from the British Library.

This book is sold subject to the condition that it shall not, by way of trade or otherwise, be lent, resold, hired out or otherwise circulated without the publisher's prior consent in any form of binding or cover other than that in which it is published and without a similar condition including this condition being imposed on the subsequent purchaser.

No part of this publication may be reproduced or transmitted in any form or by any means, electronic or mechanical, including photocopying, recording or any information or retrieval system, without the prior permission of the publisher in writing.

Printed and bound in the EU.

CONTENTS

Acknowledgements 5

Dramatis Personae 7

Organisations 11

Introduction 13

1 The Descent into Madness 17

2 The Citizen Defence Committees 29

3 The Quest for Arms Begins 34

4 The Deceiver Starts to Whisper his Lies 51

5 Clandestine Arms Flights and Military Training 61

6 Secret Bank Accounts 78

7 The CDCs and their Friends in High Society 87

8 The Bailieboro Deception 98

9 Her Majesty's Spies in Ireland 111

10 Blaney Plugs the Transatlantic Arms Supply Pipeline 131

11 Lynch Grabs Hold of the Steering Wheel 138

12 The Taoiseach Meets three Provisional IRA Leaders 152

13 The Empty Vessel from Antwerp 160

14 The Night of the Emergency Convoy 168

15 A Farewell to Arms, The Deceiver Pulls the Trigger 180

16 The Civil Servant who was a Law unto Himself 186

17 'A Pawn in a Very Strange Game' 197

18 Secret Briefings for the Opposition 204

19 The Gang that couldn't Shoot Straight 214

20 'Too Late to Have the Affair Swept Under the Carpet' 222

21 The Gardaí who Breached the Official Secrets Act 229

22 The IRA Steps into the Breach 233

23 Lynch Law 241

24 'I Am Not Going to Commit Perjury' 249

25 An Inconvenient Witness 253

26 Berry boxes Clever 257

27 The Minister who knew Nothing 265

28 Haughey Aims Carefully 271

29 Verdict and Fall Out 276

30 The Beneficiaries of the Arms Crisis 281

31 Diplomat-Spy and Black Propaganda Maestro 288

32 The 'Fruits of a Very Dirty Victory' 294

33 The Campaign to Suppress Captain Kelly's Book 298

34 The Shadow of a Gunman 306

Aftermath 323

Chronology 342

Endnotes 345

Bibliography 374

Index 377

ACKNOWLEDGEMENTS

I wish to thank all those who were instrumental in bringing this book to publication. Many people gave of their time freely to talk to me about the events in question and most of those who kindly allowed themselves to be interviewed are listed in the endnotes. Certain people for varying, but valid, reasons did not wish to be named; and their testimony is ascribed to 'private information'.

To those people who read drafts of the book along the way – thank you for your comments, suggestions and encouragement.

The endnotes show where printed sources have been used; thanks are here expressed to the authors and publishers concerned.

The photograph of Charles Haughey which appears as part of the front cover design is reproduced by kind permission of the National Library of Ireland. It was taken by the late Rex Robertson who donated his archives to the NIL.

Special thanks to Mary, Deirdre, Noel and Sarah of Mercier Press with whom it was a joy to work. Despite the difficult circumstances we found ourselves in, and the limitations imposed by the Covid pandemic, they managed to bring the project to completion on time. A special thanks also to Charlie Bird for his imaginative 'virtual launch' of the book and his camera operator Alison.

And a special thank you to my friends and family who have supported me throughout this whole endeavour with unwavering enthusiasm.

DRAMATIS PERSONAE

Berry, Peter: Secretary General at the Department of Justice in 1969 and 1970.

Blaney, Neil: Minister for Agriculture and Fisheries, November 1966–May 1970. Member of the cabinet sub-committee on Northern Ireland established in 1969. Arms trial defendant who had charges struck out against him on 2 July 1970.

Boland, Kevin: Minister for Social Welfare July 1969–May 1970; Minister for Local Government, November 1966–May 1970.

Brennan, Joseph: Minister for Labour, July 1969–March 1973. Minister for Social Welfare, May 1970–March 1973. Member of the cabinet sub-committee on Northern Ireland, which was established in 1969.

Callaghan, James: British Home Secretary, November 1967–June 1970; Prime Minister, April 1976–May 1979.

Childers, Erskine: Minister for Health, July 1969–March 1973.

Colley, George: Minister for Industry and Commerce, July 1966–May 1970; Minister for the Gaeltacht, July 1969–March 1973; Minister for Finance, May 1970–March 1973.

Cosgrave, Liam: Leader of Fine Gael, April 1965–July 1977; Taoiseach March 1973–July 1977.

Delaney, Maj. Gen. Patrick: Director of Military Intelligence, G2, April 1970–April 1971.

Devine, John: Public relations officer of the Irish Labour Party in 1969. Author of the *Devine Memorandum.*

Devlin, Paddy: CDC leader. Nationalist MP at Stormont, 1969–1972. Founding member of the SDLP.

Doherty, Paddy: Derry CDC leader.

Fagan, Anthony: Assistant Principal Officer in the Department of Finance under Charles Haughey.

Fallon, Garda Richard: Killed by Saor Éire in April 1970.

Faulkner, Pádraig: Minister for Education, July 1969–March 1973. Member of the cabinet sub-committee on Northern Ireland which was established in 1969.

FitzGerald, Garret: Fine Gael TD, July 1969–November 1992. Leader of Fine Gael, July 1977–March 1987. Taoiseach, June 1981–March 1982 and December 1982–March 1987.

Fleming, Chief Superintendent John: Head of the Special Branch in 1969 and 1970.

Gibbons, James: Minister for Defence, July 1969–May 1970. Minister for Agriculture, May 1970–March 1973.

Gilchrist, Andrew: British ambassador to Dublin, 1967–1970.

Goulding, Cathal: Chief of Staff of the IRA. Founding member of the Official IRA. Marxist in his political outlook.

Haughey, Charles: Minister for Finance, November 1966–May 1970. Leader of Fianna Fáil December 1979–February 1982. Taoiseach, December 1979–June 1981, March 1982–December 1982 and March 1987–February 1992. Member of the cabinet sub-committee on Northern Ireland which was established in 1969. Arms trial defendant.

Haughey, Pádraig ('Jock'): Businessman and brother of Charles.

Hefferon, Col Michael: Director of Irish Military Intelligence, G2, 1958–1970.

Hillery, Paddy: Minister for External Affairs July 1969–1973.

Keenan, Seán: Member of the IRA and CDC leader in Derry. Founding member of the Provisional IRA.

Kelly, Capt. James: Joined the Irish Army in 1949. He went into the intelligence directorate, G2, in 1961. He was posted to the Middle East, 1963–65. He returned to G2 and retired in 1970.

Kelly, John: National organiser for the Citizens Defence Committees, IRA member and arms trial defendant.

Lemass, Seán: Leader of Fianna Fáil and Taoiseach, June 1959–November 1966.

Lenihan, Brian: Minister for Transport and Power July 1969–January 1973. Minister for Foreign Affairs, January 1973–March 1973.

Luykx, Albert: Businessman and arms trial defendant.

Lynch, Jack: Leader of Fianna Fáil, November 1966–December 1979. Taoiseach, November 1966–February 1973; July 1977–December 1979.

MacEoin, Lt Gen. Seán: (John McKeown). Chief of Staff of the Irish Army, April 1962–March 1971.

McGrath, William: Associate of Ian Paisley.

McKeague, John: Associate of Ian Paisley. Leader of SDA in Belfast in 1969.

McMahon, Philip: The former head of Garda Special Branch who was the handler of 'The Deceiver' in 1969 and 1970.

MacStíofáin, Seán: IRA Director of Intelligence. Founding member of the Provisional IRA.

Ó Brádaigh, Ruairí: Chief of Staff of the IRA during the 1960s. Founding member of the Provisional IRA. First president of Provisional Sinn Féin.

O'Brien, Conor Cruise: Irish Labour Party TD, June 1969–June 1977. Minister for Posts and Telegraphs, March 1973–1977.

Ó Moráin, Mícheál: Minister for Justice, March 1968–May 1970.

O'Malley, Des: Chief Whip, July 1969–May 1970 Minister for Justice, May 1970–March 1973.

O'Neill, Capt. Terence: Prime Minister of Northern Ireland, March 1963–May 1969.

Paisley, Ian: Founding member and leader of the Democratic Unionist Party (DUP), September 1971–May 2008. First Minister of Northern Ireland, May 2007–June 2008.

Peck, John: British ambassador to Ireland, 1970–1973.

Markham-Randall, Capt.: The *nom de guerre* of a British spy who attempted to penetrate the CDC arms quest in London and Dublin in November 1969.

Sullivan, Jim: CDC leader in Belfast and member of the IRA. Founding member of the Official IRA.

Wilson, Harold: Labour Party prime minister of the UK 1964–70 and 1974–6.

ORGANISATIONS

B-Specials: Members of the Ulster Special Constabulary, a part-time force disbanded in 1970

Citizen Defence Committees (CDCs): A collective description of the groups which assembled in 1968 and 1969 to defend nationalist communities in Northern Ireland from attacks by loyalist extremists and the B-Specials.

Fianna Fáil: Irish political party originally formed from those who opposed the Treaty with Britain signed in December 1921. In the period under review it was led by Jack Lynch who succeeded Seán Lemass as its leader in 1966.

Fine Gael: Irish political party formed from those who supported the Treaty of 1921. During the period under review it was led by Liam Cosgrave.

Garda Síochána: The police force of the Republic of Ireland.

Garda Special Branch: The intelligence-gathering apparatus of An Garda Síochána.

G2: Irish Military Intelligence.

MI5: Britain's internal intelligence service. Attached to the Home Office. Responsible for security operations within the UK.

MI6: Britain's overseas intelligence service also known as the Secret Intelligence Service (SIS). Attached to the Foreign & Commonwealth Office.

NICRA: Northern Ireland Civil Rights Association.

Official IRA: The Marxist wing which emerged after the IRA split in December 1969. Its chief of staff in 1970 was Cathal Goulding.

RUC: The Royal Ulster Constabulary, the police force of Northern Ireland.

RUC Special Branch: The intelligence-gathering arm of the Royal Ulster Constabulary.

Saor Éire: Dissident republican movement. Responsible for the killing of Garda Richard Fallon in April 1970.

SDLP: Social Democratic and Labour Party – a nationalist political party supporting united Ireland achieved through non-violence.

Provisional IRA. The wing of the IRA which emerged after the IRA split in December 1969 with the intention of ending British rule in Northern Ireland. Its chief of staff in 1970 was Seán MacStíofáin.

INTRODUCTION

A State of Paranoia, Intrigue & Murder

In 1921 negotiations took place between the British government and Irish rebels who were seeking independence to see if a peaceful resolution could be found to settle their differences. The process culminated in a treaty which sparked a civil war in Ireland. The pro-Treaty forces prevailed and set up a political party called Cumann na nGaedheal, which held office until 1932. It later evolved into Fine Gael.

The defeated anti-Treaty forces led by Éamon de Valera put aside their arms and embraced constitutional politics in 1926 under the political banner of Fianna Fáil. With only two exceptions, they won every Irish general election between 1932 and 1973. All the while they made loud noises about ending British rule in the six counties in the north partitioned from the rest of the island, yet they never took up arms to achieve this.

After Seán Lemass succeeded de Valera as leader of Fianna Fáil and became taoiseach in 1959, he began to adopt a more conciliatory approach to Northern Ireland. He held a historic meeting with his counterpart Capt. Terence O'Neill, in January 1965. The two men who succeeded him as taoiseach, Jack Lynch and Charles Haughey, supported Lemass enthusiastically. Some hard-liners in his cabinet, such as Neil Blaney, were uncomfortable about this development, believing that Lemass was conferring *de facto* recognition on the Northern Ireland state. However, the party continued to rule without any significant internal strife.

Meanwhile, the IRA was going through a period of transformation under the leadership of Cathal Goulding, who was coaxing the movement away from militarism towards left-wing political agitation. Goulding himself had become a Marxist.

Despite the IRA's shift towards politics, militant loyalist hard-liners reformed the Ulster Volunteer Force (UVF). Men such as Gusty Spence joined it. They were convinced the IRA was about to go on a war footing. They launched a campaign of violence in 1966, in the pretence that some of it was being perpetrated by the IRA. The masquerade was not a success and Spence was imprisoned for murder in 1966 and the UVF was proscribed.

Also in 1966, Fianna Fáil politicians Charles Haughey and Neil Blaney threw their hats into the leadership ring after Lemass announced his resignation, but whipped them back out when it became clear they would not win. In Haughey's case, one of the problems he faced was that he was not perceived as someone with sufficiently good republican credentials to appeal to voters.[1] Jack Lynch emerged as a compromise taoiseach in November of that year.

Lynch pursued Lemass' policy of rapprochement with Capt. O'Neill. Haughey remained a keen supporter of the process.

In 1967 the Northern Ireland Civil Rights Association (NICRA) began campaigning against anti-Catholic discrimination in housing, employment and the gerrymandering of electoral constituencies. Militant loyalist hard-liners convinced themselves that NICRA was nothing more than a front for the IRA.

In 1968 Capt. O'Neill attempted to persuade his fellow unionists that if they embraced Catholics, they might accept Stormont and partition could be preserved. 'He is a bridge builder, he tells us. A traitor and a bridge are very much alike for they both go over to the other side,' the staunch unionist, Rev. Ian Paisley, thundered in opposition.[2]

For a while there were some indications that Capt. O'Neill's policies were bearing fruit. A number of Nationalist MPs who had been elected to Stormont, but had not taken up their seats, did so after the Lemass-O'Neill process gained pace. The Northern Ireland police force, the Royal Ulster Constabulary (RUC), had decided to disarm itself in the absence of any threat from Goulding's docile IRA.

However, this was to prove a false dawn. Militant loyalists, inflamed by Paisley's rhetoric, martialled their anger and directed it against NICRA and the nationalist community at large. This continued through late 1968 and into 1969, reaching a notorious crescendo with the 'Battle of the Bogside' in August 1969, which resulted in British troops returning to the streets of Northern Ireland. In the weeks and months that followed, the nationalist communities in Northern Ireland feared further attacks, and sought help.

It was amid this background that the tumultuous Arms Crisis of 1970 – one of the greatest Irish political scandals of the twentieth century – exploded. The Irish public awoke on 6 May to learn that two ministers, Haughey and Blaney, had been dismissed from Lynch's cabinet for allegedly attempting to import arms to the Republic. It was automatically assumed the guns had been intended for the IRA.

People who followed politics were shocked at Haughey's dismissal as he was not seen as a hardliner over Northern Ireland let alone a supporter of the IRA. His time as minister for justice was recalled, especially the steps he had taken to quell an IRA campaign in the early 1960s. He was also well recognised as a supporter of rapprochement and was friendly with Brian Faulkner, a Stormont government minister and a future prime minister of Northern Ireland. Up to this point his reputation was that of a highly competent and imaginative government minister who had focused on modernising the state, in particular the economy. The public was less shocked about Blaney, who was seen as a die-hard from a border constituency.

From the start there were whispers that other cabinet members had known about the importation plot all along, despite strong denials by Lynch in Dáil Éireann. There were also claims that MI6 had played an active part in the events, which had culminated in the Arms Crisis.

In September 1970 Haughey, along with James Kelly, a captain from G2, Irish military intelligence, and two others, were put on trial at the Four Courts in Dublin. It soon collapsed. A fresh prosecution commenced in October 1970. The evidence that emerged at the two trials electrified the nation.

It has taken fifty years for the truth about the Arms Crisis to emerge. The missing piece of the puzzle – the best kept state security secret of the last half-century – is the role played by a deceitful and mischievous puppet master who lurked in the shadows. He not only pulled the strings of the special branch but managed to convulse the political order on the island. This is the story of how he did it.

1

THE DESCENT INTO MADNESS

Ian Paisley bounded onto the political stage in the 1950s, eager to whip up a religious fervour against the Catholic minority of Northern Ireland, a community he later claimed bred 'like rabbits' and multiplied 'like vermin'.[1] No one – not even British royalty – was safe from his invective. When the Queen Mother and Princess Margaret visited Pope John in 1958, he accused them of 'committing spiritual fornication and adultery with the Anti-Christ'.

By the end of the 1960s, Paisley and his fiercely unionist supporters hurled Ireland into turmoil in the fanatical belief they were preserving Northern Ireland from a deeply mendacious pope who was conspiring against them in Rome.

Paisley's high profile and his eventual elevation to the post of first minister at Stormont in 2007 has overshadowed the pivotal roles played by those around him, especially William McGrath and John McKeague, in the events leading up to the explosion of the 'Troubles'.

McGrath perceived the Catholic church as the instrument of the anti-Christ and was determined to expunge it from the four corners of Ireland so that the Protestant community – which he believed was descended from the Tribe of Dan of Caanan, one of the Lost Tribes of Israel – could prevail. He perceived himself as a soldier in what he called the 'battles of the Lord'.[2] His self-anointed duty was to prevent the pope enslaving the

Leabharlanna Poiblí Chathair Baile Átha Cliath
Dublin City Public Libraries

Protestants of Northern Ireland and Britain. Paisley, who was nearly ten years younger than McGrath, became a British-Israelite too. The pair had met in 1949 through their involvement in the Unionist Association in the Shore Road area of Belfast where Paisley was studying at a bible college.[3]

McGrath was later convicted of the sexual abuse of teenage boys at Kincora Boys' Home in Belfast in 1981. McKeague was another deviant. He had converted to Paisley's brand of Free Presbyterianism in 1966, and acted as Paisley's bodyguard for a time. Bizarrely, he was obsessed with Satanism. McGrath and McKeague would have remained irrelevant figures trapped inside a claustrophobic loyalist cocoon but for the charisma and rhetorical flourish of the young Paisley.

Roy Garland, a one-time ally of McGrath, attended Paisley's church in the early 1960s where worshippers were led to believe the pope, his cardinals and Fianna Fáil were plotting to take over the island of Ireland as a springboard to enable Rome regain control of Britain. McGrath assured Garland that the Vatican plot would be met with determined resistance.

In 1962 McGrath produced a pamphlet that urged support for the formation of a loyalist militia and alluded to the deeds of the Ulster Volunteer Force (UVF).[4] According to Roy Garland, McGrath was 'fomenting an atmosphere of suspicion' with allegations of 'deeply laid plots to destabilise and overthrow' the Northern Ireland state. 'For at least a decade he had been predicting that blood would be flowing in the streets of Belfast. The scene was being set for the reintroduction of armed militias'.[5]

As the 1960s proceeded, Paisley, McGrath and their allies ratcheted up the level of sectarian tension. They were key figures in the Ulster Constitution Defence Committee, which was the parent organisation of the Ulster Protestant Volunteers (UPV), a Christian evangelical paramilitary organisation that would soon become involved in a bomb campaign with the UVF.

During the 1964 Westminster elections, Paisley and McGrath sparked a two-day riot in Belfast in response to the display of a Tricolour and a Starry Plough at the election campaign HQ of Sinn Féin's West Belfast candidate, Billy McMillen. Jim Kilfedder, the successful Ulster Unionist Party candidate in the contest, thanked Paisley after he won, stating he could not have done it without Paisley's help.

The 1965 meeting between Taoiseach Seán Lemass and Northern Ireland Prime Minister Capt. Terence O'Neill incensed Paisley, McGrath and their ilk. Absurdly, they convinced themselves that it was a sham and that Dublin was conspiring in the shadows with the IRA and the pope to subjugate Northern Ireland. In 1965, McGrath told Garland that the UVF was 'being re-formed to meet the perceived threat', as indeed it was.[6]

Paisley and McGrath kept the tribal drums beating. In 1966 they mounted counter-demonstrations to the Easter parades, which had been organised by nationalists for the fiftieth anniversary of the Easter Rising. McGrath, believing he was fighting for the very survival of his religion, prepared banners that bore slogans such as, 'For God and Ireland' and 'By Right of Calvary, Ireland belongs to Christ'.[7]

One of the men who joined the born-again UVF was an ex-British Army soldier called Gusty Spence who hailed from Belfast. When he joined the UVF, some of the dire predictions spouted forth by McGrath appeared to be coming true. In the real world, however, there was no threat from the rather toothless IRA, which was commanded at the time by Cathal Goulding. He had abandoned physical force violence in favour of left-wing political agitation. Hence, the hard men in the UPV/UVF decided to conjure up a *faux* version of the IRA for public consumption.

The Easter Rising had taken place on 24 April 1916. On the night of 16 April 1966, as the anniversary loomed large, gunmen from the Shankill Brigade of UVF fired two shots through the door of John McQuade, the right-wing unionist MP for Woodvale, and blamed the IRA for it. The following month the UPV/UVF 'retaliated' by attempting to petrol bomb an off-licence on the Shankill Road owned by a Catholic but set fire to the building next door, killing Martha Gould, a helpless elderly Protestant lady, instead.

On 21 May the UPV/UVF declared war against the IRA and its splinter groups, threatening that 'known' IRA men would be 'executed mercilessly and without hesitation'.[8] Six nights later, Gusty Spence and his gang threw themselves into a mission to assassinate a republican called Leo Martin who lived in a mixed nationalist-loyalist area. The assassins were unable to find him, however, as he had learned of the threat and had left his home. Instead, they torched the property and shot John Scullion, a random Catholic they found walking the streets. Scullion died a fortnight later.

Spence's gang tried for Martin again the following day but without success. Rather than return home without a scalp, they attacked four young men as they left the Malvern Arms, killing one of them – Peter Ward, aged eighteen – and wounding two others. Spence had seen them in the public house where he had been drinking himself and had ruled they were IRA gunmen and therefore pronounced a death sentence upon them.

It didn't take the police long to link Spence to the spree of violence and arrest him. In the wake of the detention, McGrath claimed that Scullion had been part of a Communist conspiracy centred on the International Hotel in Belfast, the members of which were intent upon overthrowing the Northern Ireland state. After Spence went on trial for the murder of Ward at Crumlin Road, McGrath published an anonymous pamphlet which attacked Ward, claiming he 'was an enemy agent who was working in cooperation' with 'Anti-Ulster' MPs at Westminster. In reality, Ward was simply a barman. At Spence's trial, Lord Chief Justice McDermott felt obliged to warn the jury about the pamphlet. Spence was found guilty and sentenced to life imprisonment with a stipulation that he serve a minimum of twenty years.

After the conviction, John McKeague published an article in his paper, *Loyalist News,* which portrayed Spence as the victim of injustice and police brutality. McKeague alleged that, 'Twenty-four detectives working in relays of four grilled and questioned him, threatening him, so as to make a statement, for over eighteen hours. He refused to make any statement, he was struck on repeated occasions and we have the names of the police officers who used the brutality.'[9]

There was no let-up in the tempo of sectarian scaremongering. On 25 June 1966 McGrath distributed leaflets at the annual Whiterock Orange parade entitled *The National Crisis of Faith* in which he claimed a major crisis faced Northern Ireland, one which eventually broke out into armed conflict between those who 'fight the "battles of the Lord against the mighty" and those who know nothing of "the glorious liberty of the children of God". Blood had ever been the price of liberty … Oliver Cromwell once said "choose ye out Godly men to be Captains and Godly men will follow them." We must do the same.'[10]

McGrath commanded another loyalist paramilitary organisation, which he called Tara. Some of its members were also in the UVF. Tara wanted to close all Catholic schools and outlaw the Catholic church.[11] Roy Garland, who served as the deputy leader of Tara, has explained how he and other young men were taken in at the time by the dire predictions conjured up by McGrath and Paisley. In 2014 Garland told the investigative journalist Chris Moore that they had been 'led to believe that there was this big cataclysm coming but in actual fact we were creating the problem'.[12]

When the Northern Ireland Civil Rights Association (NICRA) emerged in 1967, Paisley saw it as nothing more than a front for the IRA, as did many in the Royal Ulster Constabulary (RUC) and their political masters at Stormont. This came to a head in October 1968 when NICRA supporters organised a march in Derry to protest against anti-Catholic discrimination by the city's corporation in the allocation of houses. Unionists dominated the corporation. The Stormont government banned the march but the organisers decided to press ahead with it nonetheless. On 5 October, the day of the protest, the police attacked them. One of the marchers, Deirdre

O'Doherty, took refuge in a café: 'A door opened and a policeman came in with a baton in his hand with the blood dripping off it', she recalled to the BBC on the fiftieth anniversary of the event. 'He was young. He looked vicious. I never saw a face with so much hatred in all my life. I thought that was it. He turned, though, and walked out'.[13] Seventy-seven civilians and eleven police were injured during the upheaval that ensued.

The heavy-handed response of the police was captured on film by an RTÉ camera crew and broadcast to the world. In turn this attracted the attention of the British government, led by Harold Wilson, who exerted pressure on O'Neill to enact civil rights reforms, something that incensed extreme loyalists even further.

After the brutality in Derry, the Director of Irish military intelligence, G2, Col Michael Hefferon, who was based in Dublin, became so concerned about the festering violence occurring in Northern Ireland that he sent G2 agents across the border to monitor events. The gardaí failed to send anyone.

By now John McKeague had stepped up to the front line. On 30 November 1968, he marshalled a convoy of thirty cars and descended upon Armagh where a NICRA demonstration was about to take place. His mob took over the centre of the town. In response, the RUC stopped the march and confiscated over 200 cudgels from McKeague and his followers, some of which were studded with nails; they also seized a pair of guns and other weapons. Paisley was arrested and later sentenced to six months' imprisonment for organising the counter-demonstration. He served three months in Crumlin Road Prison.

These interventions did not quell the simmering tensions. On 1 January 1969, a group of university students were attacked by a loyalist mob who regarded them as nationalist upstarts at Burntollet Bridge near Derry while attempting to complete a march they had begun in Belfast. A student at Paisley's Free Presbyterian ministry had earlier announced that the UPV would see the march stopped. In the event this was achieved with the assistance from off-duty members of the Ulster Special Constabulary (B-Specials). Loyalist thugs hurled piles of granite stones at the students. One young woman was beaten senseless and shoved into the river. A group of men continued to attack her. One of them pierced her leg with a long nail, which he had driven through a wooden stick and as she lay face down in the water drowning, spurts of blood gushed from her calf. A group of nearby RUC officers failed to intervene, but she was saved from drowning by some of her fellow students after the loyalist gangs moved away.

After the protest, RUC officers swelled the ranks of the loyalist mob. They invaded the nationalist estates of Derry, smashing windows and breaking doors. Anyone they encountered and adjudged Catholic became fair game for a beating. One pensioner was clubbed to the floor in Woolworths. Old people were attacked in their homes. The marchers were ferried to hospital by a relay of ambulances. No one was prosecuted. The then British home secretary, and future prime minister, James Callaghan, was aghast:

> The march itself was ill-advised, but there was no excuse for the ambush of about 500 marchers at Burntollet Bridge by 200 Protestant extremists who most ferociously attacked them. That

> night groups of policemen, a few of whom had too much to drink, charged into the Bogside, the Catholic area of Derry. The verdict on their behaviour was given later in the year by a Commission of Enquiry headed by Lord Cameron, who was appointed by O'Neill to examine the causes and nature of the violence and disturbances, and who found that 'a number of policemen were guilty of misconduct which involved assault and battery, and malicious damage to property.'[14]

After Burntollet, Seán MacStíofáin, the IRA's director of intelligence, urged his colleagues on the IRA's Army Council to sanction retaliatory attacks against RUC, but received little support. However, as the violence continued, Cathal Goulding, the IRA's chief of staff, came under increasing pressure to respond in kind, something he was loathe to do as he was determined to focus on politics rather than physical force. He believed that the working class loyalists had more in common with their southern brethren than they had with the capitalists in charge of Stormont and it was his ambition to reach out to them and convince them to work together in the class struggle against their overlords.

All Goulding was prepared to do was to issue empty verbal threats. In February 1969 he found himself telling an interviewer that the IRA had not 'gone out of existence and we don't intend that it ever would'. As the tempo of violence grew more intense, Goulding found himself on BBC radio the following April spouting: 'if our people in the Six Counties are oppressed and beaten up … then the IRA will have no alternative but to take military action'.[15] It was all hot air.

Goulding's ally, Tomás Mac Giolla explained that 'what we were trying to do was to avoid getting involved in any campaign.

That's why Seán MacStíofáin was such an embarrassment. The object was to avoid military confrontation and to avoid any appearance of sectarianism'.[16]

Four weeks after Burntollet, O'Neill called an election, which his ruling Unionist Party won. Paisley stood against him in the Bannside constituency and polled favourably, an outcome that severely undermined O'Neill's standing. Weakened but back in office, O'Neill forged ahead with his reforms. On 23 April 1969, he persuaded his government to support adult suffrage in local government elections. This in effect gave the Civil Rights organisation the 'one man, one vote' they had been looking for, but led to more dissension: for example, O'Neill's minister for agriculture, Major James Chichester-Clark, resigned.

The response of McKeague and his UVF/UPV militia to O'Neill's programme of reform was savage: between 30 March and 23 April 1969, they orchestrated a series of explosions. On the eve of a crucial Unionist Party meeting to discuss leadership issues, four explosions destroyed the electricity sub-station at Castlereagh, Belfast. On Sunday 20 April, another two explosions detonated at the Silent Valley Reservoir in Co. Down, wrecking valves and supply pipes which cut off two-thirds of the water supply to Belfast. On the same night in Kilmore, Co. Armagh, an electricity pylon was damaged and high-tension wires were cut. Three days later another water supply pipe in Antrim was destroyed. On 24 April an explosion damaged yet another supply pipe. The bombs were designed to convince the public the IRA was on a war footing. They hoped to portray Capt. O'Neill as weak, ineffectual and an appeaser, thereby providing a springboard to eject him from office.

On 28 April 1969, Prime Minister Terence O'Neill resigned. 'Either we live in peace or we have no life worth living', he told his party.[17] These were prophetic words. In his memoirs, he acknowledged that the bombs 'quite literally blew me out of office'.[18] Chichester-Clark assumed his office.

***

After the UPV/UVF explosions, William McGrath orchestrated a campaign to place the blame for them on Jack Lynch, Paddy Hillery, Erskine Childers, George Colley, Charles Haughey *et al* in the Dublin government. In May 1969, in the pro-Paisley newspaper, *The Protestant Telegraph*, he declared that a source 'close to [Stormont] Government circles' had informed the paper that a purported 'secret dossier' on the Castlereagh electricity sub-station explosion contained 'startling documentation and facts. Original reports suggested that the IRA could have been responsible, but in Parliament no such definite statement would be made ... We are told that the Ministry of Home Affairs is examining reports which implicate the Éire Government in the £2 million act of sabotage. By actively precipitating a crisis in Ulster, the Éire Government can make capital, win or lose. The facts, we hope, will be made public, thereby exposing the chicanery of the Dublin regime'.[19]

McGrath had used the then deputy editor of *The Protestant Telegraph*, David Browne, a member of Tara, as his conduit to plant the story in the paper. Browne had been present at a meeting in McGrath's house at Greenwood Avenue on the Upper Newtownards Road a few hours after one of the April 1969 bombs had exploded. McGrath had told his audience that the attack had been carried out by a special unit attached to the Irish Army, nominating a figment of his imagination called Major Farrell as its leader. Farrell's mission, he alleged, was to destabilise Northern Ireland as a precursor to an invasion by the Republic. Browne later became editor of the newspaper.[20]

In May 1969 Billy Spence, a brother of Gusty, formed the Shankill Defence Association (SDA). He quickly turned it over to a trio consisting of McKeague, Alan Campbell (another child rapist) and William McCrea, a twenty-year-old devotee of Paisley.[21] Under their leadership the SDA began a ruthless and systematic programme of eviction of Catholic families from predominantly loyalist neighbourhoods. McKeague was often seen wearing a helmet and wielding a stick to direct his troops. Houses were set on fire, people were beaten up and bullets delivered as warnings to drive people out. Often families were not given an opportunity to carry their goods with them. The Army Council of the IRA did not deploy its volunteers to protect nationalist communities. Instead, ordinary nationalists began to form defence committees to defend themselves.

2

THE CITIZEN DEFENCE COMMITTEES

The citizen defence committees (CDCs) which began to spring up in nationalist communities across Northern Ireland were led by Stormont MPs, businessmen and members of the clergy. While members of the IRA were involved too, they did so in a private capacity. The CDCs were not front organisations for the IRA. James Callaghan described how the one in Derry 'represented the genuine fears of many people'.[1]

In Belfast the most prominent IRA figure involved in the defence committee structure was Jim Sullivan who, like Goulding, had repudiated 'physical force' violence. In Derry, Seán Keenan, a veteran IRA man, became chair of the Derry committee but was surrounded by a group of local figures who were opposed to the IRA.

By April 1969 there were two defence committees in the Bogside, with another next door in Brandywell, and a fourth located across the river in the Waterside. By July 1969 Keenan had established the Derry Citizens Defence Association (DCDA) with the intention of uniting the CDCs in Derry. He developed a plan to seal off the Bogside and Creggan from any further incursion by rampaging loyalist mobs.

Paddy Doherty, a friend of John Hume MP, the independent nationalist member of the Stormont parliament, attended an early meeting of the defence committee. More than 100 people were present when it commenced. In his book, *Paddy*

Bogside, Doherty recalled how, 'Even though Keenan was operating in home territory, many people began to display considerable resentment toward him' because they 'identified Republicanism with armed force'. Keenan assured them that the republican movement had no intention of exploiting the emergency for political purposes and stressed that he was the only republican on the platform, and even then, he was acting in a private capacity.[2] Additional members were appointed from the floor. According to Doherty, they were people with 'impeccable records of service to peace and the civil-rights campaign'. He felt their 'integrity strengthened Keenan's mandate'.

Keenan was elected chairman of what was then called the Bogside Defence Association. He immediately gave an undertaking to maintain the peace on what was feared would be a flashpoint date: 12 August 1969, when the Apprentice Boys' annual parade proceeded through Derry. Since it was thought likely it would inflame many Bogsiders, who would then try to attack it, the committee decided to appoint stewards to curtail them. Keenan proposed Len Green as chief marshal. Doherty recalled that he 'was a very kind and affable Englishman who had arrived in Derry in a submarine some years before. He had married a Derry girl and settled in the city, and was raising a family there. He had fully and successfully integrated himself into the community'.[3]

Dr Niall Ó Dochartaigh has argued that while republicans were involved in the establishment of the defence committee, as 'time went on, the Defence Association became even less dominated by the presence of republicans to the extent that it seemed to some republicans that Seán Keenan ended up as a "token Republican" on it'.[4]

Inevitably, there was some retaliation against vulnerable loyalist families in nationalist areas by disgruntled elements who were connected to neither the CDCs nor the IRA. Nonetheless, McKeague and his colleagues misrepresented their action as further proof of a hostile campaign by the IRA against the unionist community. In reality, as Bishop and Mallie have pointed out, Goulding had urged members of the IRA to:

> involve themselves in the citizens' defence committees that were set up in Derry, Belfast and Newry as [1969] progressed. What the leadership had in mind was not to infiltrate and subvert the [citizen defence] committees, as the Special Branch officers of the RUC had immediately assumed, but to shift the burden of defence away from the IRA and on to the shoulders of the Catholic population itself. 'The objective was,' said Mac Giolla, 'to try and help the people defend the areas rather than have the IRA come out and start a new campaign. We never wanted the role of the defenders of the Catholics' ... However, the Army Council did promise the release for defence purposes of some Thompson machine-guns hidden in farmyard dumps, but by the time of the critical riots of 12–15 August [1969] they still had not arrived.[5]

As 12 August drew closer, Doherty proposed that the Derry defence committee should approach the Irish government for help in protecting the Bogside. Keenan opposed this initially but suggested that if the motion was changed 'to an appeal to the Irish people, so as not to rule out help from any other quarter, he would support it'.[6] Doherty was satisfied with this and arrangements were set in train to get Eddie McAteer, leader of the Nationalist Party at Stormont, and John Hume to organise a meeting with Jack Lynch in Dublin. Keenan and Doherty were assigned to it while others were tasked with securing help from elsewhere in Northern Ireland.

After the Derry defence committee meeting, Keenan and Doherty went to City Hotel where they met Hume. Hume and Keenan discussed how it might become possible to involve the Irish government in the defence of the Bogside.[7]

James Callaghan observed that as 12 August 1969 approached:

> … tension grew. Some were hard at work endeavouring to allay fears. John Hume, the young, able and hard-working Stormont Member for the Foyle Division of Londonderry whose constituency included the Bogside area, spent every day and much of the night working to damp down the increasing fears. On the whole, the Catholics seem to believe that the Bogside was likely to be invaded whether the march went on or not and prepared themselves accordingly. The Derry Citizens Defence Association, which had been set up the previous month with the aim of protecting the area against either a Protestant or a police invasion, undoubtedly represented the genuine fears of many people some of the younger members of the community were quite eager to take part in any trouble that might start, and by the weekend they had erected barricades of paving stones, wooden shutters and other materials in a number of streets, leaving only narrow entrance points through which to pass. There was no doubt that they were substantially influenced by events of the previous January and April, when a number of policemen had run through the Bogside using unnecessary violence, breaking windows and smashing glass in houses. There was a general determination, by no means confined to the young, that those events would not be repeated in August.[8]

Tragically, the fate of Northern Ireland had fallen into the hands of a motley collection of murderers and bigots, not to mention a handful of paranoid fantasists and child abusers among their number. By 16 August, seven people would be dead.

3

THE QUEST FOR ARMS BEGINS

The British government and its civil service had been monitoring the turmoil that was unfolding in Northern Ireland with increasing alarm. Two subcommittees were set up to get to grips with it, both of which were independent of Stormont. Prime Minister Harold Wilson, Home Secretary James Callaghan, Defence Secretary Denis Healy, and Foreign Secretary Michael Stewart sat on the first one, which was called Misc 238. The second one, Misc 244, included senior officials from the home office, the ministry of defence, the FCO, MI5 and the cabinet office.

Wilson was informed by Gen. Sir Geoffrey Baker in May 1969 that the RUC was 'behind the times, poorly led and administered ... [and that] speculation and guesswork [have] largely replaced intelligence. ... Neither the special branch nor the Northern Ireland government have the remotest idea as to who was behind the recent sabotage', i.e. the April 1969 bomb campaign.[1] In light of Baker's report, Misc. 244 resolved to consult the Joint Intelligence Committee (JIC) 'on the means of obtaining information otherwise than through the Northern Ireland official sources'.[2] This problem was solved by the appointment of a security liaison officer from MI5 who became Britain's first independent source of information in Northern Ireland and a key part of the 'slightly better intelligence service on Northern Ireland' that ensued.[3]

Meanwhile, the Dublin government was acutely aware that the Apprentice Boys' parade was destined to become a flashpoint. Hence, on 1 August 1969, Patrick Hillery, the new minister for external affairs, paid a secret visit to London to appeal to Michael Stewart, Britain's Foreign Secretary. Sir Edward Peck, chairman of the JIC, attended the meeting where Hillery wanted the British government to intervene to ban the march. Stewart rebuffed him, stating there was 'a limit to the extent to which we can discuss with outsiders – even our nearest neighbours – this internal matter'.[4] Hillery responded by expressing his concern about the impartiality not only of the RUC but more so the B-Specials, and referred to reports that they were using weapons which had been issued to them officially for 'private purposes'. He added that if violence was to occur in Derry, it could well spill over into the Republic, and he might have to raise it at the UN.[5] Stewart retorted that if this happened, 'he was afraid' Dublin would have to accept that it would still be 'strictly an internal matter'.[6]

Paddy Doherty and Seán Keenan reached Dublin the day before the Apprentice Boys' parade for their meeting with the taoiseach and were met by 'a tall, austere-looking man' who told them that Lynch was unavailable but that he, secretary to the Taoiseach, had been asked to see them. His 'lips became dry and his face paled' when Keenan raised the prospect of violence in Derry and became even more uncomfortable when 'Keenan pressed for military assistance in case the worst happened. Whatever briefings he had received had not prepared him for this. But, like all civil servants, he had already prepared his escape route' by fobbing them off on 'two experts' at the

Department of External Affairs.[7] When they met a short while later, Doherty asked the experts, 'Will you protect the people of Derry in the circumstances we have outlined?' They told him they would and that he could take that message back to Derry. Doherty was not convinced and left the meeting 'not feeling happy'.[8]

While still in Dublin, Keenan proposed going to see his 'commander-in-chief', Cathal Goulding. Keenan did not appreciate that Goulding clearly wanted to avoid a clash with the forces of working-class loyalism, whom he saw as his natural political bedfellows. Keenan was far closer in his outlook to one of Goulding's opponents on the Army Council, Seán MacStíofáin. MacStíofáin had argued at a recent Army Council meeting that the IRA should have been making preparations to protect nationalists in 'isolated enclaves' lest an 'Orange pogrom' begin. MacStíofáin had then listened in 'utter disbelief' when one of his colleagues suggested that the British Army 'would have to protect people in the North from the excesses of the RUC!' His response was immediate: 'I put up a modified proposal which, I believe, might be more easily accepted. It was supported by others who felt as I did. I suggested that, instead of bringing up the strength of the IRA by recruiting openly, we would set up a system of auxiliary units purely for the defence of the nationalist districts, particularly Derry. There we had the services of Seán Keenan, a well-known and highly respected republican veteran who was the ideal man to take charge of the new unit'.[9]

As Keenan and Doherty walked into Goulding's builders yard, the posters of Marx, Lenin and Mao Tse-tung that 'glowered down from the walls' struck Doherty. After a few pleasantries were exchanged, Keenan told Goulding that the 'citizens of Derry call upon the people of Ireland to come to their assistance if the Bogside is attacked'.[10] Goulding was 'sitting on top of the table, one sandalled foot on the floor, the other swinging freely. What we heard next shattered a myth as the commander replied: "I couldn't defend the Bogside. I have neither the men nor the guns to do it".' Doherty described how 'Keenan stood there, motionless, as if the message hadn't sunk in yet'. Doherty, however, had had enough and stood up. 'I told you the IRA was only a myth, a fantasy army, with nothing to offer the people of Ireland,' he sneered and sat down. 'The toy soldier, the commander-in-chief of the phantom army, was shaken by my reaction. In an effort to retrieve the situation, he said, "But I will have the Chief of Police or the minister for home affairs assassinated".'[11]

Goulding's response was rash and out of character, probably no more than a ham-fisted attempt to save face with Keenan whom he perceived as a militant. Since Goulding had never met Doherty before, he probably assumed he was cast from the same mould. But Doherty was shocked: '"My God," I exploded. "As if we didn't have enough problems in Northern Ireland".' Turning to Keenan, he said, 'Let's go back to Derry, where there is work to be done.'[12]

They made it home by nightfall to a city that was on a war footing. Doherty addressed a large gathering in the Stardust Ballroom: 'We have no guns; there will be no guns. We will attempt to keep the peace, but if we fail, we will defend the Bogside with sticks and stones and good old petrol bombs'.[13]

***

On 12 August, seventy Orange bands with brass, flute, fife and drums assembled with the intention of processing through the old city. A large deployment of the RUC was present to make sure the 15,000 marchers would not be obstructed. The B-Specials, some of whom were in the UVF, were also present in force. On the ancient walls above them, a number of the unionist MPs looked down with approval. Meanwhile McKeague and two busloads of his supporters had also made the journey to Derry. They were convinced Northern Ireland was in the grip of an IRA inspired uprising. McKeague's real interests lay in Belfast where trouble was also brewing. He left Derry for there before the march began.

The clash that erupted between the RUC and nationalists in the Bogside determined to halt the march on 12 August became known as 'The Battle of the Bogside'. It was a violent and brutal affair. School children learned how to place pieces of cloth inside milk bottles partially filled with petrol before feeding them to adults to hurl at the RUC as they tried to break into the Bogside. As Niall Ó Dochartaigh has shown, Doherty was accosted by a group of younger men on the Lone Moor Road who demanded 'that guns now be supplied and used to stop the RUC advance. Essentially they were demanding that the IRA conduct an armed defence of the area. Keenan rejected these demands and argued that they should not use guns'.[14]

According to Doherty's account that night, as the battle raged outside, he received a visit at his home from a contingent of Irish Army soldiers who were based at Carndonagh, an auxiliary military base in Co. Donegal. They offered him 200 rifles and ammunition, which he refused.[15]

On 13 August in Belfast, a group of civil rights activists gathered at Divis Flats before marching to the local RUC station where they delivered a letter protesting at the behaviour of the RUC and B-Specials in Derry. A few stones were then thrown at the station with the intention of causing them to deploy and thereby stretch their resources thus relieving the pressure on Derry. Rioting ensued which continued into the next day. Others protests were orchestrated in Strabane, Lurgan, Dungannon, Coalisland and Newry over the subsequent nights. In Armagh a man called John Gallagher was killed on 14 August when B-Specials opened fire after a civil rights meeting.

On the evening of 14 August, McKeague led the troops of the SDA and the UVP on a rampage in Belfast. At first the RUC and some B-Specials attempted to separate them from a crowd of nationalists who had assembled along Cupar Street (which runs between the Shankill and the Falls), but to no avail. Alarm spread quickly across vulnerable nationalist districts in the city.

According to Billy McMillen, the republican leader in Belfast, the IRA had only twenty-four guns available to it in the city, most of which were handguns. He rejected requests to distribute them because they were only likely to justify a greater use of loyalist force if discharged.

Since early 1969 MacStíofáin had been running small numbers of arms to Belfast behind Goulding's back. 'I disliked going about this on my own, and I had to be extremely cautious in doing it. I began to collect supplies which I knew of in the South, including ammunition, an occasional weapon and a few hand grenades. I passed these myself directly to the intelligence officer in Belfast. I had the closest contact with him and could trust him to keep these transactions quiet, so that they would not leak back to the Army Council and raise hell.'[16] A small number of guns were eventually deployed in Belfast for defensive purposes.

According to the report prepared for the British government by Lord Scarman on the violence, 'Undoubtedly there was an IRA influence at work in the Derry Citizens Defence Association (DCDA) in Londonderry, in the Ardoyne and Falls Road areas of Belfast, and in Newry. But they did not start the riots, or plan them: indeed, the evidence is that the IRA was taken by surprise and did less than many of their supporters thought they should have done.'[17]

On the night of 14 August the RUC took to the streets in Shorland semi-armoured vehicles manned with Browning 0.30 medium machine guns, which had a two and a half mile range. They sprayed bullets into the nationalist Divis flats. One tracer bullet tore into nine-year-old Patrick Rooney's head. When Paddy Kennedy, MP, visited the flat, he found the boy's father scraping his brains off the wall with a spoon. Hugh McCabe, a soldier with the Queen's Royal Irish Hussars, who was on leave from Germany, was also shot dead in the flats by the RUC.

B-Specials armed with rifles, revolvers and machine guns swelled the loyalist mobs. Together they advanced on the Falls Road where the nationalists lived, and attacked their homes. In the Ardoyne, the RUC led a violent drunken loyalist mob. Samuel McLarnon was shot in his wheelchair in the front room of his home on Herbert Street.

Half of the houses on Bombay Street were gutted by arsonists but not before many of them were looted. 150 houses were burned and another 300 were badly damaged. All told, seven people were killed in Belfast.

Paddy Devlin described the semi-biblical tactics deployed by McKeague's thugs to identify their victims. Men who knew the streets 'daubed whitewash marks on the doors or windows of Catholic homes. These homes were then emptied of the people and burned. As far as I could tell around 650 Catholic families were burnt out that night. ... Police in uniform, covered in civilian coats, were recognised amongst loyalist attackers in Dover Street ...'[18]

As the sun began to rise, the Falls Road 'was filled with heavily laden prams and hand carts carrying the household utensils and furniture of the unfortunate refugee families who had lost their homes', Devlin wrote. 'Schools and halls were thrown open as temporary accommodation and school meal-making facilities, idle because of the holidays, were reactivated'.[19]

McKeague was proud of what he had achieved, boasting that if he had been given 'another forty-eight hours' his men would have burned all of the nationalists out of the maze of side streets around the Clonard.

In the absence of any preparation for these assaults, Goulding's response was to unleash another blast of grandiose fictitious bravado, this time about 'fully equipped units' of the IRA which he alleged had been sent across the border, adding that in Belfast the IRA and other organisations had 'co-operated with the Citizen Defence Groups and used their all-too-limited resources in an attempt to hold off the terrorist forces of reaction which had been unleashed upon peaceful men, women and children. The people of the Falls Road area have gratefully acknowledged this assistance in the past few days and have contrasted it bitterly with the failure of the Dublin government to act in their defence'.[20] Paddy Doherty was incensed at Goulding's bluster because many loyalists took it as confirmation that the events in Derry and Belfast had been organised by the IRA after all.

MacStíofáin had taken himself to the border, hoping to confront the B-Specials. However, his plans were thwarted by 'an amazing procession of messengers' from Dublin. 'The leadership had sent each of them to find me with the same agitated instructions. I was to do nothing, and if I was doing anything already, I was to stop.'[21] MacStíofáin developed a scheme to disobey Goulding: 'We had our plans worked out. I issued instructions to the units on the Northern side that if they ran across any B-Special patrols, they should open up on them regardless. I had made up my mind to report back to HQ that the Specials had opened fire first. It was exactly the same excuse that the RUC had put out in Belfast when they had fired on civilians, so it would even matters up a bit. But the Specials were apparently taking no chances. They did not appear, and we had no such engagements'.[22]

***

In Dublin Neil Blaney, minister for agriculture and fisheries, received a phone call from the Bogside shortly before midnight on 12 August alerting him to the upheaval across the border.

This came as no surprise to him. 'My colleagues weren't aware of what was happening in the Six Counties, even though I was feeding them at every opportunity. Partly because it was the end of the '60s, that period of optimism and idealism – everything was swinging I was told – they didn't want to hear this gobshite from the North telling them about the signs he'd been reading that were totally at variance with the euphoria at the time.'[23]

According to Blaney's biographer, he 'was up until five o'clock that morning, sitting on the stairs in his Dublin home trying to contact the Taoiseach', while others including the secretary of the taoiseach's department, were also attempting to locate Lynch. Blaney recalls that, 'He just could not be got out of his house by the phone or physically during the hours of twelve midnight and five o'clock on the morning of August 13th'. Lynch's private secretary went out to his house at around one o'clock and knocked on his door and rang the bell. 'He could hear the two phones ringing. He eventually kicked the door.' One civil servant, who worked with Lynch, was aware that he was a heavy whiskey drinker and believes he had fallen into a stupor.[24]

A cabinet meeting was scheduled for the morning of 13 August. Paddy Hillery was on a painting retreat on Achill Island and it took a number of hours for his officials to make contact with him. Despite these setbacks, the cabinet convened and then deliberated continuously over the next week. At the outset, on 13 August, they ordered the building of camps and field hospitals along the border for the thousands of refugees who were flooding across it with soldiers assigned to protect them. All told, 1,500 soldiers were deployed.[25] An implied threat of invasion lurked behind this initiative, something that was underlined by Lynch's appearance on RTÉ on 13 August when he told the nation that 'the Irish Government can no longer stand by and see innocent people injured and perhaps worse'.

As the Irish troops were settling in along the border, consternation grew at Stormont. Prime Minister Chichester-Clark wanted to seal off the road crossings with the Republic. He spoke to James Callaghan on 15 August. Callaghan argued that taking such 'a step would be ineffective' since there were 'barely enough troops available for riot control in the areas immediately affected and the closure would therefore be only a gesture'.[26]

Kevin Boland, who served as minister for local government in Lynch's cabinet, was adamant that an actual invasion was never mooted. 'There was then complete unanimous realisation that there could be no suggestion of any crossing of the border unless the situation was already so bad that no action of ours could make it worse – in other words, unless we had [what the minister for defence, James] Gibbons' [described as a] "Doomsday Situation".'[27] Boland's account tallies with that of Des O'Malley, who served as chief whip at the time, a position which entitled him to attend cabinet meetings. Their convergence is significant because these men occupied opposite ends of the Fianna Fáil political spectrum.

Irish troops on the ground had certainly been prepared to cross the border if so ordered. According to Paddy Doherty, who visited an Irish Army camp where he met 'an officer who stood over 6 feet tall' and dwarfed him said, 'My God, we should have taken Derry. There are 800 of the finest fighting men in Ireland here and for a full forty-eight-hour stretch we worked like men possessed preparing for the invasion. Not one word of protest from any one of them. When Lynch made his "we can no longer stand by" speech, we thought, "This is it". Oh, the frustration, the disappointment. Why the orders to go in were not given, we will never know. Every one of them would have given his life to free the North ...'[28]

What would have happened if the troops had crossed the border? According to John Hume's biographer Barry White, 'The Irish and British Army commanders in the north-west later revealed privately, on separate occasions, that if there had been killing on a major scale and they were ordered to go in and stop it, they had the same instructions. Both were told that if they met soldiers of the other nationality, in Derry, they should stop and hold the line'.[29] Paddy Doherty has confirmed this account. He was told by a British army officer he befriended that, 'We were instructed that in the event of meeting Irish troops, we were to hold our fire and maintain our lines.'[30]

British troops had arrived in Derry on 14 August. Members of the defence committee had gone to Doherty's house to discuss their options. Stanley Orme, an English Labour MP who was present, advised against calling London to stand the troops down. 'The man in charge today is the commander of the troops on the ground', he stressed. 'His instructions will be to restore public order and unless someone can get to him and negotiate, he may do it by force of arms.'[31]

Doherty, Orme and Michael Canavan, who worked with

Doherty, scaled the barricade in search of the commander who turned out to be Lt Col Todd. Doherty addressed him directly, telling him that he had to remove the RUC and B-Specials. Orme stepped forward, explaining he was a Westminster MP and reinforced what Doherty had said, insisting that Doherty was his 'only hope of achieving peace' and that the Bogsiders had 'suffered enough' and would respond positively to any act of generosity.[32]

Todd turned to Doherty and asked him directly if he could stop the fighting. Doherty promised him that if he pulled the RUC and the B-Specials out, he would 'cork the bottle' on his side. Todd turned to Inspector Hood of the RUC and told him to get his men off the streets. Doherty shook hands with Todd; then he, Canavan and Orme headed back into the Bogside to honour their part of the agreement.

In Belfast, the British Army managed to bring the city under a semblance of control. After the smoke cleared, McKeague boasted that if the British Army had not intervened, he would have burned many more Catholics out of their homes.

***

A few days later, Jim Sullivan, chairman of the Central CDC of Belfast, organised a trawl of the Republic to sweep up any guns that might be made available for the taking. Sullivan also happened to be a senior Belfast IRA leader loyal to Goulding. He oversaw a two-day mission involving four groups that set off on Sunday 17 August from Belfast to various parts of the Republic. The plan was to reconvene two days later in Dundalk with the haul.

IRA veterans including Joe Cahill, Danny Burke and Seamus Twomey, along with John Kelly and his brother Billy, conducted the search. There was no central record of where the arms dumped at the end of the Border Campaign in 1962 had been hidden.[33] Hence, 'searchers had to rely on the memory of local volunteers. In one case, the local activists in County Tyrone ended up dispatching a car to Belfast prison to find out where an arms dump was located'.[34] All told, they managed to gather about 75 to 100 weapons, a mixture of shotguns, sporting rifles, .22s and a few .303s along with one Thompson submachine gun. According to Kelly, 'people all around the Twenty-six Counties contributed weapons at this period, and it was not just Fianna Fáil supporters – people aligned to Fine Gael, traditionally seen as strongly anti-IRA, also helped out. Whatever they had, shotguns, old rifles, Mausers going back to the First World War, were handed over'.[35]

Neil Blaney claimed that approximately twenty-five senators and TDs handed over private weapons.

Minister Kevin Boland of Fianna Fáil disdainfully recalled one 'particularly bellicose Munster Deputy' who boasted that he had 'been running guns to Belfast' since 1956. 'Needless to say, in May 1970 [after the eruption of the arms crisis] he changed his tune with the rest and became the stoutest supporter of the "Restoration of Law and Order" policy.'[36]

In Dublin the IRA had managed to locate a supply of automatics. In addition, they purchased sporting guns and shotguns 'from sympathetic gunsmiths south of the border with money provided by Catholic businessmen'.[37]

Seamus Brady, who was close to Neil Blaney, claimed that

a 'further important Cabinet decision [taken in 1969] was that the movement of arms for defence of the minority in the Six Counties across the Border should not be inhibited by prosecution or harassment by the authorities in the South'.[38] Due to uninformative cabinet records, it is impossible to test this assertion. The veracity of the matter bears the hallmark of so much of the arms crisis: it was probably a matter of interpretation. While someone like Blaney might have walked out of cabinet believing a decision of this nature had been taken, it is equally likely Erskine Childers would have been aghast at the suggestion. Bearing this caveat in mind, Brady also claimed that a 'directive on these terms' was sent to the gardaí by the then minister for justice, Mícheál Ó Moráin. To confuse matters further, many cabinet decisions were taken in private. According to Brian Lenihan's son Conor, in 'those days the cabinet met for a period before the actual formal cabinet sessions began as a political group without officials and note takers being present'. This was a practice which had been in existence since the Lemass era. It also appears that there was a procedure to cover the situation when a sensitive issue arose during the formal part of the meeting. Lynch, it is claimed, was complicit in what might be described as the conduct of a 'Secret Cabinet'. He would step aside as chairman by physically moving out of his seat whereupon Brian Lenihan and Paddy Hillery moved around and co-chaired the deliberations. The civil servants would leave the room. Notes were never taken.[39]

Whether a directive was issued about the cross-border movement of arms or not, the mood of the gardaí was distinctly different in 1969 to what it later became in 1970, especially after the killing of Garda Richard Fallon by a republican splinter group called Saor Éire in April 1970. Mallie and Bishop believe that in 1969 the policy of the Irish government 'degenerated into the uncoordinated consideration of how they could get arms to Catholics in the North for their self-protection without being found out. Irish officials were already turning a blind eye to cross-border gun smuggling. A ship found with arms on board off Dublin was freed after it was declared that they were "supplies for the Irish army".'[40]

Conor Cruise O'Brien, who became one of the most implacable opponents of the IRA, felt that 'in these circumstances the Dublin government, understandably, was under pressure to help the Catholics get guns for self-defence, and some of its members saw that they did get guns.'[41] Samuel Dowling, chairman of the Newry Civil Rights Association, was later (January 1970) charged in the Republic with illegal possession of arms and explosives. He was acquitted, after declaring: "Those weapons were in our possession … through the work of officers and agents of the Irish government ... It was made clear between us that such arms would only be used for defence of those minority communities in the North when under attack".'[42]

When Joe Cahill and Danny Burke reached Dundalk after their search, Cahill recognised a garda special branch officer who approached them. Cahill gripped a Thompson with the butt resting on the floor between his feet. The branchman went over to the car and Cahill lowered the window. Before he was asked a question, Cahill said they had weapons, adding, 'I will blow the head off your shoulders', as he raised the Thompson.

To Cahill's amazement, the officer produced a parcel, which he put through the car window and said, 'I've come over here to give you something' and handed Cahill a Colt .45 and fifty rounds of ammunition.[43]

This incident was not the only extraordinary exchange that took place between the gardaí and the IRA in August of 1969. A senior IRA figure – someone Cahill knew well – decided to exploit his relationship with the gardaí to create mischief and mayhem for his left-wing opponents inside the IRA and the Fianna Fáil government. To him, Fianna Fáil was a nest of traitors who had sold out on their republican ideals.

4

THE DECEIVER STARTS TO WHISPER HIS LIES

The principal difficulty in establishing the truth about the Arms Crisis lies in the fact that the gardaí's most prized IRA informer was a fraud who played a devious game with his handler, Philip McMahon, the former head of the special branch. For the present, he will be referred to as 'The Deceiver'. Without him, there would have been no Arms Crisis.

At the height of the bedlam of August 1969, The Deceiver learned that Charles Haughey had met a senior IRA figure. Unfortunately, the source for this allegation, Peter Berry, secretary general at the department of justice, has provided contradictory accounts of who Haughey met. It was either Cathal Goulding or Mick Ryan, the quartermaster of the IRA.[1] Since Goulding and Mick Ryan were making a film with Yorkshire Television when the Battle of the Bogside erupted on 12 August, it is safe to place the Haughey-Goulding/Ryan meeting – if one ever took place – as having occurred sometime between then and 19 August, when the garda special branch learned about it. Berry has also provided contradictory dates as to when this alleged meeting took place: both August and September.

More attention has focused on the allegation that Haughey met with Goulding, the more senior of the two figures. He was known to be a 'relentlessly cheery' individual who made friends easily and frequented the 'fashionable bars around St Stephen's Green drinking with writers, musicians and painters and became a recognised feature of Dublin Bohemia'. Brendan Behan, himself an ex-IRA man, numbered prominently among Goulding's friends.[2]

Haughey was equally gregarious. Nonetheless, the encounter – if it happened – must have been a somewhat uncomfortable one for both men. Haughey was the IRA's nemesis, especially after his success as minister for justice in the early 1960s when he had administered the last rites to the IRA's faltering border campaign. Goulding had spent much of that time in prison in Britain. Furthermore, as a Marxist, he stood in polar opposition to Haughey's economic worldview and disdained his trappings of wealth (although Goulding ended up living in a mansion on Ailesbury Road, Donnybrook, one of most expensive addresses in Ireland). For his part, Haughey would have seen Goulding as a minor figure, certainly not someone to be taken seriously in political terms.

The fact that a minister met someone like Goulding or Mick Ryan is not as astonishing as it may now seem. During 1969–70 members of the IRA were not yet automatically shunned by 'respectable' society. Indeed, Jack Lynch met at least three IRA men in the months running up to the Arms Crisis. James Gibbons met them too, as did other cabinet ministers. Indeed, Britain's home secretary and future prime minister, James Callaghan, met IRA leaders. Moreover, as late as December 1970, *This Week* magazine – then edited by Joseph O'Malley, the brother of minister for justice Des O'Malley – asked Goulding to review *The Secret Army, The IRA* by J. Bowyer Bell for the magazine. Not only was

Goulding's glowing review published in his own name, it appeared underneath a photograph identifying him as the 'Chief of Staff, IRA'.

However, The Deceiver, who not only opposed Goulding but also despised Fianna Fáil, could not look this gift horse in the mouth and seized upon the Haughey–Goulding (or Haughey-Ryan) encounter to create some mischief. He was able to succeed in this because he had built up a deep well of trust and credibility with the gardaí as an informer during the previous decade. On 19 August 1969 he contacted Philip McMahon with an astounding – and completely untrue – story: the cabinet, he alleged, had concluded a deal with the IRA.

If we believe Berry, so stunned was McMahon that he and Chief Superintendent John Fleming, his successor as head of the special branch, went to Berry's Rathgar home, that night.[3] After their briefing, Berry prepared a handwritten memorandum for his minister, Mícheál Ó Moráin, running to 'several' pages and not completed until 1.40 a.m.[4] The next morning Berry handed it to Ó Moráin and discussed the allegation that 'the previous week a Cabinet Minister had [held] a meeting with the Chief of Staff of the IRA, at which a deal had been made that the IRA would call off their campaign of violence in the Twenty-six Counties in return for a free hand in operating a cross Border campaign in the North'.[5]

The fact that Lynch had spoken out against the IRA on 19 August did not dent Berry's confidence in the 'information' he was being fed. Instead, Berry stressed that the Army Council 'could not understand [i.e. believe] the Taoiseach's statement on 19th August as it had been accepted that the Cabinet Minister was speaking to their Chief of Staff with the authority of Government'. When Ó Moráin asked for the minister's name, Berry alleged the gardaí had not provided it. Ó Moráin then went to cabinet.

When the pair next met, Ó Moráin told Berry that 'no Minister had met Goulding' but that Charlie Haughey 'had mentioned that he had been asked to meet some fellow from the IRA but that he had not paid heed to what was said, that it was of no consequence'.[6]

No single serving member of the IRA's Army Council from this time, nor anyone associated with them, has ever claimed that a meeting of the Army Council took place in August of 1969 – or later – at which anything remotely resembling the alleged Fianna Fáil–IRA deal was struck. Two members of the seven-man Army Council, Ruairí Ó Brádaigh and Seán Garland, confirmed this to me.[7]

The notion that cabinet members like Jack Lynch and Erskine Childers would enter into such a pact with the IRA – whatever about other ministers – is not credible.[8] Might Haughey have done a deal hoping he could persuade the cabinet to agree later? Even his most severe critics acknowledge that he was an accomplished exponent of the art of politics. The concept that he would have considered that Lynch and the party hierarchy might ratify such a deal is preposterous. It is even more absurd to suggest that Berry and the civil servants at the department of justice would have gone along with it. One way or the other news of the 'deal' would have leaked to the press and the opposition within days. Significantly, Goulding and his inner circle had nothing to offer the government as the

IRA had no choice but to 'call off their campaign of violence' in the Republic or face a revolt by their support base who wanted to devote their resources to assisting the beleaguered minority in Northern Ireland.

Clearly, The Deceiver had a rather credulous McMahon eating out of his palm. As events will demonstrate, Fleming and Berry proved just as susceptible to the lies he continued to drip feed them.

The Deceiver, however, was not the only source they had. Col Hefferon, the director of G2, learnt that the gardaí had two informers during a visit he made to C3, the overarching intelligence directorate, at its Phoenix Park HQ in 1969. During the appointment Patrick Malone, the officer in charge of C3, revealed this with some pride.[9] The second informer, however, was a member of Saor Éire, a separate group, and was not in a position to contradict The Deceiver about internal IRA machinations.[10]

Kevin Boland appears to have known about the fact that there were two informers.[11]

***

Over time, Goulding's wing of the IRA developed its own version of The Deceiver's Fianna Fáil–IRA fantasy. According to them, no deal was struck. On the contrary, while intermediaries offered one, it was rebuffed. The authors of *The Lost Revolution* may very well have uncovered the root source of the yarn. Far from involving Haughey or anyone in the cabinet, a Dundalk 'businessman and Fianna Fáil supporter' was purported to be the prime mover. Nor was Goulding the point of contact.

Instead the authors have described how Bobby McKnight was approached by the 'supporter' in Dundalk and informed:

> that £150,000 would be available for arms purchases provided the IRA stopped their activities in the South and abandoned left-wing policies. McKnight had instructions to play along and 'get as much out of them as you can'. He satisfied the businessman by telling him that 'all we're interested in is defence'. The IRA leadership was aware that feelers had been put out before the trouble erupted in Belfast. A Co. Derry businessman and friend of Neil Blaney had approached Francie Donnelly, the South Derry IRA commander, and enquired whether he was interested in equipment. Donnelly reported this to Dublin and was told to continue discussions with the contact ...[12]

Goulding's account of the IRA's interaction with Fianna Fáil in 1969 was published in 1972 in a book of interviews conducted by Rosita Sweetman. Haughey is not named anywhere in connection with a purported deal. Indeed, Goulding never claimed that he met Haughey. Instead, Goulding told Sweetman that in 1969 'certain agents and members of the Fianna Fáil party were sent to infiltrate the IRA'. Goulding continued, 'When they found they couldn't get any change from us they started working on the men in the North'. The IRA men were 'told if they broke away from what [the Fianna Fáil agents] called the Marxist/ Communist group in Dublin they'd be given arms and money. We were told in the South by the same men to stop attacking the establishment of the 26 Counties, drop all socialist policies, and have an all-out attack on the unionists in the North. What they wanted in fact was a development of Fianna Fáil power into the Six Counties through a sectarian war. I told these agents we would decide how the arms and money would be used if we did decide to take them – and then all discussion stopped. We did in fact get money from Fianna Fáil people collecting in London – I'll take money from President Nixon if he offers it, but I'll spend it the way I want.'[13]

There is no substantial, nor indeed insubstantial, evidence that 'agents' acting on behalf of the cabinet, or even a rogue faction within it, made such an offer. At best, Goulding was exaggerating the meddling of a handful of peripheral Fianna Fáil busybodies. Indeed, Goulding was certainly most capable of resorting to exaggeration and deceit when it suited him as his statement of 18 August 1969 illustrates, i.e. the one that claimed that the IRA had been to the forefront of the defence of nationalist communities in August 1969.

Goulding and his supporters came to develop and cherish an even more far-fetched conspiracy theory, namely that Fianna Fáil created the Provisional IRA specifically to eclipse Goulding. In their minds Fianna Fáil did this because Goulding had become a substantial political threat to them. Yet, in the real world, Goulding had not stood a single Sinn Féin candidate in the 1969 general election and the smattering of attacks against foreign assets had not dented, let alone destabilised, the state. Indeed, Fianna Fáil had denigrated Labour in the election as 'Reds', a term of abuse in the mind of the majority of voters. In such an atmosphere, how could Goulding have expected that his party – Ireland's actual 'Red' bogeyman – were going to march democratically to political power within jig time?

Goulding and his associates even claimed that the Fianna Fáil–Provisional IRA conspiracy had been set in motion before the outbreak of the violence of August 1969. Billy McMillen, who joined Goulding's Official IRA after the republican movement split, claimed the supposed plot was hatched as early as February 1969.[14]

Goulding's supporters clung to the belief that dark forces opposed to Goulding stoked the flames of the Troubles for a further twenty-eight years to keep his hands off the levers of power. These notions were promoted by very senior party figures such as Tomás Mac Giolla, a later Official Sinn Féin leader and TD. If we are to accept Mac Giolla's analysis as sound, it means that a cabal of psychopathic taoisigh consisting of Lynch, Haughey, Reynolds and Ahern – with Pádraig Faulkner, Erskine Childers, Paddy Hillery, George Colley and Des O'Malley intermittently serving in cabinet – sustained and nourished the Provisionals so as to undermine Goulding and his supporters. How such a mendacious conspiracy was kept afloat during the administrations led by Fine Gael's Cosgrave, FitzGerald and Bruton, with ministers like Paddy Cooney serving at justice and later at defence, is a mystery best not contemplated by a rational mind.

During he course of this alleged marathon plot, Goulding rebranded Sinn Féin as Official Sinn Féin, then Sinn Féin the Workers' Party, and finally the Workers' Party. At Goulding's oration in 1998, Mac Giolla maintained that the puppet masters of the Troubles – Fianna Fáil and Fine Gael – had only begun to wind down the violence of the Provisional IRA a few years earlier because they believed a breakaway group from the Workers' Party (the Democratic Left) – which became part of a coalition government with Fine Gael and the Labour Party under John Bruton – had finally completed the mission: the eclipse of Goulding and the left-wing policies he represented. Mac Giolla's actual words were that Goulding had:

> recognised the bloody events of the past 28 years as a counter-revolution designed to smash the growing power and strength of The Workers' Party which he was in the course of building. When it seemed that the treachery of Democratic Left in 1992 had finished off The Workers' Party … moves began in 1993 to end the counter-revolution and call off the Provisional Dogs of War.
>
> However the Workers' Party is far from finished. As Cathal brings the 200th Anniversary of 1798 to a dramatic close, by exiting left, some may feel he has abandoned us or left us in the lurch. But it is quite the opposite. He has told the next generation to make a new beginning, in a new age of exploitation, to the struggle of the working class, nationally and internationally against oppression; and he has left us the means to do so in a strong and vibrant Workers' Party ready to take up the Republican space and the socialist space recently abandoned by 'traitors and slaves'. You can hear him shouting at us 'It's up to you now, and fuck the begrudgers'.[15]

On the other hand, Bishop and Mallie have provided a lucid and entirely objective account of how the Provisional IRA emerged in their book on the organisation. Their analysis was based on decades of experience as frontline reporters and numerous interviews with key historical figures:

> In fact, the division of the republican movement had been ordained long before 1969. In quiet times, with give and take on both sides, the habitually bickering traditions of revolutionary socialism and romantic physical force of nationalism could just

> about get along under the same roof, [but] faced with the crisis of any dimensions, the union was bound to fall apart. The events of August 1969 merely accelerated a process that had begun with the attempts by Goulding and his supporters to modernise the movement. The theory of a [FF] government-inspired conspiracy to remove the dangerous leftists of the new IRA and replace them with manageable stooges of the old tradition was characteristically fanciful and vain. There was scarcely any evidence in 1969 that the Goulding camp's political strategy was making significant progress in the South nor that it had any potential to do so. Even if it had, Lynch and his government had much more immediate preoccupations than the neutralisation of a minor political nuisance.

Despite this, traces of The Deceiver's mischief lingered for decades. Des O'Malley attended cabinet meetings in his capacity as chief whip in 1969, and as minister for justice after 5 May 1970. In his 2014 autobiography he alleged that while Haughey 'was relatively silent during government discussions about the North, *reliable informants* [my emphasis] told the Gardaí that a government minister met Cathal Goulding, the IRA's Chief of Staff, in August 1969. It was alleged that they discussed a deal whereby, if the IRA agreed to stop the destruction of foreign-owned property in the South, it would be facilitated in moving weapons in the North. The Special Branch learnt the identity of the minister: Charles Haughey.'[16]

While the special branch was being side-tracked by The Deceiver's fabrications, a far more important development was about to take place at Dublin Airport, one about which they knew nothing.

5

CLANDESTINE ARMS FLIGHTS AND MILITARY TRAINING

A group within the Irish cabinet was aware that a cargo of arms was about to fly from London to Dublin in September 1969. Those who knew were prepared to turn a blind eye. Dr Roy Johnson, a member of the IRA's Army Executive, knew about the flight before its arrival. He had spent the previous number of years trying to rid the IRA of its weapons with the support of Goulding. Now, he was arguing that the 'political response to the pogrom [in August 1969 should] have been to let it run its course and turn all attention to getting the world media to report it, and thereby show up the nature of British rule; to get the democratic forces in Britain out on the streets; to get the Dublin government to get at the British and complain at the UN, with US support. To go for guns was to do what the enemy wanted ... Anthony Coughlan and I resolutely held out for a totally political response, but increasingly no one was listening'.[1] Johnson believed Goulding only became involved with the London cargo to keep the weapons out of the hands of militants in the IRA like MacStíofáin, and 'as an insurance policy in case he might need them later'.[2]

When asked about the flight decades later, Seán Garland, a Goulding ally and member of the Army Council, did not deny that it had occurred.

Minister Kevin Boland had no difficulty in recounting

rumours about a consignment of small arms he maintained had the blessing of the Dublin government. In his book, *Up Dev,* he recorded how reports about it 'became so insistent as to amount to a virtual certainty at least insofar as the members of the Government were concerned'. As far as he could see, 'everyone assumed everyone else knew' and it was treated as if it was a case of the government helping the nationalist communities in the only way the cabinet could 'without a diplomatic breach'.[3] The odds are that Boland was describing the consignment coming from London to Dublin Airport.

Des O'Malley, who became minister for justice the following year, has stated that in the 'autumn of 1969 the Special Branch received further information that small consignments of arms were being imported through Dublin Airport at times when a sympathetic customs officer was on duty. The belief in Garda circles was that [Charles] Haughey was involved; there were also suspicions that Blaney was active in this'.[4]

John Kelly, a CDC organiser said, 'Pádraig [Haughey] went out to the airport and collected them in a van and delivered them to Cathal [Goulding]. There were two boxes of short arms. Maybe 20 or 50 weapons, something like that'.[5]

The consignment was collected by Pádraig ('Jock') Haughey, Bobby McKnight and a third individual.[6] McKnight, born in Belfast in 1936, was an IRA member, a veteran of the Border Campaign and an unsuccessful candidate in the 1966 Westminster general election.[7] In a letter written in May 1973 to Garda Commissioner Malone, Detective Patrick Crinnion of the garda's overarching intelligence unit, C3, identified the third participant as Richard Timmons.

Bobby McKnight's recollection differs from the account provided by John Kelly insofar as the size of the consignment was concerned. 'Two of us went down (and) Charlie's brother brought us into the airport, we'd a wee pickup truck we got a loan of, (and) he brought us in, and they put these big boxes on the truck, we had to take it away, the truck was fucking swaying from side to side [but] we had the right of way'.[8]

According to McKnight, they drove to 'a rendezvous nearby where Goulding had assembled a team who divided up the cargo – handguns and automatic weapons – and moved them to separate dumps.'[9]

John Kelly said the guns 'weren't supplied to the North. They certainly weren't supplied to volunteers in the north so I would say that Goulding sat on them … Pádraig [Haughey] told me he gave the guns to Goulding and then we were wondering "where are they".' Joe Cahill also confirmed they never reached Northern Ireland.[10]

If Boland was correct that members of the cabinet knew about the arms flight, it is difficult to conceive that Jack Lynch did not. None of this implies that Lynch was enthusiastic about the endeavour, merely that he was aware of it and did not halt it. It solved a problem that was besetting him: guns were now getting to Northern Ireland without his government's fingerprints on them.

***

While doubts still surround the cabinet's knowledge of the September 1969 flight, there is no confusion about the government's decision to train men from Derry in the use of arms in October 1969.

An interim Irish Army report marked 'Secret' was furnished to the government by the Army's Planning Board on Northern Ireland Operations on 27 September 1969. It anticipated four scenarios in which the nationalist minority might be imperilled. First, an attack 'by Protestant extremists', which the RUC and B-Specials would prove incapable of repelling. In this eventuality, it was envisaged that an incursion by Irish troops could reach into areas near the border such as Derry and Newry while colleagues would engage in a 'wide range of unconventional operations' across the border designed to draw the extremists away from the vulnerable nationalist areas. Significantly, the report suggested the Army should supply 'arms, ammunition, equipment, and medical supplies to [the] Catholic minority in accordance with availability'.[11] In this context 'unconventional' operations anticipated deploying Irish soldiers who would wear civilian clothing and might be aided by locals living across the border.

A second scenario involved a potential conflict between the 'Catholic minority' and the RUC and/or B-Specials would be met with a similar response involving a 'supply of arms, ammunition, equipment and medical supplies to Catholic minority, in accordance with availability.'

A third situation contemplated attacks by the IRA on the RUC or B-Specials, sparking retaliatory attacks against the minority community. Once again, there would be direct intervention and a supply of arms to the minority.

Finally, the report considered an overspill of violence against the minority in the wake of a conflict between 'Protestant extremists' and Northern Ireland's 'security' forces. Here it was envisaged that the Army would:

> a. Infiltrate elements armed and equipped to [organise], train and advise Catholic and Nationalist groups in vulnerable areas far from the Border (e.g. BELFAST).
>
> b. Deploy sub-units up to [company] level across the Border prepared to keep routes open for refugees moving South.

Part of the report focused on 'guerrilla operations', which envisaged:

> (1) Organising and conducting military training in the Republic for nationalists living in Northern Ireland.
>
> (2) Supplying arms, ammunition and equipment in accordance with availability to nationalist elements in Northern Ireland.

Areas which might be attacked by Irish troops included Belfast Airport and key installations such as television studios. Since these were located far across the border, 'unconventional type' military operations were considered appropriate.

The planners pointed out that the adoption of a mission involving 'active intervention in Northern Ireland' would demand an intensive intelligence effort, both before and during operations. Of significance, the report warned that a 'number of the courses suggested would involve support of and cooperation with various movements in Northern Ireland such as civil rights and republican groups. This could also lead to cooperation with illegal groups in the Republic. These contacts,' the report continued with a warning, 'would have serious political implications on the national and international scene. They could also pose serious problems in the aftermath, particularly where arms and equipment have been supplied'.

The board recommended the 'desirability of supporting the minority in the North by training and by the supply of arms and equipment be considered, and if found to be acceptable, the development of plans for the implementation of these courses'.[12]

Shortly after receipt of the report, the Irish military reserve, An Fórsa Cosanta Áitiúil, better known as the FCA, began training civilians from Derry at Fort Dunree in the use of arms. Irish military Intelligence, G2, was deeply involved in the programme.

While the Irish Army was developing its plans, Paddy Doherty and Seán Keenan approached the nearest Irish Army post to them at Rockhill House, outside Letterkenny in Co. Donegal. 'The young sentry at the gate grew a little agitated on seeing the old red Morris Oxford with the Derry registration number. "Is the commanding officer available?" I asked.' Doherty was told he wasn't but that the officer in charge was 'up in the canteen'.[13] The pair went into the canteen where the soldiers recognised both of them. They were offered drinks – a fruit juice for Doherty and whiskey for Keenan. They were told that Lt Col Buckley, the officer in charge of the Northern Command, was at Army HQ in the Curragh, but was due to return. When he did, he shook hands with them and invited them to his office. He revealed that his intelligence officers were in contact with people inside the Bogside and the Army had considered the possibility that British troops might yet attack the Bogside.

Doherty told Buckley that they wanted training in small arms for the men of Derry. 'There was a long silence. The O/C of the Northern Command of the Irish army shook his head in disbelief. His sympathy went out to the people of the North, but in no way could the army get involved in the ways we had requested'.[14] An embarrassed silence followed, which Doherty broke with a request that Buckley send their request 'up the line'. The OC agreed but warned that it would take several days to obtain an answer. Doherty surmised from the look on his face that he believed it would be rejected. They drove back to Derry in silence. Keenan was not optimistic and expressed his contempt for the Dublin government.

Yet, when the request reached his desk, James Gibbons, the minister for defence, sanctioned it. Less than a week later, Doherty received a summons to Rockhill Barracks where an officer he had never met told him to 'prepare my men for military training' which was to take place at Fort Dunree, on the shores of Lough Swilly in Co. Donegal.

Men were also trained at Finner Camp near Ballyshannon, likewise in Co Donegal, which was being used as a refugee centre.[15] The Finner camp programme has largely been kept a secret.

A myth has grown up over the decades that the men chosen for training at Fort Dunree were handpicked IRA men. Yet, foremost amongst the trainees was Paddy Doherty along with members of his family and Michael Canavan, who had worked in the credit-union movement and was a civil rights campaigner. Canavan had acted as the CDC's principal negotiator with the British Army with great success.[16]

According to Doherty, 'The first batch of men to be trained by the Irish army were chosen with considerable care. I knew that the Irish government would be severely embarrassed if it became known that men from the North were being trained in the use of firearms. Everyone was briefed on the need for secrecy. My two sons, my elder brother and six others working out of [my house at] Number 10 formed the first unit.'[17] At the time his house was serving as the HQ of the Derry CDC.

Irish military Intelligence, G2, used the training programme as an enticement to close down the IRA drilling that was taking place elsewhere. According to *The Lost Revolution*, in September a 'County Derry businessman' who was a friend of Neil Blaney 'arrived with Captain James Kelly of Irish army intelligence, who had ... made contact with Keenan, Johnny White ... in Derry. To White he offered Army instruction for volunteers in Donegal with the proviso that independent training would cease'.[18] Capt. Kelly became a co-defendant at the Arms Trials alongside Charles Haughey, John Kelly and Albert Luykx the following year.

Capt. Kelly had been in Belfast during the turmoil of the previous month. One of his brothers was a priest on the Falls Road. In a report dated 31 August 1969, which he submitted to Col Hefferon, he concluded that, 'Extreme Protestantism and extreme Republicanism are the two elements likely to upset N.I. at the present time, with the former more likely to be the immediate troublemakers. Political developments to date are more favourable to extreme republicanism, which is one factor likely to hold its hand, the second one would be the shortage of arms. This does not eliminate the possibility of some Catholic/IRA hothead taking action which would precipitate an escalation, thus playing into extreme Protestant hands. On balance, however, the next move would seem to be up to the extreme Protestantism and if the Catholic/IRA element does not oblige by taking action first, it is practically forced into the position of taking the initiative itself.'[19]

Many commentators, ranging from those sympathetic to the Marxist wing of the IRA, to leading Fine Gael figures such as Garret FitzGerald, have portrayed Capt. Kelly as a rabid supporter of militant republicanism. They have labelled him a 'hothead' and a 'troublemaker'. The Information Policy Unit (IPU), a British intelligence black propaganda machine which operated in Ireland, also circulated smears about him.[20]

***

If Gibbons and others had hoped to deter the independent arms training, they were not successful. Eamonn McCann recalls that from the beginning of September, 'Republicans and some members of the Labour Party' received training from a 'Republican training officer' who came up from Cork. The activity took place in a tiny house in the Brandywell district. McCann has written about how 'people who had perhaps joined the Labour Party a year or two ago out of admiration for the political principles of Harold Wilson (this is possible) learned how to dismantle and reassemble the Thompson and the Sten and how to make a Mills bomb.[21] We went across the border into the Donegal hills for practice shoot-outs. It was exciting at the time and enabled one to feel that, despite the depressing trend of events in the area, one was involved in a real revolution'.[22]

Capt. Patrick McGonagle enrolled Doherty and his fellow trainees into the FCA at a temporary recruitment building in Buncrana, twelve miles from Derry. According to Doherty, 'No one ever swore the oath of allegiance to the Irish Republic more sincerely than we did … My brother and I had to knock ten years off our ages to satisfy the regulations …'[23] A blind eye was turned to the questionable fitness of some of the recruits. Nine men were lined up with shirts in their hands. Two of them were bare-chested while the others wore various types of singlets for inspection:

> With an unlit cigar in his mouth, the doctor pushed his stethoscope against the men's white skin. 'Pass! Pass!' He came to my eldest brother. 'Too much smoking and drinking. Pass.' The formalities over, the doctor re-lit the shredded end of his cigar. 'I could do with a good drink,' he quipped, perhaps in sympathy with my elder brother. Or maybe the remark reflected his disbelief at what was happening. I reported for duty every morning but was allowed to return to Derry in the evening while the other men remained in the camp.[24]

Doherty's group had enrolled for a further one-week course and were due to return to Derry on Friday 3 October. Capt. Kelly was with Col Hefferon in his office when they were informed that the training was 'likely to be the subject of newspaper comment over the weekend'.[25] The director, Colonel Hefferon, attempted to contact the minister or the chief of staff, but without luck.' As a result, 'The colonel decided to cancel it on his own initiative'. He contacted the G2 officer based in Donegal and ordered a postponement and added that his instructions would be confirmed or countermanded by a telephone call at ten o'clock that night. A secure line was established between the office of the garda chief superintendent in Letterkenny, Larry Wren, and Col Hefferon's office in Dublin. Both phones had scrambler devices. It was then confirmed that a group of about twenty men due for training on the following morning would not leave Derry. On Monday morning, Col Hefferon reported on his action to the chief-of-staff and Gibbons was subsequently brought up to speed.

One actual report about Fort Dunree made it to print: London's *Private Eye* magazine revealed on 24 October 1969, that 'a number of volunteers have taken the road from Derry to Lettakenny [*sic*], across the Border, and thence to the FCA (territorial army) training grounds at Rockhill Camp and Dunree Camp. Members of the citizens defence committee in Derry handpicked the men, many of whom are unemployed. The men were taken to two camps and put on a "crash" course in the use of rifles and machine guns. They are then dispatched back to Derry with assurances that in the event of serious civil strife in the town, guns will be made available. "The purpose of this training from the point of view of the Southern Government is not to provoke violence but to ensure that, if violence does break out, the right people have guns".'[26]

Peter Berry claimed in his 'diaries' that he did 'not know then and I was not to know until the arms trial in September 1970 of the Fort Dunree episode' which had been carried out 'with the approval of the Minister for Defence'. Berry alleged that it 'was immediately cancelled when brought to the Taoiseach's notice'.[27] This is a puzzling and problematic statement. News of such a dramatic development should instantly have reached Berry through the garda network. Regrettably, Berry had an imperfect relationship with the truth and, while the information may have reached him, he might have become embarrassed that he took no steps to thwart it. Another problem with Berry's account is the existence of the report that appeared in *Private Eye*, a magazine that was readily available in Dublin. A third problem is the discrepancy that it was Col Hefferon who stood the second wave down, not Lynch.

Richie Ryan of Fine Gael raised the events at Fort Dunree in the Dáil in May 1970. Ryan pointed out that military training had been 'given in at least one military camp to civilians in the use of arms'. Ryan's reference to 'civilians' gave Gibbons an opportunity to conceal the truth. He interrupted Ryan with the words: 'That is not true'. Strictly speaking he was telling the truth, for the Doherty family and the other trainees had sworn an oath of allegiance and had joined the FCA and hence were not technically civilians. Naturally, this created the misleading impression that no training had taken place. As late as 2018, Ryan would simply shake his head in bewilderment when reminded of this incident.[28] Gibbons' economy with the truth did not survive cross-examination at the Arms Trial.

Gibbons was also chairman of the secretive Council of Defence. One of its more intriguing meetings took place on 13 October 1969 and included Gibbons, Lt Gen. MacEoin chief of staff of the army, as well as the army's adjutant-general and quartermaster along with a number of civil servants. Gibbons used the occasion to instruct Lt Gen. MacEoin to 'submit a program', covering 'intensive training' for regular troops and special courses for 'elements of the F.C.A.'[29] The reference to the FCA may have been a coded reference to the reactivation of the training of CDC members.

That same Council of Defence meeting was intriguing for another reason: a discussion that took place about the purchase of naval vessels. The minutes record the 'urgent necessity to provide vessels in order to maintain a fishery protection service'.[30] Gibbons decided that efforts should be undertaken to locate 'suitable trawlers or other vessels in Britain and the Continent'.[31] This makes little sense as a trawler would be a most unsuitable vessel for 'fishery protection' where speed is of the essence. Having reviewed a number of formerly secret military documents, Angela Clifford, wrote in 'Military Aspects of Ireland's Arms Crisis':

> We have seen the Planning Board on Northern Ireland Operations suggest that Britain might cut off the Army stationed in Donegal, in which instance there would have to be a supply by sea ... There have also been several references to arming nationalists in the above reports, something that could be done by sea. All in all, it is easy to see why acquiring a new vessel is treated with such urgency, and why 'trawlers' might fit the bill.[32]

***

All of this was happening against a background where relations between the British Army and the nationalist community were also good. One British soldier quoted by Peter Taylor in his book *Provos* recalled that he had felt 'like a Prince in shining armour' after his arrival in Northern Ireland. 'It was a day of great sadness', he recalled of the end of his tour in early 1970. 'I was leaving friends, people we knew. Leaving the girls behind was probably the saddest thing of all. The [nationalist] girls lined up to wave goodbye. It was like the Wailing Wall of Jerusalem. I remember a hit at the time – "Leaving on a Jet Plane". You know, the lines about "packing my bags and hating to go and don't know when I'll be back again". We were all singing our head off and girls were waving and throwing their knickers at us. God bless –'em! And they were all shouting, "We'll wait for you!"'[33]

By the time he returned, however, Wilson and Callaghan had been replaced by Heath and Whitelaw; the unionist government had gained more control over the British Army, and incidents like the Falls Road curfew had taken their toll.[34] The soldier recalled how everything 'had changed. Attitudes have changed. It was sad. People were frightened. [They didn't] want to know us. No tea. No scones. No breakfasts. People shunned us'.[35]

Before the atmosphere changed for the worse, it was the IRA that felt the contempt of the nationalist community. Fr Marcellus Gillespie told the Scarman Tribunal that following mass at Holy Cross church in Ardoyne on Sunday 17 August 1969, a meeting of residents had taken place at a nearby school. Those in attendance wanted guns. '[I] did not agree with guns and [said] that they should not have guns, and they accused me of being a cheek-turning fool.' After the meeting, some of those who had attended it 'raided the houses of people who were supposed to be IRA men by repute and found nothing, and after the riots they called the IRA, the "I Ran Away".'[36]

By way of contrast, British Army weapons were largely safe from thieving hands. One Belfast publican with premises on

Leeson Street, recalled soldiers 'coming into my bar with their faces covered, with their little tin hats with camouflage on. I served them and they left the guns and bayonets up against the counter when they went off to the loo.'[37]

Initially, the uneven deployment of British troops across Belfast had let a number of loyalist attack gangs slip through the sectarian demarcation lines. One of the areas the troops failed to reach in sufficient time was the nationalist Ardoyne. The Catholic bishop, William Philbin, had appealed to the British Army to come to the defence of the area but without success. Militant loyalist gangs from the Shankill Road had launched an attack on Unity Walk flats. After it began, a smattering of British troops outside the flats withdrew, seeking reinforcements. In their absence the assault was repelled by a man armed with a submachine gun and a colleague with a revolver, positioned on a balcony in the flats. The next day the British commander in the area, an English colonel, complained to the locals about the shooters. In response, they accused him of having created the vacuum, which the pair had filled, by abandoning them in their hour of need. Rather than order an immediate search for the weapons, he explained that although he was under pressure from Stormont to confiscate them, he would not be back for four days. This allowed the locals to spirit the guns to safety.[38]

A lenient attitude was also taken to the possession of guns in Derry where Eamonn McCann joined a delegation which went to Victoria Barracks on the Strand Road where they met Brigadier Leng and Col Millman. Leng told them he 'quite understood that we might have certain things in the area which we wished now to move out and, to facilitate this, there would be no check on vehicles on one of the roads to the Republic for the next twenty-four hours. We thought he was talking of our radio transmitter, which shows that at that point we were almost as naive as the army.'[39]

Brendan Hughes, a future Provisional IRA leader, was attending gun classes conducted in kitchens and bedrooms on local streets in Belfast. 'I remember one particular night sitting in a house in the Lower Falls with six or seven others and a well-known British army officer opened the door and just walked in and said, "what weapons are you training on tonight lads?" That sort of thing happened during the honeymoon period. The army was basically gathering intelligence and we weren't as yet on a war footing.'

Hughes also recalled how soldiers in 'a wee pub just down Leeson Street' would tell them about weapons. 'We used to ask them about their weapons and how they worked and very often they would give you a whole run-down on the weapon ... A lot of my training came from pubs, you know, from the British army, British troops, young lads of eighteen and nineteen. We weren't much older than that ourselves though. They were quite happy to give you a run-down on the workings of the SLR [Self-Loading Rifle]. We used to steal the ammunition all the time. We used to sit in the pubs and lift a magazine or something like that. A few rifles were stolen as well. They used to leave them sitting at the corner of the street. That used to happen because they were so naive at that period and they weren't in a hostile environment either.'

John Kelly, an activist who was involved with the CDCs and stood trial with Haughey and Capt. Kelly at the Four

Courts in 1970, was another IRA man who had a similar experience.[40] He received weapons training from a British Army officer in Belfast a few weeks after the troops had settled in. 'He stripped down a machine gun and demonstrated how we should put it together again. He probably did it because he was an intelligence officer and wanted to find out how much we knew about weaponry. I was a little surprised but in those days it was a sort of one-to-one relationship and we took it as a matter of course.'[41]

Clearly, neither the IRA nor young nationalists with guns were seen as a threat to the British Army at this juncture.[42] James Callaghan wrote in *A House Divided*, 'In fact the IRA at that time was almost dormant and had little support'. He had personally observed the well-known taunt which had accused them of ineptitude and cowardice: 'One of the slogans I saw sprayed on walls in the Catholic areas was: "IRA – I Ran Away".'[43]

While the British Army was providing *ad hoc* arms training, the Irish government was trying to forge links with those who could be considered responsible citizens inside the nationalist communities of Northern Ireland. Ostensibly, while the fund approved by Dáil Éireann was for the relief of distress, some ministers appeared to be happy to let the CDCs siphon off some of the money for the purchase of arms.

Brainse Fhionnglaise
Finglas Library
Tel: (01) 834 4906

6

SECRET BANK ACCOUNTS

Col Michael Hefferon of G2 had responded early to the violence that was festering in Northern Ireland. 'I had many, many people working inside and outside the area and from October 1968 it was apparent to us that the trouble was going to erupt sometime'. He felt the situation that developed in August 1969 'was one, which from our point of view down here, was of such a terrible nature and I had fears if such a situation developed again, then I would like to know the trustworthy people in certain areas, the people who could be depended upon to organise resistance to mass onslaught which was one of the things that was very much on in view of the experience in Belfast'. Capt. Kelly had a network of contacts in Northern Ireland. 'It was in view of this background that I asked Capt. Kelly to keep his contacts', Col Hefferon added.[1] Another person who was developing contacts was Seamus Brady, a journalist who was sent to Belfast by George Colley to gather information for the Irish government as part of a propaganda campaign which it ran for a few months in 1969. Brady learned the UVF was smuggling guns across the Irish Sea from Scotland. When he reported this to Dublin, he was put in contact with Col Hefferon and Capt. Kelly.[2] At their first meeting Brady agreed to introduce the captain to his contacts. They were primarily members of the CDCs. A number of them were, or had been, in the IRA. Foremost amongst them was Jim Sullivan.

Another key figure who emerged as a contact of Capt. Kelly was Tom Conaty, the chair of Belfast's Central Citizens' Defence Committee. Conaty was not a supporter of the IRA, nor ever became one. In an interview on RTÉ on 21 June 1973, while he was still chairman, he criticised the IRA, stating that while it was pursuing the type of objectives the majority of Irish people wished for, what separated them from the rest of the Irish population was their methods, their 'use of violence'. Conaty was also close to Canon Pádraig Murphy, another man committed to non-violence and described by British Home Secretary James Callaghan as 'a wonderful leader of his flock who constantly strove for peace'.[3]

Capt. Kelly was also put in contact with Paddy Doherty in Derry, another leader who had little time for the IRA. Kelly was determined to deter militants who might aggravate the situation. In one of his reports he spoke about how 'arms and support seem to have got into the wrong hands in Belfast'. He was also concerned about the type of people he described in his book *Orders for the Captain* as 'psychopathic'. He had no concern about the general membership of Central CDC, nor about Jim Sullivan who believed that the old 'brute military stance' as exemplified by the Border Campaign 'would never achieve anything in Ireland. It was as simple as that. The [border] campaign had bloody well proved it for us'.[4]

***

A number of important cabinet decisions were taken on 16 August. One was to set up a sub-committee to deal with the Northern Ireland crisis. It consisted of Haughey and three ministers with border constituencies, Blaney, Pádraig Faulkner and Joseph Brennan.[5]

Also that day the Dáil voted to make £100,000 available for the relief of distress in Northern Ireland. Haughey, as minister for finance, was placed in charge of the distribution of the fund.

Capt. Kelly assumed the task of liaison officer between the Irish government and the CDCs and became central to the distribution of these funds. One of his tasks was to identify those who might best administer it.[6] Haughey came to rely on G2 in his considerations about its distribution. Some of these funds would be used in an attempt to purchase arms by the CDCs.

Around October the captain was introduced to Anthony Fagan at the Department of Finance. They met at regular intervals, sometimes twice a week in addition to exchanging telephone calls as part of a vetting process for the distribution of the relief fund. A bank account was opened in Clones, Co. Monaghan, near the border, to assist in the circulation of the money.

One name furnished to Haughey was that of Paddy Doherty in Derry. One day Doherty received a call from a voice which was 'unmistakably Southern Irish, slightly nasal but with an air of authority'. The caller identified himself as Charles Haughey. After the exchange of some pleasantries he said, 'You will need some money up there. How much do you need?' Doherty couldn't believe it: 'the Irish Minister for Finance was offering me money over a phone line which the authorities must have been tapping ... To me, the minister's apparent lack of concern for secrecy indicated a commitment on the part of the government, something which was more important to me than money.'[7]

Doherty paused before giving Haughey an answer. As he hesitated, 'Haughey said he would send five thousand. "No," I replied, "one thousand would be plenty. Any more could prove to be an embarrassment." Next day a banker came to my door to tell me that a sum of money had been deposited and that the bank awaited instructions for the management of the account.' He contacted Michael Canavan, who asked Tommy Carlin, a director in Derry credit union, to set up a book-keeping system for the Defence Association. 'The two men's ability, integrity and financial experience eased what would have been an onerous burden on Keenan and me. Soon we received another thousand pounds. We agreed to forward this money to the Bishop, who was overwhelmed with requests for assistance.'[8]

Haughey seemed to be doing everything in his power to help. He even opened the doors of his house in Dublin to Jim Sullivan in September 1969. While Sullivan was a supporter of the Marxist Goulding, he was calling on Haughey in his capacity as a senior figure in the Central CDC of Belfast. His companions were Paddy Devlin, MP, and Hugh Kennedy, the latter a Belfast man who had been working for Bord Bainne. If there was any truth in Goulding's conspiracy theory that Haughey was trying to divide the IRA by seducing some of its members with the promise of guns in return for toppling him, this was Haughey's opportunity to test the waters with Sullivan who was the second-in-command of the IRA in Belfast. Haughey did nothing of the sort.

Devlin provided an account of the meeting in his memoirs at which he and his colleagues impressed on Haughey the 'great need that existed and he indicated his willingness to help. Not long afterwards I received a letter from Madame de Barra, president of the Irish Red Cross, setting out the terms on which help would be given, and giving the names of some people who had appealed for assistance. I was also told that £10,000 was available to be picked up at a bank in Baggot Street, Dublin, but for convenience, the account was later transferred to Clones, a town in the Irish Republic close to the border. My recollection is that we needed two out of three authorised signatures on every cheque. Those nominated were myself, Paddy Kennedy and a respected Belfast lawyer'.[9] The lawyer Devlin chose not to name was Patrick McGrory.[10]

Later, when Devlin was alerted that a cheque book had arrived, he contacted Paddy Kennedy, 'who set off with the signed cheque to collect the money and have it distributed amongst those in need. I gave him the Red Cross letter. I only ever signed three or four cheques and made just one pick-up myself on a date when Paddy couldn't go, but I passed the £2,000 cash on to him immediately afterwards'.

Devlin had called for guns at a rally in Dublin yet claimed in his memoirs that this was out of character, an aberration he regretted. However, a family member of Capt. Kelly recalls how Devlin visited their home 'and sat in a big leather armchair where there were two wooden lions-heads mounted on the armrests. At one stage he lost his cool, became red faced and demanded guns while slamming the lion-heads on the armrests with ferocity. I was bringing in refreshments. He was a big man and so intense was his conduct, I thought for a moment that he was about to attack my father and that the lions-heads were going to implode'.[11]

These funds were not being channelled to the IRA. Some IRA men later kidnapped Paddy Kennedy and forced him to draw a cheque for £2,000 under duress. He was held while one of them drove to Clones and cashed it. During October 1969 a Belfast IRA officer managed to withdraw a further £4,000 from the fund. Bishop and Mallie tracked down someone who knew the culprits and who revealed that while most of the money was 'used for the stated purpose' the Belfast IRA had been able to 'con them out of a few thousand quid'.[12]

Capt. Kelly subsequently came to believe that Clones was not a suitable location for the account and Fagan opened a series of accounts on Baggot Street in Dublin instead.

The Dublin government was keeping a few plates spinning in the air. While it did not want to invade Northern Ireland or supply the CDCs with weapons which could be traced back to it, it was prepared to let the CDCs – not the IRA – siphon off some of the relief of distress fund to purchase arms on their own volition. Despite clear evidence of this, Jack Lynch later painted a picture which implied the Dublin government had been resolutely opposed to the procurement of arms at all times. 'People have been coming down frequently from all parts of the Six Counties ever since and even before 12th August last year [1969]', he told the Dáil the following year. 'Some of them have come down asking for ammunition and for guns. They have seen me and other ministers ... I told successive groups too – and they came I am sure in genuine fear and in the conviction that they needed guns – that we could not supply any guns either because I felt possession of arms on any side would be dangerous'.[13]

Kevin Boland painted a rather different picture of what was afoot. According to him, the ministers met deputations which 'consisted of people who would be looked upon as "responsible members of the community" – members of [Stormont] Parliament, surely all the [Stormont] Opposition members must have come at some time and to my own knowledge each of the SDLP men came, priests from all the attacked areas came, and other prominent citizens, some who had previously been regarded as "Castle Catholics" and some who have lately reverted to that role. Their request was always the same. They asked for the means to protect themselves, their families and their homes. They wanted respirators to protect themselves from CS gas and guns to repel enemies – these and the money to buy them – and they asked for nothing else'.[14] Boland insisted that no one 'refused them, everyone's heart was in the right place', and even when eventually the Taoiseach could side-step them no longer his attitude seemed favourable: "He would bring the matter to government". And, of course, the deputations could count heads – the aid they asked for had been promised'. Pessimistically, Boland gave them as 'little encouragement' as he could because he had no confidence that 'any help would be forthcoming from the Government'.[15]

According to John Kelly, 'initially our contacts were with the Irish government as we understood it. We met Brian Lenihan and Paddy Hillery, Jack Lynch and Jim Gibbons – there were others'. The discussions with the taoiseach and his foreign minister took place in Dáil Éireann. He recalls how the 'main thrust was whether they provided the soldiers to defend nationalist areas or they provided the weapons that IRA trained people could use'. The general 'burden' of the discussions with Lynch and his ministers revolved around what:

> could they do to help the Northern situation? What were we asking them to do? What were the requirements; how urgent was the need? Central to the whole thing was the defence of the Nationalist community, the Catholic community. I said, 'There is no need for blankets or feeding bottles. We need arms to defend the people.' They accepted all that. It was open, transparent and above board, there was no subterfuge, no winking and nodding and no cute hoorism. It was straight forward, they understood the need and to us they were willing to co-operate and supply those needs. I don't think there was any member of the Cabinet we did not meet at that early stage ... Money was never a factor.[16]

John Kelly only met Haughey 'twice at that time'. The first occasion was:

> at the beginning when we met other members of the Cabinet in delegations that went down with [the solicitor] PJ McGrory, Paddy Devlin, Tom Conaty and people like that. We met Charlie Haughey on that occasion. We were meeting him as Citizens' Defence. The second time I met him was when we were told the decision had been made by the Government to go ahead with the project of supplying arms to Northern Nationalists. That would have been in early September of 1969. We met in Leinster House. Neil Blaney told us of the decision in the presence of Jim Kelly [of G2]. After that the only person we had contact with at governmental level was Neil Blaney. He was the driving force of that whole arms procurement mission on behalf of the Irish government.[17]

The next time John Kelly encountered Haughey was 'when we were charged [in 1970]'.

According to Capt. Kelly, one of the accounts on Baggot Street – in the name of 'George Dixon' – was to be used as an arms account by the CDCs, while the main purpose of another account – in the name of Ann O'Brien – was for the publication of a weekly newspaper called *The Voice of the North*.

At his trial Capt. Kelly stated that it 'was the money out of these accounts that was used for the purchase' of arms. He also explained that £3,000 had been withdrawn from Baggot Street 'sometime around Christmas of 1969' by the CDCs so it could be used as the first down payment on a possible purchase of arms.[18]

7

THE CDCS AND THEIR FRIENDS IN HIGH SOCIETY

The CDCs were not looking for arms to wage war with the British Army. On the contrary they had established good working relationships with its top brass and their political masters in London.

In *A House Divided (*1973), James Callaghan wrote, 'The IRA had few members in August 1968 [*sic.*] and it was not until later that it reorganised and mobilised. I believe that if events had not gone so tragically wrong in the summer of 1970, the IRA might have broken fresh ground with an entirely new policy of recognising Stormont and of working through the Civil Rights Association and similar organisations.[1] This may sound a bold claim, but I believe we were within a touch of this happening.'[2]

Callaghan had forged his own relationship with the CDCs in August 1969. At the end of that month, he had ditched his British Army escort before heading into the Bogside where he received a rapturous welcome. The Derry CDC honoured the occasion by having the 'Free Derry' sign re-painted professionally. 'The vigilantes were mobilised to escort Mr. Callaghan,' Eamonn McCann wrote, 'but when he appeared they, and he, were swept along by a surging crowd of thousands up Rossville Street and into Lecky Road. Mr Callaghan took refuge in a local house, where four members of the Defence Committee – Seán Keenan, Paddy Doherty, Michael Canavan and I – were to talk to him.'[3]

Keenan, while a member of the IRA, was there in his CDC capacity. Doherty recalled that John Hume 'formed the reception committee. Our job was to greet Callaghan and to escort him to a meeting with the leaders of the Defence Association, who were waiting in the Bogside Inn. The three of us represented different strands within the nationalist community: Keenan, the republican, with his belief in armed struggle; Hume, the constitutionalist; and me, the pragmatic wheeler-dealer. It said a lot for Keenan's integrity that he carried out the Defence Association's instructions, despite his lack of faith in British politicians.'[4]

Eamonn McCann was also part of the group. He recalls how they told Callaghan about 'the unemployment problem and he said that, yes, it was very serious, unemployment was always very serious and that, indeed, he and his colleagues would have to see what could be done about it. Seán Keenan said that Mr Callaghan could see we were all reasonable people. Mr Callaghan agreed that indeed we were. He went upstairs and addressed the crowd outside from an open window'.[5]

On the other hand, when Callaghan met Ian Paisley, he was told that the 'incidence of unemployment and the shortage of houses can be attributed exclusively to the Papist population. These people breed like rabbits and multiply like vermin'.[6]

Callaghan wasn't the only British cabinet minister who got to rub shoulders with members of the IRA at this time. Denis Healy, secretary of state for defence, wrote in his memoirs that when he 'flew over to Northern Ireland a few weeks' after the violence he had been 'greeted by crowds of cheering Catholics as I walked down the Falls and Crumlin roads – accompanied, without knowing it, by two leaders of the IRA.'[7]

Ted Heath dispatched Quentin Hogg (later Lord Hailsham), his shadow home secretary, to visit Belfast and the Bogside. 'But my most poignant visits', he wrote later, 'were to the Bogside in Londonderry, at that time a no-go area designated by its inhabitants as Free Derry (or Doire) and the scene of the riots in Belfast, whose pitiful inhabitants, Protestants and Catholics, showed me the burned-out rooms of their homes. At that time by far the worst damage had been caused to Catholic homes by Protestant mobs ... In Derry I was handed over by my guards to the representatives of the no-go area in the Bogside. I was utterly alone and unprotected, but they all treated me hospitably, feeding me lavishly with chicken sandwiches and beer as they aired their grievances, imaginary and real. For me, the whole experience was a searing one and, spiritually, tore me apart. I had immediately afterwards to report what I had seen to the Tory conference, and I almost broke down in describing what I had seen and heard. My own family connection with the place no doubt explains the depth of my feeling, but what chiefly shocked me was the sheer evidence of mutual hatred exposed by the burned-out living-rooms and shattered windows ...'[8]

Hogg was escorted around the Bogside by Doherty and also got to meet Keenan. Doherty was unimpressed by Hogg who 'insisted that Catholics in Northern Ireland were exaggerating their woes and that their lives were considerably better than those of many other people throughout the world'.[9]

In his memoirs, Hogg said that when he visited 'the Protestant areas of Londonderry', he was shown places 'by the families where people had actually been done to death'. Yet during 14–16 August 1969 no Protestants were killed in Derry. Two Protestants were killed in Belfast.[10] Meanwhile James Callaghan had no faith in the RUC and was relying upon two police officers he had sent to Northern Ireland, Robert Mark and Douglas Osmond, to act as his eyes and ears. They had reported back to him that the RUC 'was obsessed with the belief that the rioting was the result of a deep IRA plot'.[11] Callaghan's men also noted that the RUC had a siege mentality which was 'a hangover from the IRA menace of the past'.

The unionist politicians at Stormont shared the RUC's fixation about 'a deep IRA plot', including the new premier, Chichester-Clark. During the 1956–62 Border Campaign, Stormont had interned IRA suspects. Brian Faulkner, who was now in Chichester-Clark's cabinet, had served as minister for home affairs in 1959 when he had deployed internment, a tactic unionists believed had crushed the IRA.

In August 1969 Chichester-Clark ordered the RUC to round up suspected republicans under the Special Powers Act, as the Stormont government believed the IRA was responsible for the upheaval that had broken out across Northern Ireland. One of those arrested was Billy McMillen from West Belfast who had taken part in the Border Campaign, and had been interned previously for four years.

Also arrested were Malachy McGurran, an IRA man from Lurgan who later joined the Official IRA; Prionsias Mac Airt, a Belfast IRA volunteer who helped found the Provisional IRA and edit its newspaper, and Martin Meehan, an Ardoyne IRA man who became a senior Provisional leader.

Callaghan had been informed of the arrests by Keenan, during his visit to the Bogside in August 1969 and had agreed to intervene to secure their release. Callaghan also met with the Stormont cabinet during the visit. He found he could get along with most of them just fine. One person he didn't warm to, however, was Stormont's attorney-general, Basil Kelly, a key figure in the roundup of McMillen and the others. Callaghan found him to be a 'most difficult right-wing gentleman'. Callaghan recalls how he had to be 'very rough with him the next day over some men they had arrested under the Special Powers Act after the rioting and whom I suggested should either be charged or released. That was one of the few occasions when the iron fist came out of the velvet glove'.[12]

During this visit, Callaghan identified Brian Faulkner as a force to be reckoned with. He noted how he 'sat at the end of the table and said very little at that meeting, although it was clear from his occasional intervention that Chichester-Clark knew even then that he had got to carry Faulkner with him in everything he did.'[13]

A few days later Callaghan dined with the Stormont cabinet. 'We talked about our hobbies and interests and the state of the harvest and who was going sailing that weekend – all far removed from the real problems. The only item of political interest during lunch was that Faulkner, who was sitting on my right, leaned over and whispered that since my last meeting with them the Cabinet had agreed to release those detainees held under the Special Powers Act who were not going to be charged. This was good news because it was something I had pressed for and it suggested that I might have an easier passage with the Cabinet than I feared.'[14] The men were soon released.

Despite these promising signs, after Callaghan returned to London, the expulsion of nationalists from their homes in Belfast continued. A number were burned out in September. That same month thousands of loyalists gathered on the Shankill intending to march on Unity Flats, but were stopped by British soldiers.

***

The following month Callaghan brought in Sir Arthur Young, a former commissioner of the City of London Police, to take charge of the RUC as inspector-general. When Callaghan returned to the Bogside on 9 October for a two-day visit, a favourable wind was gathering behind his back. Paddy Devlin recalls that he met Callaghan and Young in the Conway Hotel at Dunree the following morning 'The civil rights MPs had been invited for breakfast. As we were leaving this, Callaghan gripped my arm and called Sir Arthur Young over. "This is my man. I want you to look after Arthur. He should be in retirement but is staying on to sort out Ulster for me. He cannot do it without your help".'[15]

Callaghan brought Young into the Bogside where he introduced him to a cheering crowd. 'This is Sir Arthur Young. He's going to look after you. "Oh no," said Sir Arthur, all London bobby and affability, "they are going to look after me." There were more cheers'. Unarmed British military police were sent into the Bogside until a reformed RUC was ready to take over.[16]

Young sought to win over the confidence of the minority community in Belfast too. Jim Sullivan was instrumental in inviting him to address the Central CDC at the Long Bar in the middle of republican Leeson Street, along with District Inspector Frank Lagan. Tom Conaty, a businessman and the Andersontown delegate to the Central CDC, collected him in his car in Springfield and brought him down to the meeting. 'You had to walk up a dusty staircase to get to the room where we met and it was hung with a photograph of the McMahons, a family who had allegedly been murdered by the RUC. He walked into the room – you could hardly see the walls for cigarette smoke – a big fellow, well over 6 foot. And when he walked into the room, I don't know why it was, but every man got up and applauded.'[17]

On 10 October 1969, the Hunt report, which had been commissioned by the British government, recommended disarming the RUC and the disbandment of the B-Specials. This ignited loyalist rioting during which RUC Constable Victor Arbuckle was shot dead by the UVF. Two other civilians died in Belfast. 300 people were arrested. Eamonn McCann wrote:

> It was, by any estimation, a victory for the Catholics. Any lingering doubt was removed on the night of 10–11 October, when the army in Belfast smashed a riot on the Protestant Shankill Road. The Hunt report had driven the Protestants raging mad. It had castigated and disarmed their police force and abolished their B-Specials and, by extension, humiliated their whole community. They came out now in their thousands and flung themselves down the Shankill to vent their wrath and frustration on Unity

> Flats. A policeman who stood in their way was shot dead. The [British] army moved in and battered its way up the Shankill with bloodthirsty enthusiasm. In the shooting two Protestants were killed and a dozen wounded. Many others were beaten or kicked unconscious. Who in the Bogside could now doubt that at long last law and order was being administered impartially?[18]

Three days after Young's visit to the Central CDC in Belfast, further rioting broke out in the Shankill. By then Young was in London. In his absence, Robert Porter, the Stormont home minister, raised the temperature by declaring that the RUC would return to the Falls with military backing if the unrest continued. Young returned the following day, 16 October, and cooled matters down by going on a walkabout along the Falls where television cameras filmed him in discussion with Jim Sullivan.

Callaghan entertained a delegation from the Central CDC in October 1969 in London to deal with the pronouncement by Chichester-Clark that barricades in nationalist areas were going to be torn down. Jim Sullivan accompanied them. Callaghan was keen to avoid inflaming unionist tempers, which had already been roused by newspaper reports of a CDC meeting attended by Sullivan and Lt-Gen. Sir Ian Freeland which had appeared in an article by Tony Geraghty in *The Sunday Times*. In *A House Divided,* he describes how the meeting took place without Sullivan:

> The building of the peace line was announced by Chichester-Clark on September 8 and the Royal Engineers began work immediately. They erected a 6 foot-high curtain of corrugated iron and barbed wire which ran intermittently for about a mile and a half across

> streets and waste grounds between the Falls Road and the Shankill. Chichester-Clark then said rather peremptorily that all other barricades would have to come down at once and a deputation of Catholics promptly flew to London to demand my support for their retention. The party included three MPs – Paddy Kennedy, Paddy Devlin and Gerry Fitt – and also Father Pádraig Murphy, the parish priest of St Peter's in the Falls Road, a wonderful leader of his flock who constantly strove for peace, and Tom Conaty, a businessman. They were accompanied by Jim Sullivan, whom I knew to be a member of the IRA and whom I therefore refused to see; he waited in an ante-room.[19]

The meeting ended with a personal assurance from Callaghan that if the barricades were taken down, there would be soldiers at the end of every vulnerable street to prevent further attacks by loyalist extremists.

Tom Conaty provided a more revealing account of the meeting when he said that while Kennedy and Sullivan had left Westminster for the Irish Club they had returned later. When they did, Callaghan met Sullivan in the ante-room.

In Derry relations between the British Army and Keenan were cordial and unaffected by his membership of the IRA. As Niall Ó Dochartaigh has noted, local commanders acted 'with a great deal of autonomy and the army became immersed in the local political scene, to the extent of trying to attend meetings of the local political parties'. They became 'a political force, developing its own priorities and analyses and at times acting almost as a local administrative body'.[20] Ó Dochartaigh also points out how Keenan, 'the most prominent of the older Republicans, was one of those who was now involved in regular contacts with the army and British politicians'.

Ó Dochartaigh believed the level of harmony between soldiers and locals evident at this time was 'possible not only because the IRA accepted the authority of the DCDA [Derry Citizens Defence Association] but also because there was little opportunity for friction to develop on the ground ... these troops did not stop or search or question people ... The almost total absence of "policing" by the army was crucial to the maintenance of friendly relations ... If anything, people in the Bogside and Creggan seem to have been more annoyed at being stopped and questioned by DCDA Peace Corps members in their own areas who were often local youths, identified only by the white armbands they wore.'[21]

Doherty recalled that Col Todd, the officer who had accepted his offer of a truce in August 1969, 'bid farewell to Derry, and Brigadier Leng took command of the West of Northern Ireland. I soon built up a good relationship with the new commander. "Jobs are what you need around here," he said. "We have got to get jobs for the young people".' Doherty developed a high regard for the brigadier. 'There was no doubting the well-bred soldier's sincerity, or his concern for the people whom he believed history had thrust into his care.'[22] Doherty took Leng for a farewell dinner in Donegal at the end of his tour.

After Leng left, Lt-Gen. Freeland followed the practice of negotiating with the Defence Association. 'This small man, who had a twitch at the corner of his mouth, which created an illusion of a perpetual grin, had been dubbed "Smiling Death" by his soldiers'.[23]

Doherty arranged a meeting with him in the school in the heart of the Bogside. 'He arrived in a military convoy and entered the room flanked by his aides. [Tom] Canavan and I represented the Defence Association.'

However, strains were beginning to show as Seán Keenan no longer wished to engage in the talks. According to Doherty he 'was now developing his own strategy'.[24]

Unlike Belfast, the threat to the nationalist areas of Derry had primarily come from the outside. On a day-to-day basis, nationalists were far less vulnerable to the threat posed by extreme loyalists. The arrival of British troops the previous August had deterred the external threat. In addition, some of the reforms imposed on Northern Ireland by Wilson and Callaghan, such as the abolition of the B-Specials, had diminished the need for a Derry Defence Association. (It disbanded on 10 October.)

One of Keenan's last acts as a CDC leader was to participate in a meeting of defence committees which Capt. Kelly arranged for on 5 October at his brother's hotel in Bailieboro, Co. Cavan, a meeting that still generates controversy in the narrative of the Arms Crisis to this day.

8

THE BAILIEBORO DECEPTION

The deployment of the British Army by Harold Wilson had not instilled much confidence in nationalists that they were going to be protected from further attacks. Capt. Kelly was acutely aware of this. He described how there were still many nationalists, especially in 'isolated rural areas', who feared the troops might not always be on hand to rescue them. They feared that the British Army:

> was too thin on the ground to withstand concerted attacks in many widely-spaced areas. It was against that background that delegations came south to the government of the Republic looking for support. Having gone away feeling that in the last analysis the south would not leave them defenceless, they were psychologically prepared to withstand greater pressure without resorting to the extreme of violence. Indeed, many people in close touch with the situation in the North were aware that this psychological link had already been as effective as a restraining factor in some potentially ugly situations.[1]

It was against this background that a meeting between the CDCs and G2 was arranged for 5 October 1969 at Bailieboro, Co. Cavan. The meeting took place in the Republic because of the order Col Hefferon had issued to his officers not to cross the border. The colonel and Capt. Kelly met Charles Haughey at his home on 3 October 1969. 'The proposed

Bailieboro meeting and the question of how much it would cost was discussed,' Capt. Kelly wrote later. 'I suggested that £150 should cover it. In the end, Mr Haughey arranged that I be paid £500 to cover the meeting, with any balance to be used for other subsequent expenses'.[2]

At the meeting on 5 October Capt. Kelly met with fifteen representatives of the various CDCs to listen to their pleas for help. The delegates included Seán Keenan, Jim Sullivan and Billy Kelly. In his evidence at his trial, the captain explained that all but one of the Six Counties had been represented but that one of the other delegates stood in for it. The representatives reiterated that their communities urgently required arms, training and protection. After the meeting finished, he was satisfied that any distribution of arms to the CDCs would be used for defensive purposes only.[3]

In the report he submitted to Col Hefferon, he described how the issue of training was considered of 'paramount importance' and that a lot of time was spent on a discussion of the training course which had taken place at Fort Dunree 'particularly, the reason for its abandonment'. His explanation that it was only being postponed due to media interest 'was accepted, but the meeting emphasised that it would have to be resumed under some other guise. Very rationally, all present considered training essential before there could be any question of distributing arms, and this request for training was the second major element of my report'.[4]

The Deceiver became aware of the Bailieboro meeting in advance and seized the opportunity to feed Philip McMahon a confection of deceit about it. Peter Berry was in Mount

Carmel hospital when he learned on Saturday 4 October from Fleming that it was about to take place:

> I received information which alarmed me. It was to the effect that the egregious Capt. Kelly had had meetings with the Chief of Staff of the IRA, Cathal Goulding and that he had set up a meeting for that weekend in Bailieboro with persons from both sides of the Border with a known history in the IRA. From the information already communicated in recent weeks it looked as if an officer group in the [Irish] Army were collaborating with members of an organisation which had been proclaimed by government Order to be unlawful and who were engaging in violence contrary to the declared views of Government.[5]

This information was erroneous in a number of respects. First, Bailieboro was not a meeting of the IRA. Second, Goulding did not organise it. Third, the delegates were from the 'Six Counties', not 'from both sides of the Border'. Alarmed, Berry phoned Ó Moráin but got no reply. He then rang the Taoiseach's number but without success. 'I phoned Mr Haughey: he would be with me within the hour. His arrival, in time for afternoon tea, caused more excitement amongst the nurses than the visit of the President. I told him of Capt. Kelly's goings-on and of the visit planned for Bailieboro. He did not seem unduly perturbed about Capt. Kelly but was quite inquisitive about what I knew of Goulding. I felt reassured.'[6]

Haughey undoubtedly kept Berry in the dark about his familiarity with the meeting because he knew full well that it was a G2 operation and, as such, was none of Berry's business. Berry had tried and failed to take over military intelligence a few years earlier but to no avail and hence was the last person

G2 wanted sticking an oar into their affairs. In addition, Haughey would have been in breach of the Official Secrets Act had he disclosed details of a G2 operation to Berry. It is also possible that Col Hefferon warned him about his suspicions that Patrick Crinnion, a C3 officer at Garda HQ, was an MI6 agent.[7] Berry worked hand in glove with C3. Hence, by talking freely to Berry, MI6 might have learned about the government's secret activities *via* C3 or some other leak.

If, as was to be alleged later, the IRA *qua* IRA was meeting at Bailieboro – which it wasn't – and if Haughey was in league with any faction of the IRA – which he wasn't – he would surely have cancelled the meeting upon discovering Berry knew about it. Instead, he let it proceed. His behaviour demonstrates that he knew it was a meeting between G2 and the CDCs, not the IRA. Moreover, Haughey's decision to let it go ahead protected the special branch informer from exposure. Ironically, it was The Deceiver he was protecting.

On 16 October, Fleming paid another visit to Berry at Mount Carmel hospital and provided a report which purported to describe what had transpired at Bailieboro. Berry was so alarmed he 'felt that the Taoiseach should be told immediately'. Lynch visited him the following day:

> I did not have a 100 per cent recollection of my conversation with the Taoiseach [on 17 October] as I was a bit muzzy and bloody from the medical tests but I am quite certain that I told him of Capt. Kelly's prominent part in the Bailieboro meeting with known members of the IRA, of his possession of a wad of money, of his standing drinks and of the sum of money – £50,000 – that would be made available for the purchase of arms. I remember a

> conjecture of the Taoiseach as to where could they possibly get it and my suggestion that perhaps Mr Y or Mr Z, two millionaires of the Taca Group, might put up the money and the Taoiseach's observation that those boys didn't give it up easily.[8]

When Fleming testified before the Dáil's Public Accounts Committee (PAC) in 1971 he portrayed the delegates at Bailieboro as bedfellows of Goulding's dominant Marxist wing of the IRA:

> First, in about the last week of September 1969 Captain Kelly met Cathal Goulding, Chief-of-Staff of the IRA, in Virginia, Co. Cavan, and he agreed to get him a regular supply of arms and ammunition for use in Northern Ireland. He also promised to provide training facilities for Northern members of the IRA in Gormanston Camp. Captain Kelly attended an IRA meeting in Cavan in the first week of October 1969 and he then promised the IRA to give them £50,000 by instalments. To prove that he was not bluffing he promised to pay the first instalment within three days.

There has never been any evidence of such a payment, aside from the word of The Deceiver. Fleming continued to tell the PAC that:

> On or about October 7, 1969 [Capt. Kelly] paid over £7,000 at Cavan Town to Cathal Goulding. During the last week of November 1969, he paid over a further sum of £1,000 ... As far as I know it was to Cathal Goulding. I cannot swear to that, though. In the early part of December 1969, he paid over a further £1,500. Again, I am not sure, but I think it was to Cathal Goulding. Those are the sums which as far as I know Captain Kelly paid over.[9]

Fleming told PAC that since all of his information emanated from confidential sources, he was not at liberty to reveal them.

Capt. Kelly pointed out that Fleming 'said that he knew "for a fact" of at least one meeting attended by Rory Brady [i.e. Ruairí Ó Brádaigh], a senior colleague of Cathal Goulding's at the time and, later, President of Provisional Sinn Féin'. Capt. Kelly stressed that:

> All the above evidence was false. It was assumedly fed to Mr Fleming and his confrères by the IRA 'informants', because it suited the purposes of an element of the IRA to do so in the fraught circumstances of an impending split in that organisation. It is worthy of note that all the 'crimes' of which the Chief Superintendent [i.e. Fleming] accused me, allegedly took place during the pre-Christmas period of 1969 in the run-up to the end of year, the time of the IRA split. From then on, this particular, well-nurtured line of disinformation went out of operation. One could speculate and come up with many answers as to why that happened, but, one thing is certain, Chief Superintendent Fleming's aptitude for peddling hearsay as genuine straightforward evidence was not as avidly fed, if fed at all, from then on.[10]

Ruairí Ó Brádaigh was adamant that he did not meet Capt. Kelly until long after the events surrounding the Arms Crisis, and then at an unplanned, chance encounter at the Four Courts in Dublin in the mid-1970s.[11]

In addition, a local Special Branch man stumbled upon the meeting at Bailieboro accidentally and rang in a report to Dublin Castle. This officer, who was a heavy drinker, was not sober at the time and was less than discreet: he made his report within earshot of passing members of the public at Kelly's hotel.[12] This minor débâcle, however, served to protect The Deceiver as many believed the drunken officer was the source of the leak about the meeting. Clearly, the officer did not supply the advance information about the meeting.

The false, but alarming, reports about Bailieboro instigated a merry-go-round of enquiries which rotated all the way back to Capt. Kelly. The carousel began with the Taoiseach quizzing Gibbons about Bailieboro. Next, Gibbons spoke to Col Hefferon who in turn questioned Capt. Kelly. Col Hefferon's testimony to PAC reveals: 'I am not clear specifically on that date – it could be November – Mr Gibbons asked me to see him and told me that the Taoiseach had had a report from Mr Berry that Capt. Kelly had attended a meeting at Bailieboro ... at which there were IRA people present, that he had waved a wad of notes around promising money to them.'

Capt. Kelly was aghast at how he was being portrayed:

> There was talk of a table and of my moving money across it or over it. There was a suggestion that there was a surfeit of alcohol consumed ... Even the factual details were wrong. As far as I recollect there was no table available in the room, and I certainly sat on a chair in the corner without the benefit of a table. There was no money whatsoever produced at the meeting, and as regards a surfeit of alcohol, the cost of the meeting alone indicated otherwise. Fifteen people attended, some of whom stayed overnight, while there was a meal available for those who required it on the evening of the meeting. The total bill came to £35, which did not give much scope for extras apart from the fact that those at the meeting were all mature men who had come long distances on very serious business and to whom the availability or otherwise of alcohol was of minor consequence.[13]

Having clarified what actually happened from Capt. Kelly, Col Hefferon reported back to Gibbons and assumed that Gibbons then 'reported back to the Taoiseach'. Nothing further was heard about the issue leading Capt. Kelly to the conclusion that Berry's 'complaint had been rejected by both Mr Gibbons and the Taoiseach'.[14]

Kevin Boland described in his book *Up Dev* how, during the period August 1969 to May 1970, 'the activities of Captain J. Kelly, as an [Irish] Army Intelligence Officer, in relation to the Six Counties were discussed several times at government meetings and they were answered for by the Minister for Defence. My recollection is that he was first mentioned in the early stages, probably as early as August, when background information in relation to what we read in the papers came mainly from Neil Blaney. The Minister for Defence, Mr Gibbons, gave a generally similar picture based on Captain Kelly's reports'.[15]

Somewhere along the line the gardaí asked their minister, Mícheál Ó Moráin, to raise their concerns about Capt. Kelly's activities at cabinet. In *Up Dev* Boland recalls that Ó Moráin's officials, i.e. Peter Berry and his deputy Andrew Ward, were complaining that Capt. Kelly was meeting the 'wrong kind of people and this struck a sympathetic chord in the Taoiseach and some Ministers. The Minister for Defence always contended that it was what the besieged community were thinking and feeling we needed to know and that information from the "authorities" would be useless'.[16]

Specifically, the meeting at the hotel in Bailieboro came up at least once while Gibbons was describing the role of Capt. Kelly to his cabinet colleagues in terms of information gathering. According to Boland, 'This made sense to me. We could read British propaganda in the British papers and hear it from the B.B.C. and any "information" from the Department of Justice, through regular channels, would be in this category. It was as a result of one of these discussions (probably, I think, in connection with the meeting of representatives from all parts of the Six Counties held in a hotel in Bailieboro) that it was decided that the Minister for Justice should arrange for the collection of information also by his department and [Ó Moráin] informed the Government that two detectives had been sent to the Six Counties for the purpose.'[17]

Despite this, when Gibbons testified in the Four Courts against Capt. Kelly, Haughey and the other defendants the following year, he denied any knowledge of the Bailieboro meeting. When he appeared at the Public Accounts Committee (PAC) inquiry into the distribution of State funds to those in Northern Ireland in 1971, he maintained this position, claiming: 'I am absolutely certain that I was never informed of the Bailieboro meeting and that the reference to it in the Four Courts is the first reference I can recall.' Also that, 'There was no question of a complaint from the Taoiseach that I can recall – absolutely none'.[18] The taoiseach and many of his ministers knew well that Gibbons was committing blatant perjury yet only Boland ever called him out for it, at least in public

In 1980 Lynch acknowledged that he visited Berry at Mount Carmel but offered an alternative account of what had transpired. His version has been faithfully relayed by his biographer, Dermot Keogh and argues that Berry, who was receiving medical attention after suffering a series of seizures, was too disorientated to have had a proper recall of the exchange that took place whereas Lynch – who was not on medication – had a clear mind and his recollection was that Berry had not informed him about Bailieboro.[19] However, the foregoing explanation fails to account for the testimony Col Hefferon gave to PAC, namely that Gibbons told him that Lynch 'had had a report from Mr Berry that Captain Kelly had attended a meeting at Bailieboro'.[20]

The disinformation from The Deceiver continued to flow thick and fast after Bailieboro. In a further instalment, delivered on 22 October 1969, the special branch reiterated to Berry that Haughey and Blaney were involved in an operation to obtain arms for the IRA. Peter Berry later alleged to the attorney-general's office that:

> This information in detail was given from time to time to Ó Moráin who said that he hesitated to believe that Mr. Haughey and Mr. Blaney could be actively associated with the IRA. I suggested to him (I was then in Mount Carmel Hospital) to have a conference with the Commissioner and the top Special Branch officer in order to hear the details direct from them. He did so and saw the Commissioner and Chief Superintendent Fleming in the week following 7th December. Chief-Superintendent Fleming says that he showed the Minister his notes ... Afterwards the Minister informed Mr Ward, Assistant Secretary, who, as he knew, was aware generally of these matters, that he had asked the Commissioner to have matters relating to names and exact dates of payment of monies to the I.R.A. checked. He commented adversely on the fact that the Garda officers did not know the occupation of [redacted].

Berry was discharged from Mount Carmel on 3 November but went on convalescent leave until 12 January 1970. Yet his mind remained occupied by his work. In early December, he contacted Garda Commissioner Michael Wymes and urged him to submit a formal report to Ó Moráin about Blaney and Haughey. A number of meetings involving Ó Moráin, Wymes and Fleming took place. In his statement to the attorney-general, Berry stated:

> On my return from sick leave on 5th January 1970, I was informed by the Assistant Secretary that, as far as he knew, the foregoing matter had not been followed up. I checked with the Commissioner who said that the information as to persons, dates and payments had been checked and confirmed by the S Branch and that he had been awaiting an indication from the Minister that he wished to resume the discussion. I drew the matter to the Minister's attention who said that in a serious matter of this kind involving Mr. Haughey and Mr. Blaney he felt that he would like further time to think the matter over. I said that I would bring the matter to his notice again in a couple of week's [*sic*] time and I reminded him of the danger that Special Branch might start "leaking" information in view of the spate of armed robberies that had taken place in which the lives of Gardaí were endangered. At the end of January or early February I again reminded the Minister of the alleged involvement of the two Ministers and that I had been warned that within the Special Branch and in Garda Headquarters criticism of Government was becoming caustic and was mounting.[21]

Ó Moráin probably suspected – or knew – that Capt. Kelly's activities had been sanctioned by Gibbons and were therefore none of his department's business. If nothing else, Ó Moráin would have heard the captain's name being mentioned by Gibbons at cabinet meetings in connection with intelligence gathering missions and realised he was about G2's work.

Ó Moráin was also keeping Lynch apprised of what he was being told.

When Col Hefferon was told the garda version of what had allegedly happened at Bailieboro, he described it as 'pure poppycock'. When Berry 'related this back to the "S Branch" the comment was: "Christ, Hefferon must be in the swim, too".'[22] It speaks volumes about the mesmerising sway The Deceiver held over the special branch that they were prepared to believe that a distinguished officer with an unblemished record was a traitor.

Put simply, the behaviour of Lynch, Ó Moráin and Gibbons throughout this period indicates that they knew about the Bailieboro meeting; more significantly, that Capt. Kelly's attendance at it was part of a legitimate G2 intelligence gathering exercise. They must also have realised that the special branch's informers were, at best, unreliable.

Decades later, Capt. Kelly uncovered the Planning Board on Northern Ireland Operations report of 27 September 1969, and pencilled a number of remarks on the copies he made for himself. When he came to the section which envisaged infiltrating 'elements armed and equipped to [organise], train and advise Catholic and Nationalist groups in vulnerable areas far from the Border (e.g. BELFAST)' he noted that: 'My job [was] to pinpoint such "elements".' He wrote 'N.B.' against the proposal to supply 'military training' and 'arms, ammunition and equipment ... to nationalist elements in Northern Ireland'.

The Deceiver – now long since deceased – must be laughing in his grave that his yarn about the pledged sum of £50,000 for the Marxist wing of the IRA is still doing the rounds with no less a figure than Des O'Malley reporting it as fact in his memoirs. O'Malley pronounced that in:

> October 1969 [Capt.] Kelly met senior IRA figures at a meeting in Baileyborough (*sic*), County Cavan, and pledged £50,000 for the purchase of weapons.[23]

The special branch was not the only intelligence-gathering organisation that was trying to monitor the covert manoeuvres of Capt. Kelly and his political masters. An old foe had awoken from a slumber with a renewed and vigorous interest in what was now afoot in Ireland.

9

HER MAJESTY'S SPIES IN IRELAND

Sir Dick White, the Intelligence coordinator at the cabinet office, 1968 to 1972, sat at the summit of Britain's sprawling intelligence community, the various branches of which were monitoring the dealings between the Irish government and the CDCs. Uniquely, White had served as both director-general of MI5 and chief of MI6, two of the main players in Ireland once the *Troubles* got underway. MI5 (attached to the Home Office) led the intelligence march on Northern Ireland in 1968 while MI6 (attached to the Foreign and Commonwealth Office) concentrated on the Republic. White worked with Sir Edward Peck, the chairman of the JIC, who had attended the meeting between Patrick Hillery and Michael Stewart, Britain's foreign secretary, in early August 1969 in London.

Another of the big beasts roaming about the thickets of the intelligence jungle was Sir Maurice Oldfield, who had served as White's deputy chief at MI6 in the 1960s and was still in that post when the *Troubles* erupted. Oldfield assumed control of Irish affairs because his new boss, Sir John Ogilvy Rennie, did not share the same experience as he in the dark arts of the secret world. Rennie, who had been a surprise replacement for White, had a diplomatic and propaganda background whereas Oldfield had participated in deception campaigns during the Second World War; fought anti-British forces in Palestine after it; and monitored the flow of weapons and money to the communist guerrillas fighting the British in Malaya in the 1950s. And, if all this wasn't enough to square up to the unruly Irish, he had a good idea of what it took to run a paramilitary operation due to his knowledge of MI6's guerrilla campaign against Albania in the 1950s gleaned during his stint as deputy chief of MI6's counter-espionage directorate, R5.

As a constituent part of the UK, the British government could not send an ambassador to represent its interests in Northern Ireland. Instead, the cabinet dispatched a hybrid diplomat-civil servant with the bespoke title of 'UK Representative of the British Government to Northern Ireland', who became known as the UKREP, to Belfast. The office of the UKREP soon assumed an espionage role. The first UKREP, Oliver Wright, was a Foreign Office diplomat who had had extensive dealings with the British Intelligence community. He later became ambassador to Washington.

Ronnie Burroughs, a card-carrying member of MI6, followed Wright in March 1970. What did he do to merit the posting to Northern Ireland? From what little we know, Burroughs was a rather devious operator. In the late 1960s MI6 was supporting Nigeria's military against Biafran secessionists. Independent observers were assigned to monitor breaches of human rights. Burroughs managed to plant at least one MI6 agent inside the observation team to feed intelligence back to London, which was exploited to advance the interests of the Nigerian military. James Callaghan, who appointed both Wright and Burroughs, chose not to mention Burroughs in *A Divided House*, whereas Wright was featured. Sir Howard Smith who went on to become D-G of MI5 in 1978 replaced Burroughs.

Robin Ramsay of the Northern Ireland Civil Service (NICS) dealt with all three UKREPs. He describes in his memoirs how the office they ran was 'more like an embassy of the Soviet Union in a satellite state' than a liaison office with London and began to notice that 'the people who ran it had intelligence backgrounds.'

One of the thornier issues to confront the UKREPs and the various British Intelligence agencies hovering around them was the presence of G2 officers on their terrain. Amongst other things, G2 was trying to gather information about the RUC. MI5's official historian, Christopher Andrew, noted that G2 did not 'even possess an organisation chart of the RUC and made strenuous efforts to assemble one based chiefly on gossip of varying reliability – only to discover that the information it required was freely available in Northern Ireland official publications which were on sale in Dublin'.[1] Contrary to Andrew's condescending portrayal of G2 as bungling provincials, G2 was busy reporting to the Irish government about what nationalists were thinking and forging links with the CDCs, not to mention talent spotting for fifth columnists lest the Irish Army should ever be directed to cross the border. In another success, in December, G2 learned about attempts by a Liverpool arms dealer to purchase a stock of bolt action .303 surplus Irish Army rifles and ammunition from the Irish Army for the UVF.

Despite the shock waves generated by the Arms Crisis in May 1970, G2 continued to spy on Northern Ireland and, as a result, we now know that MI6 had at least one spy in Dublin at the time of the crisis. On 17 June 1970, UKREP Burroughs wrote to the FCO making reference to a delicate 'source' who had supplied information about Irish military intelligence activities in Northern Ireland:

> If the function of these [Irish military intelligence] Officers is as innocent as is suggested [their work] can be carried out by ordinary political observers operating quite openly. If there is a clandestine element then I do not see how we can tolerate them. We certainly would not do so in any other part of the UK … Owing to the *delicacy of the source* it would of course not be possible to reveal to the Irish their own acknowledgement of the presence of these Officers.[2]

The Dublin source had probably been reporting to London long before June 1970. The use of the word 'delicacy' about his position raises the prospect that the informer was the holder of a senior position within the Irish state security apparatus.

Before all this, in late September and early October 1969, Charles Haughey tried to open a back channel to the British government. His emissary was Constantine Fitzgibbon, a former British military intelligence officer who was then living in Killiney. Fitzgibbon, born in 1919, had served in the British and American armies during the Second World War. By the end of it, he had become a major in military intelligence and a specialist on the subject of the German general staff. He was the author of a number of books and in 1969 he published *Out of the Lion's Paw, Ireland Wins Her Freedom*, a book about the War of Independence. He also published *High Heroics*, a fictional account of the activities of Michael Collins. Haughey's proposal was that London should drop the pretence that 'Stormont still existed' and talk with Dublin instead.

Haughey made little progress with London *via* Fitzgibbon and subsequently concentrated his efforts on Ambassador Andrew Gilchrist in Dublin. Gilchrist was an experienced diplomat-spy. Born in 1910, he had served with Force 136 of the Special Executive Office in Siam during the Second World War. After his retirement in 1970, Gilchrist wrote *Bangkok Top Secret Force 136 At War* about his experiences. Gilchrist was also a propaganda expert and had worked hand in glove with the Information Research Department (IRD), the Foreign Office's black propaganda machine. Gilchrist also served for a while as chairman of the Asian Joint Intelligence Committee. He had become ambassador to Ireland in 1967 and in June of the following year the special branch learned that Saor Éire, a republican splinter group, intended to kidnap or attack him, and he was placed under heavy armed guard. He accepted this with humour, reporting that his imposing bulk made him a good target. He described his special branch bodyguards as 'not merely efficient but tactful and friendly in a high degree".[3] He also developed an excellent relationship with the head of the special branch, John Fleming, an officer he deemed to be highly efficient.

***

As Downing Street continued to focus more on Northern Ireland in 1969, Sir Burke Trend, cabinet secretary at Downing Street, instructed the JIC to set up a sub-committee to deal with the emerging developments. It became known as the Current Intelligence Group on Northern Ireland and was up and running by 30 April 1969. By June 1969 it had concluded that the potential for further disorder emanated from the 'interaction of three distinct groups': the IRA, the Civil Rights movement and the 'ultra-Protestant' supporters of the Rev. Ian Paisley. Sharing the all-pervasive obsession of the intelligence community with Soviet intrigue, it noted the 'increasing Communist influence in the IRA and Trotskyite infiltration of the Civil Rights movement' as if the KGB was trying to manipulate NICRA.

Gilchrist was able to provide London with an accurate picture of Goulding's efforts to shunt the republican movement, of which the IRA was the central cog, towards left-wing political agitation. In September 1969 Gilchrist was invited to share his views with the JIC in person. When he did, he emphasised that after the turmoil of the previous August, the IRA had become a threat to the stability of Ireland and therefore to the UK. His views were met with genteel scepticism. He also argued that the willingness and ability of the Dublin government to counteract the IRA had been affected by the loyalist violence in Northern Ireland, again something that was met with doubt. Gilchrist also felt that Britain should explore a new arrangement for Northern Ireland with which the Dublin government could be associated and which would be acceptable to all sides.

Haughey succeeded in luring Gilchrist to his home 'Abbeville' for discussions in early October 1969. On 4 October 1969, Gilchrist reported to the FCO in London that Haughey had argued that the reunification of the island was the best solution to the overall problem. He impressed upon Gilchrist that there was nothing he would not sacrifice, including the position of the Catholic church, in order to achieve a United Ireland; he would even support re-joining the Commonwealth and the granting of access to Irish military bases to the Royal Navy and also NATO membership.

Haughey was hardly acting as a back channel for Lynch. According to Gilchrist, 'It was impossible for me to discuss such a question [i.e. the negotiations Haughey was suggesting] since I did not know what the Irish government had in mind'. Further, Gilchrist advised London that 'if it came to a planned contact for serious discussion, Haughey's rivalry with Lynch would raise a question'.[4]

Haughey called upon Fitzgibbon again a few weeks later in an effort to forge a link with Anthony Crossland, a member of Harold Wilson's cabinet, but nothing came of that endeavour either. Secretly Fitzgibbon was also acting as an 'agent of influence' for the British embassy. Gilchrist gave the game away in a communication to London, which has been released by Britain's National Archive:

> After leaving Haughey Fitzgibbon met me and asked how in the circumstances he could best angle his articles or which points he should emphasise ... I know Fitzgibbon well enough to be sure he is not in the pay of the Irish ...[5]

It is not clear what, if anything, Haughey knew about Fitzgibbon's secret role as a British agent and whether or not he spied on Haughey for the British.

On another occasion Gilchrist tempered his faith in Fitzgibbon a little by advising London that:

> Though [Fitzgibbon] has so far been of considerable use to me, he is now applying for Irish nationality so that he is an interested party as well as being emotionally involved.[6]

Meanwhile, Gilchrist was in receipt of intelligence about a number of people from Northern Ireland with whom Haughey was in contact. A lot of Gilchrist's information had been supplied by Conor Cruise O'Brien, an Irish Labour Party TD who shared a constituency with Charles Haughey. [O'Brien was the Labour Party's then spokesman on Northern Ireland, and later a government minister in the FG-Labour coalition, 1973–77]. He had obtained the information from a report compiled by John Devine, the public relations officer of his party. O'Brien passed the details in the report – if not actual copies of it – to Gilchrist.

G2 had established a base in Monaghan, almost certainly as a result of the order which Col Hefferon had issued at the end of September 1969 forbidding his officers from crossing the border. It masqueraded as an office of NICRA. Members of the Irish Labour Party soon observed the secretive goings-on at it and by the time their perception of what was afoot percolated through their grapevine to Gilchrist, it had become a pot pourri of facts, distortions, speculation and political bias.

In fairness to Devine he acknowledged, in the report – which he entitled *Aspects of the Six County Situation* – that 'Much of the information which follows has been checked out by me, and found to be fairly accurate. What is contained, unchecked, is passed on because it comes from what are described as 'usually reliable' sources. The historical significance of the document is therefore not that it is an accurate record of the events it purports to describe, rather that it provides an insight into the type of information that was reaching Gilchrist and therefore MI6 about the alleged intrigues of Blaney, Boland, Haughey and Gibbons.[7]

With the benefit of the passage of time, however, it is possible to sift some diamonds from the rough scattered about the Devine Memorandum. For example, Devine had managed to get wind of the fact that the first edition of the *Voice of the North*, a propaganda publication sponsored by the Dublin government, was about to be launched:

> On Friday next the first of a series of weekly propaganda newspapers will be circulated and distributed in the North. The paper will be bitterly anti-Unionist. The committee of management involves some of those named on the Monaghan committee; Blaney, Boland and Haughey's agent, and others, also known to me. The paper will be printed in the *Anglo-Celt*, Cavan. Five or six vans, necessary for transporting the newspaper, have already been acquired.

Since the *Voice of the North* was first published on Sunday 12 October, the Devine Memorandum was probably completed in early October 1969. The 'agent' of Messrs Blaney, Boland and Haughey was Seamus Brady.

The document also contained a number of references to G2 activities:

> 3. In the first (and current) issue of the magazine 'This Week', it is reported that Irish Army intelligence officers and British Army intelligence have exchanged visits into each other's territory. Whatever about the British, the Irish certainly have been visiting the North regularly since October 5 last (1968).
>
> 4. Since the recent major outbreaks of trouble an 'agent' of Messrs Haughey, Blaney and Boland, has been conducting these military intelligence personnel (Captains Doolan and Duggan) on trips behind the barricades. Contacts are being built up and

ammunition and money has been distributed. Generally the contacts are among the Republican element in the North, who have more or less broken with the Dublin HQ of the IRA, principally because this 'agent' can deliver what the IRA cannot. The [Goulding faction of the] IRA is highly worried and indignant at the influence of which these Fianna Fáil people are having among Northern Republicans; the possibility of retaliation is likely from the Dublin end. Fianna Fáil have now established a chain of links from Belfast and Derry, including places like Dungannon, Newry, Armagh, Coalisland, Omagh and in other places where their sphere of contacts up to now has been negligible. Their aid is being accepted.

5. The 'agent' (for want of a better word) has now spread his net to broaden the scope of his activities. He is set up, in Monaghan town, with the approval of the Government Ministers already mentioned, and with the aid of their finance, what is known as the Monaghan Civil Rights Office of the Northern Ireland Civil Rights Association. This office is located in what was the Monaghan HQ of the Fianna Fáil Party. It is understood that the Northern Ireland Civil Rights Association has no control over the activities of this office and the link with the NICRA is only established in that the committee members are also members of NICRA. The link with Fianna Fáil is only established by (1) the building in which it is located and (2) that NICRA has no overriding control or responsibility and (3) because I know it was set up with the aid and connivance of Blaney, Haughey and Boland. This fact is only known by others, including Sinn Féin and the IRA. It is doubtful if many, (or any) of the people who are associated with this Monaghan organisation are very aware that it is a front organisation for Fianna Fáil.

12. Meanwhile the activities of the Monaghan Civil Rights Office continue to proliferate. Last Saturday week it organised a

> meeting outside the GPO at which a wide range of northern political thought (and non-thought) was represented right across the board from Eamonn McCann to Ivan Cooper and Austin Currie. There were some calls to arms from the platform.

Another passage described how Currie was allegedly involved in an attempt to take over the NICRA in a conspiracy with Fianna Fáil, albeit that at 'this stage it is difficult to tie in Currie with the Fianna Fáil front, especially on the Blaney, Haughey and Boland side.' The irony is that Currie became a Fine Gael TD and, in 1990, its candidate for the presidency of Ireland.

On 10 November 1969, Gilchrist sent a confidential telegram to the FCO, describing the mysterious machinations in Monaghan. He identified O'Brien as his informant and the information reflected the content of the Devine Memorandum. It described an 'organisation in Monaghan' which was 'quite a small one' and that it had been 'set up by Haughey with party funds'. Shrewdly, O'Brien or Gilchrist, or perhaps both of them, had deduced that: 'It contains an Intelligence Unit, where Irish Army Intelligence Officers brief and debrief visitors to and from the North.'[8]

Gilchrist's interest also focused on the allegation that Haughey and his associates had prepared lists of civil rights Defence Units (*sic*) in Northern Ireland and of their requirements 'for self-defence' should 'further disorders break out'. This was a fair stab at what G2 was up to, save that G2's tendrils were reaching out to the CDCs, not civil rights groups, though there was an overlap between the two.

Gilchrist proceeded to explain how, according to O'Brien, the Monaghan organisation was hoping to provide support to the defence units 'by way of weapons, radio sets and personnel'. O'Brien also reported that, 'numerous weapons have already been supplied, not on the responsibility of the [Monaghan] organisation itself but by people who have been given access to its lists.' This however, was unconfirmed, 'being only my own attempt to reconcile conflicting rumours and reports'.

O'Brien's information was particularly welcome to Gilchrist as he had, in his own words, been 'trying to probe for some time reports linking [Haughey] with an organisation in Monaghan devoted to trans-border activities'.[9] Gilchrist told the FCO that O'Brien did:

> not believe in the seriousness of Mr Haughey's organization in the sense of effective military or subversive plans. In his view the activities in Monaghan were intended to come to public knowledge as more internal politics designed to bolster the image of Fianna Fáil as the patriotic party, still fighting for Irish unity. He may be right but we should keep our eyes open to this threat on our flanks.

Having met Haughey at Abbeville, Gilchrist was aware that he was interested in moving matters forward at an inter-governmental level and, while he was a 'hard man', he was not a 'wild man'.[10] He advised London: 'Mr Haughey's passion for Irish unity being greater than that of Jack Lynch and Patrick Hillery, he is even more certain than they are that the UK government cannot hold the position in the North and that further disturbances will break out.' Clearly, if the ambassador had believed that Haughey or anyone in Fianna Fáil was arming the IRA, he would have said so. In fact, he believed that most of the gunrunning that was afoot was unrelated to the IRA. Less than a week later, on 4 November 1969, he advised London that:

> There has certainly been some very considerable gun-running for the benefit of the Catholics in the North, but it is by no means sure that the IRA as an organisation is responsible for it.[11]

According to Gilchrist, O'Brien, had advised him that 'Mr Lynch, until a few days ago, was quite unaware of the range of Mr Haughey's activities, and is much perturbed'. This implies that O'Brien or someone on his behalf had spoken to Lynch and was given the impression that he was apparently 'perturbed'. Yet, since Lynch did nothing to curb these alleged activities, he cannot really have been that 'much perturbed'. Someone must have put his mind at rest, if indeed he had ever been unsettled.

On 19 November Gilchrist took an opportunity to ascertain what Lynch knew about what was afoot in Monaghan when the pair met. Lynch spoke first about a loyalist arsenal which was being maintained on the Shankill Road and pressed Gilchrist to get the British to break it up. Gilchrist seized this as his opportunity to reveal that:

> It had come to my notice that there were alleged to be activities on this side of the frontier which, if reported back to the people and Stormont, whom he had just criticised, would strengthen them in their suspicion of the Republic and furnish them with arguments in support of their old-fashioned attitude. I had no reliable information whatever and what if anything was actually going on: my concern was with the rumours, some of them plausible enough

> on the surface, and with the political effects which might arise from them.
>
> Lynch at first denied all knowledge of the rumours, even when I mentioned the word 'Monaghan': but rather gave himself away by asking if the rumours might relate to activities by a certain member of his cabinet.[12]

By 10 November Ambassador Gilchrist was advising London that there were questions which required answers. He was also beginning to fall for the notion that Haughey was in league with the IRA. This was exactly what Berry, McMahon and Fleming had come to believe as a result of the lies being peddled to them by The Deceiver. According to Gilchrist:

> An important question is how far Lynch/Hillery and Haughey (and the IRA) are succeeding in their efforts, how far the Civil Rights movement in the North is becoming orientated towards the south and away from loyalty to and participation in the Northern administration, even a reformed one.[13]

When Gilchrist's 10 November 1969 telegram emerged from Britain's National Archives in January 2000, O'Brien stated, 'I recognize the Ambassador's report as an accurate record of my views at the time.' No one, however, seems to have asked him why he had felt it appropriate to inform the British government that there was an office in Monaghan which contained an 'Intelligence Unit', where Irish Army intelligence officers briefed and debriefed visitors to and from Northern Ireland.

O'Brien's disdain for Haughey was deep-seated and may provide a partial explanation for his willingness to talk to

Gilchrist. He once reported Haughey to gardaí at Howth station for vote buying and pressed for his prosecution. The complaint was recorded in the station log and became the source of much amusement in garda circles for many a year afterwards. The nub of O'Brien's complaint was that he had seen Haughey give one of his constituents, an elderly woman of limited means, a small amount of money to help her out. Suffice it to say, no charges were levelled against Haughey.[14]

***

In November 1969 British Intelligence launched an operation to penetrate the on-going efforts of G2 in assisting the CDCs in their quest for arms. They began by seducing Blaney with the prospect of securing arms in London. Blaney fell for the bait and informed John Kelly about the offer. Jock Haughey became involved too. 'The first meeting I had with Pádraig Haughey, Jock as he was known, was through Neil Blaney who told us he had a contact in London who was prepared to supply arms', Kelly revealed in 2005. Blaney he explained, had been led to believe that a London contact 'was equipped to buy arms within 48 hours. Arrangements were set in place with the banks and whatever else had to be done'.[15]

Kelly went to London where he and Jock Haughey tried to find out what was on offer from a man who operated under the *nom de guerre* Capt. Peter Markham-Randall.[16] However, they were followed from the moment they arrived in the city and photographed as they left Oxford Street tube station. The unit trailing them owed more to Monty Python than Smiley's People. Kelly spotted a man at a bus stop, 'standing on his toes looking after them, with a radio to his ear'. Further down, he saw a woman standing at the tailgate of a station-wagon. When they passed, she pulled a radio from her bag 'and seemed to say a few words before replacing it'.[17]

Jock Haughey returned to Ireland while Kelly remained behind and met the mysterious Markham-Randall. The encounter only served to make him more suspicious and he hightailed it back to Dublin where he joined Capt. Kelly at Buswell's Hotel and told him of his suspicion that they were being 'set-up'. However, behind the captain's back, the Belfast Kelly and some of his associates were scheming to assassinate 'Markham-Randall'. In furtherance of the plot, John Kelly rang the British spy in London and informed him that he had returned to Dublin. 'I invited [Markham-Randall] to Dublin to meet us along with Jim Kelly in the Gresham Hotel. We were going to assassinate him; that is why we arranged the meeting'. Markham-Randall agreed to take a flight over and rendezvous with them at the Gresham Hotel.[18]

Unaware of the assassination plot, Capt. Kelly went out to Dublin Airport to see if Markham-Randall would arrive on board a passenger flight. He proved a no-show at the arrivals gate. Yet, when Capt. Kelly reached the hotel himself, the spy had already checked in. The captain deduced that he had taken a military craft to Northern Ireland and was indeed a spy.

At the hotel, John Kelly and Markham-Randall went upstairs to negotiate. According to Capt. Kelly:

> When the small, dark-haired, goatee-bearded man [Markham-Randall] finally got down to talk with John [Kelly] in an upstairs bedroom, he claimed to be a former British army

> officer, introducing himself as Captain Markham-Randall. Whatever he was, he turned out to be very well informed on behind-the-scene events [in] Ireland, throwing around the name Kelly in an obvious manner, which John took to refer to me. He was also very interested in Ministers Haughey, Blaney, Boland and Gibbons, whom he intimated were strong supporters of Northern nationalism.

Capt. Kelly proceeded to describe how the reference to him 'on which Markham-Randall harped, also indicated inside knowledge which could only have come from an Irish source'.

Markham-Randall's pitch was bizarre if not downright gauche. He proceeded to tell John Kelly that:

> ... what is not so obvious is that I feel like an Arab; think like an Arab. My father may have been an Englishman, but I am one of my mother's people. I served with the British army. So did many Irishmen. That does not make them any less Irishmen, as it does not make me any less an Arab ... I trust you understand me. There are many Irish and many Arabs who do not like the English. I am Captain Markham-Randall and I am here to help you.[19]

Markham-Randall proceeded to tell him he was an expert in guerrilla tactics and had completed many courses in counter-revolutionary warfare. 'I could be a big help to you people,' he declared. 'If I visited one or other of your training camps I would be very useful: small arms, fire and movement, tactics and that sort of thing.' Kelly insisted he was only interested in arms:

> 'Arms, okay, okay,' he shrugged his shoulders. 'A consignment of automatic weapons, grenades and LMGs for thirty thousand

> [pounds]. It's cheap. It's the market price. But I am on your side. You may have the lot for three thousand.'

At this Kelly had had enough and accused the man of being an agent. 'Maybe I am,' Markham-Randall conceded, 'but what difference does it make to you? You get the guns and you can keep the money. All I want is access to the training camps.'

Capt. Kelly and three men from Northern Ireland were downstairs in the lobby of the Gresham Hotel awaiting news of the discussions upstairs. John Kelly came down and told them he was convinced Markham-Randall was a spy. '[Capt.] Jim Kelly didn't know anything [about the murder plot] till Markham-Randall arrived'. The captain now assumed that the talk about killing Markham-Randall was a spontaneous reaction to the confirmation he was a spy. According to John Kelly, the captain 'said no to it' and he was left unharmed.[20] This one incident, more than any other, highlights the exceptionally dangerous and thin ice upon which G2 was skating.

According to John Kelly, when 'we questioned Blaney [afterwards] about Markham he said, "It was a mistake, I'm sorry John but we were put on a bum steer." He didn't go into too much detail …'

Capt. Kelly reported the Markham-Randall's fiasco to Col Hefferon who made inquiries with garda intelligence. 'Word came back that Markham-Randall was a person of ill-repute; some type of underworld figure, who was not particular how he made his money; just the type of person who would involve himself in selling arms or any other underhand activity for that matter,' Capt. Kelly wrote.[21] While it is entirely possible the gardaí were fed this humbug by London, it is difficult – though not impossible – to accept they swallowed it whole.

In February 1970 Capt. Kelly learned that a large dossier on the London farce had been sent to garda HQ and he was given an opportunity to inspect it. Among the papers, he found a photograph of John Kelly and Jock Haughey climbing up the steps of the Oxford Street tube station. Jock Haughey was instantly recognisable as he had played for a Dublin All-Ireland winning GAA football team. According to Capt. Kelly, 'Obviously, the Irish police had been briefed on the affair by their British counterparts. Interestingly, while the Gardaí recognised [Jock Haughey], they did not identify John Kelly. Presumably, neither did the British. Apart from filing the information, the security agencies here took no action on the matter, but the file confirmed that [Markham-Randall] was a British agent.'

***

John Kelly has described how, the night after he and Jock Haughey had been trailed around London, they had separated, fearing arrest 'but nothing [had] happened. I figure that British Special Branch knew exactly who they were dealing with and that this was part of an Irish government escapade. Maybe they were trying to suss out how far this was going to go or maybe they were told to lay off it for a while'. The pair met up later at the Irish Club in Eaton Square. Gerry Fitt was present with 'a guy from the Irish embassy, a Clare man with reddish hair, Con somebody'.[22] The group sat and 'talked about what had happened and they knew all about it. Gerry [Fitt] was aware of it from a meeting in his house with [Capt.] Jim Kelly, which was the first meeting we had with the Irish government. He [had] asked for guns very histrionically. My brother Billy was there and so was Tom Conaty'.[23]

'Con' could hardly have withheld details of the discussion he had witnessed at the Irish Club from his superiors in the Department of External Affairs. If he furnished a report, it would surely have landed on Patrick Hillery's desk. In turn, Hillery was unlikely to have withheld it from Lynch.

The captain's notebook shows that the British spy stayed at the Gresham between 25 and 28 November with a comment that he may have stayed a little longer, perhaps moving to another hotel. In any event, on 30 November Markham-Randall wrote a letter addressed to 'G. Dixon' at the Munster and Leinster bank in Baggot Street. G. Dixon was the fictitious name employed by the CDCs for the account they were using to fund the arms quest. The odds are that the source of his information about Dixon was the informer referred to in the memorandum prepared by Ronnie Burroughs on 17 June 1970. The individual in question was probably an official in the Department of Justice or garda special branch.

Following this, Capt. Kelly became so concerned about the safety of the British spy that he availed of official funds to expedite his departure from the country on a flight from Dublin Airport.[24]

The conspirators now began to look further afield for arms. There was one country where they knew there were people who would be willing to help.

10

BLANEY PLUGS THE TRANSATLANTIC ARMS SUPPLY PIPELINE

'Instead of dealing with people we don't know, why not go to those we know and can depend upon amongst the Irish Americans?' John Kelly suggested after the Markham-Randall fiasco. Seán Keenan had set his sights on the US too. He was hoping that the remnants of a US arms supply network from the Border Campaign might be revived. He and Kelly arranged to fly to the US in December 1969.

Keenan collected his dole as normal one Thursday after which Paddy Doherty collected him in his car and drove him at speed to Dublin Airport. 'He never told me whom he had met or what he had achieved during his visit, and I never asked,' Doherty later wrote. 'The gulf between us was widening. There was no bitterness between us: we simply realised that our different backgrounds and the different roads we had been travelling – which had temporarily converged during the defence of the Bogside – were again taking us in separate directions'.[1]

Blaney provided the passports Kelly and Keenan used to travel to the US. Joe Cahill joined them in America. Keenan toured Boston, Philadelphia and New York where he met with members of Clan na Gael, an organisation which had provided support for the IRA and some of its splinter groups in the past. Keenan began by contacting a number of Irish republicans he knew personally. 'In Philadelphia, for example, Seán Keenan and Joe Cahill contacted members of the local Clan na Gael chapter. These include Bridget Makowski, a member of a prominent republican family in the city. She had close links with the younger radicals in Derry, had joined the republican club in Derry and knew Keenan personally. In Philadelphia, many of the Clan na Gael members (though not Makowski) backed Keenan.'[2]

In Boston Keenan phoned a Derry republican, Liam Deeney, 'who had been active in the 1950s and had left Derry in 1965. Keenan asked him to organise support. Although Deeney, like Makowski, was reluctant to become personally involved, a group of a dozen or so Irish-born republicans living in Boston met Keenan and arranged to help him.'[3]

Another republican Keenan knew from old was Liam Kelly who had been in the IRA but had been expelled in 1951 after which he had set up Saor Uladh (Free Ulster). After it had failed to gather any momentum, he had emigrated to the US and Keenan contacted him in New York. According to Ó Dochartaigh, 'In recent months, [Liam] Kelly had been working with people such as Mike Flannery in civil rights groups in New York and with the republicans in the New York chapter of Clan na Gael. Keenan now met Clan na Gael members in New York.[4]

According to John Kelly, some of the Americans he and Keenan encountered, such as Michael Flannery, reacted with 'horror' when they discovered he was involved with the Dublin government, telling him there was 'no effing so and so way' they were going to 'deal with the Free State Government and De Valera and Fianna Fáil and all that.' Kelly recalls that a meeting took place 'in the Bronx, it was really the beginning of Noraid [the Provisional IRA fundraising organisation in the US], and it was in November or December of '69. They were reluctant to get involved because they wouldn't trust Fianna Fáil after what De Valera did and so on. I said to those guys, "Well look, I agree with all you are saying in terms of not trusting the Free State government but who else? Can you supply the money that will get this deal put together? Have you got it now?" The answer was "no" so reluctantly they agreed'.[5]

The question they should have been asking themselves was whether the Dublin government would ultimately decide to deal with them.

John Kelly's group proceeded to organise an arms shipment in Canada. According to him, there was an arrangement 'through the Irish Seamen's Union that whatever container arrived in the port in New York would go on to Dublin. We met the guy from the Longshoremen's union in New York. A small guy. He was on the docks in New York and Liam Kelly arranged the meeting'.[6] On the Irish side of the Atlantic, Willy Stacey, the general secretary of the Seamen's Union, cleared everything for them in Dublin Port.

John Kelly was keeping Capt. Kelly apprised of the progress he was making in America. 'I was delighted to report to him that everything was in hand. The weapons were available; the money was transferred from Dublin to an account in America held by Alan Clancy who is dead since but who owned a chain of pubs in New York. £75,000 was involved. This was okayed by [Neil] Blaney, so we thought, but the next communication from Dublin was that Blaney had cancelled it. He had a contact closer to home who could deliver the goods. The money had never been transferred after all'. The Americans 'blew a fuse and said "We fucking told you" and we were very annoyed but we were the servants and what could we do. Clancy had exposed himself for nothing'.[7]

When he returned to Dublin, John Kelly was a 'very angry man but [Capt.] Kelly said, "Blaney has it all set up. Blaney has this guy in Belgium who will be in contact and the weapons will be here in a couple of days".' John Kelly came to believe that the reason Blaney cancelled the American operation was because 'he was afraid that we would take [the arms consignment] and that he wouldn't see it. Which leads me on to believe that this was a government operation. He thought, "We had to have this under our control".'[8]

***

As the attempt by Keenan and Kelly to establish a US arms supply pipeline was imploding, the IRA was in the throes of a split with two factions going their own way. An aggravating factor in the schism was the rift between Goulding and Keenan. Goulding was aware of the trip Keenan made to the US and as a result expelled him from the IRA. Keenan's involvement with the *Voice of the North* newspaper, which was being financed by Dublin government funds, was another factor in the expulsion. After this, Goulding went to the US where he provided a Clan na Gael convention with a presentation of his theory that Fianna Fáil was manipulating Keenan in an effort to split the republican movement. Few were swayed by his interpretation of what was afoot.[9]

Two factions emerged from the rupture. On one side stood the 'Officials', who were led by Goulding with Seán Garland, Tomás Mac Giolla, Jim Sullivan and Billy McMillen. On the other side, the 'Provisionals' formed up, led by Ruairí Ó Brádaigh, Seán MacStíofáin, Dáithí Ó Conaill, Joe Cahill, Seán Keenan and others.

Inevitably, the division ripped Sinn Féin (SF), the political arm of the republican Movement, asunder. The SF fracture took place after a walk out by the Ó Brádaigh faction from the party's Ard Fheis at the Intercontinental Hotel in Dublin, 10–11 January 1970. As Cathal Goulding drove away from it with a colleague, the latter asked him what he reckoned would be the impact of the latest wrench. 'The movement has had a good shite and is all the better for it,' Goulding replied as they drove towards their Gardner Place HQ in Dublin where armed men were taking up defensive positions.[10] The Provisionals headed towards Kevin Barry Hall on Parnell Square.

There were now at least three groups vying for nationalist support in Ireland: the CDCs, the Officials and the Provisionals. The CDCs had come to enjoy widespread approval and often advocated a line which those around Ruairí Ó Brádaigh opposed. In particular, the CDCs offered nationalists an opportunity to protect their communities without having to join either wing of the IRA and they had a working relationship, if not actual allies, in the British home secretary, the RUC chief constable and Lt Gen. Freeland. Many of those who later became involved with the SDLP were involved in CDC activity.

The dismantling of barricades in Belfast had exposed a significant rift between the CDCs and the hawks who later sided with the Provisionals. It had come to the fore at a meeting of the Central CDC in Belfast after the talks with James Callaghan in London in October 1969. More than 100 people attended and opposition to the London deal was led by Billy McKee, Prionsias Mac Airt (aka Francis Card) and Leo Martin, all of whom wanted the barricades to remain in place. The moderates had the support of clerical figures such as Canon Pádraig Murphy who in turn enlisted Dr Philbin, bishop of Down and Connor, to support the barricade deal. The bishop's intervention swung the Central CDC behind it. On the day of the dismantling, the bishop was escorted around the Falls in a British Army land rover and one of the future Provisionals denounced him publicly for it.

After the barricades were removed, loyalist gangs torched three nationalist houses. Replacement barricades sprang up promptly. Canon Murphy then engaged in further negotiations with Lt Gen. Freeland and secured further promises of protection from British troops. The barricades came down again. Clearly, the CDCs were not – as has been claimed – a front for the emerging Provisional IRA. They were a wholly separate and distinct organisation.

In the meantime, the Provisional's Army Council instructed their volunteers to maintain no more than a defensive stance and hold it until told otherwise. In the period running up to the Arms Crisis, the Provisionals embarked on a secret canvass of the IRA units scattered across the country, seeking their allegiance. It began in January 1970 and while it had been intended to call a new Provisional Army Convention in June 1970, it did not take place until September 1970. So secret was the canvass, Martin McGuinness was not aware the IRA had split into two camps when he joined it in Derry. He found himself in the Officials but soon left for the Provisionals.

There was little indication the Provisionals were going to wage a campaign against the crown. In a frank admission, James Callaghan revealed in 1973 that: 'We did not know it at the time, but [the Ballymurphy riots of April 1970] marked the emergence of the Provisional IRA as a separate force'.[11] Dublin knew no better because the gardaí were relying on the ever-cunning Deceiver, now a leading Provisional, who was hiding what he knew about the Provos from them while directing their attention towards Goulding's Officials.

When the Provisionals eventually commenced some tentative military operations, it was still not appreciated by the public exactly by whom they were carried out. The activities of an active – and highly secret – unit did not emerge until much later, long after the eruption of the Arms Crisis and then only by accident.[12] Hence, it can be argued that G2, Gibbons, Blaney and Haughey could not have foreseen just how volatile and incendiary Northern Ireland would soon become. Their actions should be assessed in context, i.e. the absence from the view of an IRA intent upon going to war with the British state and their alliance with the CDCs who had no intention of instigating violence.

Taoiseach Jack Lynch, however, appears to have developed a far more wary view of what might happen if the CDCs were to secure a supply of arms. This analysis offers an explanation for the dramatic intervention he made at the start of the new year.

11

LYNCH GRABS HOLD OF THE STEERING WHEEL

The policy of making funds available to the CDCs, some of which could be siphoned off to purchase arms, while the Irish government turned a knowing blind eye, was not working. Hence, in December 1969 the CDCs approached Capt. Kelly: '…I was formally requested to assist in the proposed Continental purchase. I agreed to help on condition that the Dublin Government approved. Accordingly, I put the proposition to Colonel Hefferon, who approached the Minister for Defence, and my understanding was that my active co-operation with the Northerners had the full and unequivocal approval of the Minister'.[1] The captain later described Gibbons as 'the originator of the plan as the competent authority here was the Minister, Mr Gibbons'.[2]

At a political level, Gibbons was in the habit of taking advice from his friend George Colley. Back in 1966, Gibbons had acted as Colley's campaign manager in the latter's ill-fated leadership bid. The pair invariably dined together while the Dáil was in session. Ben Briscoe, a Fianna Fáil TD from Dublin, and Billy Kennelly TD from Waterford, also Fianna Fáil, completed a table of friends who were at ease in each other's company. According to Briscoe, 'Gibbons had spoken to Jack Lynch before Christmas 1969, or closely after it', to inform him about the on going attempts to import arms and obtain his direction.

According to Briscoe, Gibbons left that particular meeting with Lynch 'none the wiser' about what to do than when he had gone into it. It is likely this meeting took place before Capt. Kelly had been approached by the CDCs with the request to take over the quest for arms.

Gibbons was still in a quandary three weeks later and raised his concerns with Colley in the Dáil restaurant. Briscoe, who was also present, recalls that Colley's advice was to 'go back to talk to Lynch' and press him for an instruction, which is exactly what Gibbons did. Although it is not possible to be precise about the timing, this approach was very proximate to the request the CDCs made to Capt. Kelly, the one which he sent up the line to Gibbons. All the evidence indicates that Gibbons communicated the new request to Lynch, who gave Gibbons the green light for the state to take over the arms quest at this juncture, i.e. in January 1970.

On the surface, Lynch appeared to have been acting out of character. However, by acceding to the request, Lynch was seizing back control of what had become a runaway train. With this one bold move, he had accrued the final say on when – if ever – the arms might be released to the CDCs and, in the meantime, could ensure they were held safely under Irish Army lock and key in perfectly legal circumstances in the Republic. The prospect of ever having to release any arms that might be purchased to the CDCs was a small one indeed. The move also made sense in circumstances where it was patently obvious to him that Gilchrist had a shrewd idea as to what was afoot. Furthermore, Capt. Kelly had undoubtedly told Col Hefferon about the near assassination of Markham-Randall in Dublin. The colonel must have relayed this to Gibbons. Assuming Gibbons knew, he would hardly have withheld the information from Lynch. If Lynch knew about the assassination plot, it provided yet another layer of explanation for his decision to take control of such a volatile set of affairs.

The captain was soon explaining to John Kelly that any arms that were to 'be brought in, if brought in at all, [would be done so] under the control of the Department of Defence, and they would be distributed at the discretion of the authorities here, and on foot of which I advised some of my Northern contacts that they should come down and see the Government about it.'[3] The CDCs had no choice but to accept these terms.

***

On 6 February 1970, Gibbons called Lt Gen. Seán MacEoin, chief of staff of the Irish Army, and Col Hefferon, to his office. He asked them to sit down and told them he was about to say something which was for their ears only. He then proceeded to issue a verbal directive which caused them to look at each other in astonishment. After they left the room, Gen. MacEoin turned to Col Hefferon and advised him to go back to his office straight away and write down the order exactly as they had heard it. MacEoin had the directive recorded by the Plans and Operations Officer. It read:

> The Government directs the Army (1) prepare for incursions into Northern Ireland, (2) to make weapons available and (3) make gas masks available

The reference to making 'weapons available' was not and could not have been a directive to furnish the Irish Army with weapons since it already possessed an adequate supply – indeed it had a surplus of .303s rifles, which it had nearly sold to the Liverpool arms dealer acting on behalf of the UVF. Clearly, the directive was designed to ring-fence the supply of weapons to be made available – if the need arose – to the CDCs.

Four days later a second document addressed to the chief of staff or Ceann Foirne (CF) of the Irish Army was prepared. It referred specifically to the taoiseach and was entitled *Addendum to the Memo of 10/2/70, Ministerial Directive to CF*:

> The Taoiseach and other Ministers have met delegations from the North. At these meetings urgent demands were made for respirators, weapons and ammunition the provision of which the Government agreed. Accordingly truckloads of these items will be put at readiness so that they may be available in a matter of hours.[4]

A military intelligence record marked 'secret' reveals that on 18 February 1970 the following items were assembled in Dublin and Athlone:

> 500 rifles;
>
> 200 Gustav machine guns;
>
> 3,000 respirators;
>
> 80,000 rounds of 303 ammunition;
>
> 99,000 rounds of 9 mm ammunition.[5]

While the cabinet never passed a formal resolution during which it 'agreed' to supply 'weapons and ammunition' to the CDC 'delegations from the North', Gibbons, Haughey and Blaney supported such a policy, as did other ministers. The significance of the directive is that it shows that Lynch joined their number, or at least went along with the policy for strategic purposes. Combined, this quartet encompassed the office of the Taoiseach, the office of the minister of defence and the remaining ministers on the cabinet sub-committee on Northern Ireland which had been set up by the full cabinet and unto which responsibility for dealing with the crisis in Northern Ireland had been delegated. For reasons which are unclear, Pádraig Faulkner and Joseph Brennan, both of whom had been appointed to it, had dropped by the wayside. A further alternative, of course, is that there was a meeting of the 'Secret Cabinet' in the absence of civil servants.[6]

Only the ministers for defence and justice could sanction the importation of arms. No other minister enjoyed such a power. The involvement of Gibbons therefore rendered the G2 operation, which commenced in January 1970, a lawful exercise. Lynch may also have told Gibbons that it would not be necessary to bring the matter to the full cabinet because he and the relevant key ministers had approved it. This explanation would be consistent with Lynch's overall reluctance to raise the activities of G2 at a full cabinet session despite requests to do so from his justice minister. Suffice it to say, the actual distribution of weapons – as opposed to their importation – was another question altogether. Distribution was something that required cabinet approval.

Lynch's almost invisible involvement in the quest for arms offers a perfect explanation for his decision to shield Gibbons from the political storm that erupted in May 1970 and the criminal prosecutions that followed.

***

At the Arms Trials, Col Hefferon confirmed that Gibbons gave Capt. Kelly his approval for the purchase of arms. While the operation involved G2 personnel, it was not a normal G2 action because Col Hefferon was not in overall charge of it. It had been transformed into what Capt. Kelly described as a government operation. Capt. Kelly testified that the colonel 'did not think that as a serving officer it would be wise were I to become involved in an operation of this sort'. According to the captain, one of the colonel's concerns, was that 'I was subject to a corporate body such as an army, and if they found out I was doing this [meaning if it became public] it would expose what would be a very top-secret operation'. The colonel, he explained, felt 'I would have to resign, but, however, he would refer to the Minister for Defence. In the meantime, [Col Hefferon] told me to make out the [resignation] forms'.[7]

Capt. Kelly placed the completed forms on Col Hefferon's desk before the end of January, to take effect on 13 February, a date which marked the twenty-first anniversary of his military commission. Col Hefferon brought the forms to Gibbons who, having considered them, decided he should not resign from G2.

Capt. Kelly arranged for a string of CDC delegations to meet him, the Taoiseach and other ministers during this period. One group visited Leinster House on 14 February 1970, to see Lynch, Gibbons and Blaney. It provided Gibbons with his first opportunity to meet the captain. At that meeting Gibbons instructed him to report to him directly.

Capt. Kelly also spoke to Haughey on 14 February. 'I put him in the picture, I told him the essentials. I was satisfied he knew what I was talking about.'[8]

Two days later Capt. Kelly told Col Hefferon that the CDCs had made contact with Otto Schlueter, a licensed arms dealer in Germany who had already received some monies for arms.[9] But now there was a pressing urgency: a CDC representative had been due to travel to the Continent to make a further payment but was unable to go. Capt. Kelly suggested that he would go instead 'to find out, first, if arms really were available and second, what exactly was going on'.

The mission was financed by a payment made out of one of the two subsidiary Baggot Street accounts. 'I had a sister living in Frankfurt at the time', Capt. Kelly said later, 'and it was agreed that I should say I was visiting her … My passport was out of date, but within hours I obtained a new one and on, 19 February, I went to the Continent ... As I boarded a plane at Dublin Airport, I was secure in the knowledge that the Minister for Defence was fully briefed on this, my first direct involvement in the proposed arms importation'.[10]

A day or so later he met Otto Schlueter in Dortmund for about two hours. 'He assured me that there were arms available including pistols, bullet-proof vests and machine-guns but I was somewhat disappointed to find that I could not inspect them then. We discussed transport and prices; there was still some money outstanding, and I returned to Dublin having seen neither arms nor ammunition'.[11] Nonetheless, he concluded that Schlueter was probably genuine and that weapons were available in Hamburg. He stayed overnight and returned home the following day.

Capt. Kelly met Schlueter on all four of his visits to the Continent.[12] Unfortunately, he destroyed his records about these trips and it is not possible to be precise about dates, times and the extent of the payments made. What we do know, however, is that during one of his visits he had handed money over to the German; also we know that he eventually managed to inspect a number of the weapons.[13]

***

Blaney arranged another meeting between Capt. Kelly and Gibbons in Leinster House on 4 March. 'I made it my business to go to Mr Gibbons to make sure he knew what was going on ... so there would be no doubt and, if you like, you could call it a form of self-protection', the captain told the jury on 16 October 1970. He informed Gibbons that the plan was now to bring the weapons in by ship to the Port of Dublin, something about which Gibbons was already aware.[14]

He also testified that at either this or another meeting with Gibbons, he discussed the fact that the arms should be untraceable, a stratagem Gibbons favoured. He also explained that the arms were to be stored in the Republic.

Capt. Kelly returned to the Continent on 10 March for three or four days during which he met Schlueter again, most probably in Düsseldorf. A plan was put in train for the arms to be shipped from Antwerp to the Port of Dublin on 25 March 1970. Albert Luykx, a Belgian whom he had met through Blaney, assisted him. The consignee of weapons now destined for Dublin Port was Weluks Limited, a company owned by Luykx.

On his return, the captain saw Gibbons again, once if not twice. At one of these meetings Gibbons suggested to him that he should take up residence in Northern Ireland but he explained that he was able to meet people in the south and that it would not be necessary to move.

In all of the discussions about the Arms Crisis, a manifestly obvious detail is frequently neglected: clandestine military intelligence operations by their very nature must be conducted secretly. Cabinet ministers in the UK are not told about covert British Intelligence operations, no more than their counterparts in the US are kept in the loop about CIA transactions.

G2 was naturally aware of the need for secrecy. Capt. Kelly had driven around in his blue Renault in civilian clothes for about six weeks during August and September 1969 gathering intelligence and forging contacts in nationalist communities. Even at that, Col Hefferon was concerned lest the RUC or loyalist militants might realise who he was and detain and question him.

At the political level, Haughey and Gibbons also gave some consideration as to how best to cloak Capt. Kelly's activities from British eyes. During his evidence at the Arms Trial, Haughey told the court that Gibbons had wanted the captain to continue in his role but was worried and 'wanted to find some post for him inside the public service, where he would be able to continue with his activities. I suggested a good cover for him would be to become a special customs officer with responsibility for pig smuggling, which was then a very serious problem ... I do remember Mr Gibbons telling me of his fears that Capt. Kelly [must have come to the attention] of British Intelligence and that he wanted to get some position for him where he could carry on his valuable work.' This discussion most likely took place on 17 March 1970.[15]

The need for secrecy permeated all levels of the operation. Seamus Brady wrote that the 'whole exercise in importing of arms from the Continent for the defence of the minority in the North of Ireland revolved on the need to ensure that the British did not find out'.[16] During his 'speech from the dock' John Kelly described his 'concern' that 'the British Authorities should not know' about what he had been doing.

With the benefit of hindsight, Gibbons would have been well advised to bring Berry inside the tent whereby any misgivings he and the gardaí were harbouring about his operation could have been assuaged. At one stage Berry had considered that he and the gardaí might have been 'intruding on a secret Government mission', which was exactly what they were doing. Had they been brought into the loop, they probably would have counselled against what was becoming an increasingly reckless and ill-advised operation, and possibly even brought it to an end. Instead, Berry remained in thrall to The Deceiver, who had plenty more mischief to create.

Logically, the inner workings of Gibbons' operation were not disclosed to cabinet ministers who did not fit into the rarefied category of 'need-to-know'. Pádraig Faulkner, a Lynch supporter, who had briefly been a member of the cabinet subcommittee, later propounded the erroneous notion that the importation of arms required the sanction of the cabinet 'as a whole'. Faulkner also failed to pay attention to the evidence at the Arms Trials that the weapons were to be stored in a monastery in Co. Cavan until the government instructed otherwise. Somehow, Faulkner managed to persuade himself that the plan had been to dispatch them across the border upon their arrival.

In his memoirs he wrote that, 'As to any suggestion that in some way the Government authorised or condoned *supplying arms to civilians in the North* [my emphasis], the evidence is to the contrary.'[17] As others such as Kevin Boland have stressed, the distribution of arms to Northern Ireland nationalists might have arisen in the context of a 'Doomsday scenario'.

In a similar fashion Des O'Malley assumed G2's plan was for the immediate distribution of the Schlueter arms consignment. 'I should make it clear from the outset: there never was a Government proposal or any intention to buy arms or *to supply arms to people in the North*,' [my emphasis] he wrote in his memoirs.

At the second Arms Trial, Charles Haughey was asked if he had known that the Schlueter cargo was 'intended for possible ultimate distribution to civilians in the North [and if so] would that have made any difference?' He replied: 'No, not really, provided, of course, that a Government decision intervened. I would have regarded it as a very normal part of Army preparations in pursuance of the contingency plans that they would provide themselves with, and store here on this side of the Border, arms which might ultimately, if the Government said so, be distributed to other persons.'[18]

As spring lengthened, the taoiseach was refusing to engage with Mícheál Ó Moráin, who was trying to get him to raise the arms quest at cabinet. It should be stressed that Ó Moráin had his doubts about what Berry had been telling him since the dubious report he had presented about the Haughey-Goulding encounter in August. If anything, he was even more doubtful by the time he attended a meeting on 10 December 1969, with

Garda Commissioner Wymes and Fleming, at which they relayed to him The Deceiver's latest bundle of lies about the activities of Capt. Kelly along with allegations that Haughey and Blaney were involved in a plot to import arms for the IRA. Ó Moráin asked them to recheck the information provided by their source.

Ó Moráin also tried to get Lynch to talk about the issue to him 'privately', but again without any success.[19] 'I know this is true,' Kevin Boland wrote, 'because [Ó Moráin] sat beside me at government meetings and he asked me on more than one occasion if I had heard the rumours. When I said I had heard some rumours, he told me he had asked the Taoiseach to have the matter raised at the Cabinet so that he would be able to instruct his department on the matter. He failed to get the Taoiseach to do this.'[20] Overall, Boland established that Ó Moráin made 'a number of requests' to Lynch but had been unable to get him 'to clear the matter up'. All the while, Ó Moráin was being pressed by 'his Department' – that is to say Peter Berry and Andrew Ward – for an answer to the questions which they were raising.[21]

According to Boland, Ó Moráin 'knew all about the principle of collective responsibility. He knew of the delegated authority [by the cabinet to Blaney, Haughey, Faulkner and Brennan] and no doubt he knew also of the statutory authority vested in the minister for defence [to import arms]. He also could see the need for secrecy, if such an operation were decided on, but he felt it was necessary that he should know the position and the only way to find out was to ask the Taoiseach to raise the whole question of what was being done under the delegated authority at a Government meeting. This he could not get the Taoiseach to do, nor could he get him to tell him even privately'.[22]

Lynch also gave Berry the impression that he had not received a briefing from Ó Moráin. In his memoirs, Berry described a phone call he says he received from Lynch on 13 April, asking him to come to government buildings that evening because Lynch wanted a run-down on the IRA situation vis-à-vis Northern Ireland. 'When in the course of conversation with the Taoiseach I mentioned [Ó Moráin's] meeting with the [Garda] Commissioner and the Head of the "S Branch" in the previous December and the police information about the participation of ministers in supplying arms to the IRA he seemed to be genuinely surprised'.[23] Yet, Ó Moráin told Boland he had informed Lynch what the gardaí were relaying to him. Assuming Ó Moráin was telling the truth, why did Lynch appear to act 'genuinely surprised' in his conversation with Berry? If Lynch was not playing a game, why did he not take action to intervene to halt the activities of Blaney and Haughey? Of course if Lynch was playing a game, i.e. he knew perfectly well from Gibbons what was afoot, he would have had little choice but to act 'genuinely surprised' in front of Berry but do nothing about it later – which is exactly what happened.

It is abundantly clear from Boland's account that his – Boland's – discussions with Ó Moráin concerned the efforts by the state – not the earlier failures of the CDC – to acquire arms and hence at least one of Ó Moráin's approaches to Lynch must have taken place after Gibbons and G2 had assumed control of the operation in January 1970.

According to Boland, Lynch was:

> playing a devious game, which a conscientious man like [Ó Moráin] could not be expected to suspect. Either the importation

> was right or wrong. If it was wrong, it should be stopped and the Taoiseach should take whatever action seemed to him to be appropriate in relation to the members of his Government. If it was right, the Minister for Justice should know so that he could direct his Department in the matter … but he had asked the Taoiseach and he wouldn't tell him, nor would he raise the matter at Government level.[24]

It would be easy to castigate Lynch for behaving in a deceptive manner but the threat posed by Paisley *et al* had cast him into a deeply invidious situation where he had little choice but to keep as many plates spinning in the air as he could, ever hopeful none would fall. Whilst his behaviour often fell below what could be described as entirely honourable, his overriding concern must have been the avoidance of unnecessary violence. Perhaps when Ó Moráin had approached him, he tried to give him – and through him Berry – a subtle hint to back off; not to ask questions; that he knew about the operation and that it was being run by Gibbons with assistance from G2 but he did not want to verbalise it.

Lynch knew full well that anything he said would be relayed to Berry and recorded in an internal Department of Justice memorandum. In addition, there was the ever-present danger of leaks from cabinet reaching London *via* the department of justice or garda special branch sources. As part of his plate spinning exertions, Lynch continued to meet with delegations from Northern Ireland, including at least two which consisted of members of the Provisional IRA.

12

THE TAOISEACH MEETS THREE PROVISIONAL IRA LEADERS

The taoiseach held private meetings with at least three members of the Provisional IRA in early 1970, all of whom were or had been members of the CDCs. John Kelly was one of them. Kelly met Lynch in Dublin on 3 March as part of a CDC delegation. After the meeting ended, the delegation was escorted to the Parliamentary Secretaries' dining room where Blaney introduced them to Patrick Hillery and Jim Gibbons.[1] During his 'speech from the dock', in October 1970 Kelly said:

> I myself accompanied delegations which met the Taoiseach and Mr Blaney, delegations which met Dr Hillery and Mr Haughey, delegations which met Mr Gibbons and Mr Lenihan ... I want to be very emphatic that we were coming from all parts of the Six Counties not to indulge in tea-parties, not to be entertained, but to elicit, insofar as we could, what was the opinion of this Government in relation to the Six Counties.[2]

John Kelly's overall recollection was that 'no one from Taoiseach Lynch down refused that request [for arms] or told us this was contrary to government policy'. Insofar as the meeting with Gibbons was concerned, 'it was a serious discussion on matters which we considered to be of vital importance, and we discussed very thoroughly with the Minister, Mr Gibbons, the position in the Six Counties, and the necessity for arms being provided against any break-down in society there'. He was dismissive of Gibbons' subsequent claim to have not known precisely who he was:

> I find it hard to understand that whereas Mr Gibbons remembers that I sat at the end of the table – where I did sit – that he could have mistaken me for Capt. Kelly, because, when that discussion ended, Mr Gibbons called me aside, and another member of that delegation, he called two of us aside, and he told me in very express terms that he wanted me to keep in touch with him, and to keep him abreast of the situation.

Capt. Kelly also revealed that Gibbons and John Kelly had held a lengthy discussion at the meeting of 3 March. 'Actually', he testified, 'after the meeting of March 3 which John Kelly attended, there was no necessity to put John Kelly in the picture. Mr Gibbons had told him everything he would want to know and more.'[3]

At the meeting with Hillery and Gibbons after leaving Lynch, the delegates spoke of their fears of a renewal of what they described as a 'pogrom' and their desire for arms for their defence. 'They were putting a proposition to Mr Gibbons as Minister for Defence who was a man in authority meeting these people', Capt. Kelly testified. 'They put forward various suggestions and the end result of their suggestions was that, as far as Mr Gibbons was concerned, and if he for instance, had been Taoiseach, there would have been no difficulty in getting the guns … He did say that ... I am trying to give you the sense of what Mr Gibbons was conveying to the delegation, that if he was Taoiseach in Ireland these people would have guns ready for distribution in the morning'.[4]

Gibbons 'attitude to me and to the others,' Capt. Kelly added, 'was that he would do all in his power to assist them. In fact, when he got up to leave for his Kilkenny home at about 10 o'clock that night he was challenged by an older member of the delegation who made a remark to the effect that he hoped the meeting was "not so much water under the bridge", with the clear implication that Northern republicans had been hoodwinked by previous Fianna Fáil governments.[5] The minister's reaction could only be described as restrainedly aggressive. Apparently grievously insulted by this questioning of his integrity he came back from the centre of the room where he was settling himself into his overcoat, and standing over the table where we were sitting he vehemently declared that he was not that sort of man, that his word was his bond and that what he said he would stand over'.[6]

Capt. Kelly felt that the 'delegates accepted Mr Gibbons' assurance and in fact some of them felt that there had been no need for one of their number to adopt such a cynical attitude to a minister who had been so forthcoming. The incident had the effect of reinforcing the delegates' confidence that Mr Gibbons would do everything possible to meet their requests. Indeed, the delegates and I left Leinster House that night convinced that the Dublin Government, as represented by its Minister for Defence, would provide aid to the minority in the North if the situation demanded it'.[7]

According to the captain, Gibbons 'discussed guns being available for distribution and told these people that he had held guns back specially for this very purpose and that he kept the guns under his control for this very purpose'.[8] Furthermore,

'Gibbons went beyond the question of the supply of weapons. He had gone past the stage of discussing the weapons that were needed in the event of attack to the question of the follow-up action that [the] Irish Army would take'.

Gibbons admitted at the Arms Trial that he met this group, but denied it had anything to do with providing arms to them. Insofar as his claim that he had mistaken John Kelly for Capt. Kelly, the captain rounded on him when he got into the witness box: 'There was no question or doubt about' making such a mistake he stated firmly.

***

Another meeting between Lynch and members of the Provisional IRA took place in either February or March 1970. One of those present was Seán Keenan who had been chairman of the Derry CDC, though he had retired from it more than three months earlier and was now devoting his energies to helping MacStíofáin and Ó Brádaigh develop the Provisional IRA. The Derry CDC had also been disbanded since 10 October 1969.

In *Paddy Bogside*, Doherty describes how he had received a message from Blaney to come to Dublin with Keenan. The pair were brought into Blaney's office where the minister gave them a detailed account of the recent attempt by the UVF to acquire a 'massive number' of surplus Irish Army rifles. Blaney then escorted them to the Shelbourne Hotel. Over lunch he told them that he wanted them to apply pressure on the government to hand the surplus stock over to the CDCs.[9] After lunch, he invited Haughey to join them. Haughey absorbed the information and suggested that Gibbons, Boland and Ó Moráin, should also be included. However, Boland wasn't available and Ó Moráin was ill. According to Doherty, Blaney and Haughey were confident the absent men would have been supportive of the delegation's petition.

Gibbons attended within minutes. Doherty noted that he was very tall and had 'a swarthy complexion and a long hooked nose'.[10] Doherty and his colleagues were concerned by the attempt by loyalists to accumulate arms. They also discussed the gun clubs which had been set up by the disbanded B-Specials and the support they were receiving from unionist MPs. Doherty believed that loyalists had about 100,000 legally held guns. 'Another pogrom against the Catholic population in Northern Ireland was on the cards'.[11]

In addition, the Dublin government knew that the UVF was smuggling guns from Ardrossan in Scotland by trawler to Lough Foyle and Sheephaven.

Insofar as the surplus Irish Army rifles were concerned, the key figure to convince was Lynch and the Northern Ireland visitors were eager to talk to him. Blaney addressed Haughey, 'You'd better ring him. I can't stand the man.' Haughey agreed and soon reported that Lynch would see them in the morning.

The abandonment of the training at Fort Dunree was another issue which had caused the CDCs great concern. Gibbons now promised that 'as soon as it was safe to do so, it would begin again'.

Keenan proposed to tell Lynch 'in no uncertain terms where his responsibility lay'. Doherty was more cautious. 'You can't walk in on the leader of a country and make demands, no matter how important or how just those demands might be,' he reasoned. Gibbons sided with Doherty who suggested that the best approach would be to place the facts before Lynch and hope he would ask Blaney, Haughey and Gibbons for their view which would be supportive of the delegation's request for the surplus rifles.

The idea of storing the rifles on the southern side of the Border instead of supplying them directly to the CDCs was mooted by Doherty during a discussion between the group ahead of the meeting with Lynch. Doherty was aware that Keenan was now committed to the IRA, an organisation he – Doherty – opposed. Since the Derry CDC had disbanded, any arms delivered to Derry might have fallen into the hands of the IRA. Doherty suggested that they ask for the weapons to be held by the Irish Army somewhere close to Derry so they could be distributed quickly in the event of an attack 'and play the rest by ear'.[12]

No one from Belfast was present and it was decided to call a representative down to support the petition. Keenan and Doherty spent the night at Capt. Kelly's home. Billy Kelly, a representative of the Belfast Defence Association, joined the group. He was an IRA veteran who had sided with the Provisionals and was a brother of John Kelly.

***

The meeting with Lynch took place the following morning. During it Doherty noticed that Billy Kelly deferred to Keenan who urged Lynch 'to prepare for the inevitable confrontation' between nationalists and loyalists. Doherty could sense that

Keenan 'was pushing too hard' and so he – Doherty – suggested that 'guns were not necessary in Derry'. Keenan took the hint and asked that the guns might be stored in Donegal where they would be easily accessible if required.

However, Billy Kelly then took up the running, contradicting them. 'I was amazed at his approach. He demanded guns and he wanted them right in the heart of Belfast. He said that not only were the ghetto Catholics frightened, but many professional and business people were also appealing for guns'.[13]

Doherty watched Lynch flinch under the demands and tried to calm Billy Kelly down by turning the discussion to Derry, which he felt was more manageable.

Eventually Lynch said, 'Gas masks I can give you, even for humanitarian reasons, but guns I will have to think about.'

Aside from Doherty, the other northerners were jubilant, something which puzzled him. They were confident that the taoiseach was going to supply the rifles. Doherty accused Billy Kelly of having frightened off Lynch: 'We blew it. That man has no intention of getting involved in Northern Ireland,' he said with some prescience.

One significant problem does not appear to have been broached at the meeting: the fact that any rifle that Lynch might have released to them could have fallen into the hands of the British Army or RUC, with the attendant risk of being traced back to the Irish Army. Such an outcome had the potential to create a diplomatic furore between Dublin and London and provoke more loyalist violence. It is inconceivable that this did not occur to Lynch. Not surprisingly, he turned down the delegation's request for the rifles when the meeting resumed in the morning.

Meanwhile, Gibbons may very well have informed Lynch that a consignment of unattributable arms was about to enter the country by sea.

Brainse Fhionnglaise
Finglas Library
Tel: (01) 834 4906

13

THE EMPTY VESSEL FROM ANTWERP

By March 1970 the engines driving the arms quest appeared to be warming up nicely. On 19 March Capt. Kelly approached Anthony Fagan at the Department of Finance and told him G2 wanted to import a cargo without it being inspected. He was quite satisfied Fagan was aware he had arms in mind. When he went back to Fagan the following day, he was ushered in to see Haughey briefly. The minister told him clearance had been approved.[1] Outside, Fagan gave him the names of the appropriate officials who would see the cargo pass through at customs without any fuss.[2]

The plan that crystallised was to ferry the consignment on board the *MV City of Dublin* from Amsterdam to Dublin Port. Col Hefferon and Capt. Kelly discussed where they might store it. The captain suggested Cathal Brugha Barracks, which Col Hefferon felt would be unsuitable because too many people would learn that 'a secret, a top-secret operation' was afoot.[3] The captain suggested storing the arms in a monastery in Co. Cavan, near the border. The colonel gave this the green light. It seems that while the monastery was being prepared, the arms were to be taken to the west of Ireland. 'The lorry to transport the goods was supplied by a Dublin Fianna Fáil man. The intention was to transport them to the yard of another Fianna Fáil man in the west of Ireland.'[4] Gibbons asked Col Hefferon 'where the arms were to be stored when they came in on the *City of Dublin*. I told him the location and he smiled and quoted the line of poetry.'[5]

On 4 March Capt. Kelly briefed Gibbons 'on developments and told him that it might be necessary for me to go to the Continent again'. On 10 March he went to Antwerp 'where I met Herr Schlueter [the arms dealer]. The arms, I was told, were crated at the docks, and I was assured that they would be shipped to Dublin on 17 March'. In the event, the *City of Dublin*, the vessel on which the arms were to be transported, arrived in Dublin on 25 March.

***

Meanwhile, The Deceiver was plotting to seize the cargo, something he denied for a long time before finally admitting the truth. In 1975 while he was still in full deception mode, he disingenuously alleged that:

> Early in 1970 we were informed that a consignment of weapons, paid for out of Dublin government funds and meant for the Belfast Defence Committees, would be arriving within a matter of weeks. I had no other information except that the consignment would consist of various types of weapons suitable for defensive action and a considerable quantity of ammunition. I was told that there would be no difficulty about importing the material as all arrangements had been made the previous autumn, prior to the formation of the Provisional Army Council.
>
> My attitude was that if weapons were being imported for defensive purposes in Belfast, well and good, no matter who got them. If, for once, the Dublin politicians were doing the right thing, even with a token amount of help, it was not too early. Even so, I had serious reservations about whether the undertaking would materialise.

Years later, he told an RTÉ interviewer the truth: he had a unit standing by poised to seize the shipment. 'Certainly', he explained, 'the [Provisional] IRA was going to take the guns for itself.' If the consignment was actually destined for the Provisional IRA, as some conspiracy theorists have propounded, he would not have had to go to such dramatic lengths to 'take' them for himself.

Des Long was an IRA volunteer who sided with the Provisionals after the IRA split. He knew The Deceiver well. While Long was on the run from the end of 1971 until 1973, he found himself in his company for extended periods of time during which the pair had many discussions about IRA activities. Long confirms that The Deceiver told him about the attempt to seize the weapons at Dublin port. 'The plan was to seize them, he told me – no doubt about it. They were not coming in for us.'[6]

The four-man unit The Deceiver dispatched to hijack the cargo included Paddy O'Kane, Michael Kane and Harry Canavan, all of whom were now in the Provisional IRA, albeit that the organisation had not yet declared its existence to the world.[7]

Michael Kane hailed from Ballymurphy. 'He was part of a secret unit that was planting bombs but not declaring them' on behalf of the Provisionals, according to Kieran Conway, the former Director of IRA Intelligence.[8] Kane died on 4 September 1970 while handling a device during a non-attributable mission at an electricity pylon located on the New Forge Lane, off the Malone Road which exploded prematurely. The Deceiver later described him as the 'first casualty of the campaign'. Kane came from a traditional Republican family. His grandfather, Jack Coogan, was an IRA member who had been killed in Valentine Street in the 1920s. His nephew, James O'Neal, would be killed in February 1976.

Paddy O'Kane hailed from North Belfast. He had joined the Parachute Regiment in 1957 serving in its ranks until 1964. During this time he saw action in Cyprus and Jordan. He joined the IRA in 1969. He was part of the unit which lured three Royal Highland Fusiliers, John McCaig, 17; his brother, Joseph, 18, and Dougald McCaughey, 23, to their deaths a year later in a 'honey trap' apparently using two young women as bait. Their bodies were found in North Belfast on 10 March 1971. Conway recalls how 'he made no secret of his involvement' in the killings. He then went on the run in the Republic, established a home in Shannon, County Clare, and set up a unit in Armagh. O'Kane is believed to have been behind the infamous Tullyvallen massacre in September 1975 when five men were murdered during a ceasefire, and the equally egregious Kingsmill massacre in January 1976 when ten workmen were ordered out of a minibus at gunpoint and murdered. In 1976 *The Times of London* described how the British Army in Armagh was facing 'the best trained, best equipped IRA active service unit in Ulster, led by Paddy O'Kane, an ex-soldier sergeant in the Parachute Regiment'.[9] During his time as an active IRA member, he trained other volunteers in the use of rocket propelled grenades. In 2003 he was refused an 'on the run' letter to exempt him from arrest in the UK. He was finally granted such an exemption in 2007. He died in 2009.

According to Kieran Conway, while O'Kane had been in the Parachute Regiment, he had sought entry to the SAS only to be rejected. Conway has described him as a 'psychopath', and says the SAS 'failed him on psychological grounds but he was okay for the paratroopers'.[10]

The third man in the unit, Henry 'Harry' Canavan, was also involved in the March 1971 killing of the Scottish soldiers and other Provisional IRA activities alongside O'Kane as well as The Deceiver. He died in 2015 aged 72.

The actions of a fourth man involved with the Dublin Port hijack operation will be discussed later.

This IRA unit drove down to Dublin Port on the morning of 25 March. Independently, Capt. Kelly made his way there at 7 or 7.30 a.m. unaware of the presence of the IRA unit. At some point he linked up with John Kelly. Hence, there were two groups of eyes on the *MV City of Dublin* as it berthed on the quays.

Diarmuid Ó Riordáin, the custom surveyor in charge of the port, knew in advance that Capt. Kelly would be coming to collect a secret consignment for the Army. The two Kellys were standing at the boat, looking into the hold with deep frustration, when Ó Riordáin arrived. Capt. Kelly introduced him to John Kelly and he took them over to his office. They were there till about ten o'clock without any sign of the arms being found on board.

Capt. Kelly remained at the docks until the afternoon when it became certain that no weapons were on board. Only 'forty bullet-proof vests had arrived. The surveyor arranged with the shipper to have a telex message sent to Antwerp, asking what had happened to the arms. Sometime later we were shown or given a copy of a telex message explaining that because of a procedural technicality the arms cargo had been off-loaded at Antwerp'.

The Provisional unit at the docks clearly received an alert that arms had not arrived because it remained out of sight. By a process of elimination, the fourth man, an individual who had the ability to move between both groups, was most likely the messenger who alerted his colleagues that there were no arms. In the captain's eyes, the fourth man was a CDC activist and, while he undoubtedly knew of his IRA background, had no inkling he was playing a dual role, with a primary loyalty to The Deceiver and would have been prepared to hijack the arms had they arrived. As such, it would have been the first armed Provisional IRA operation had it gone ahead.

At the Arms Trial the captain only provided a vague outline about what had become of the flak jackets on the ship. During his cross-examination on the issue, Seamus Sorohan, SC, who acted for John Kelly, interjected to say that his client 'had had the courage to admit that he was the person who had collected' them.[11] In any event, the captain came to exercise control – if not actual possession over them – until a day or two after his retirement from the army at the end of April 1970. Vincent Browne, a particularly well-informed authority on the Arms Crisis, has written that the IRA got hold of them.[12] It is not known if the captain handed them over under duress or was content to get rid of them as the gardaí were looking for evidence that he had been involved in what they were characterising as an illegal plot to import arms. In either event, they had passed out of his possession before his arrest on 1 May.

John Kelly retained some hope that the arms might yet arrive at Dublin Port. 'I returned to Mr O'Riordan some four or five days later and asked him if the arms had arrived yet' only to find out they had not.[13]

***

A few days after 25 March, Capt. Kelly met Gibbons again and told him that 'a message had since arrived saying that the arms would be shipped from Trieste at some future date'. The captain then 'grew more dubious about the whole operation' and felt he should go back to the Continent to investigate'.[14]

A decision was taken to bring the arms in by air next time. Capt. Kelly obtained from Fagan the names of the customs officials at Dublin Airport who would wave them through. He was satisfied that whatever difficulties might arise, there would be no obstacles with customs clearance.[15]

In what must rank as one of, if not the most bizarre, yet revealing – sequences of the Arms Trials, Gibbons admitted that Capt. Kelly told him about an attempt to import arms through Dublin Port. From Gibbons' perspective, this admission made no sense since by this time he was denying any involvement in the importation. Yet, he admitted to the jury that the captain had discussed the next proposed importation with him. Even more baffling, he conceded that he did not voice any opposition to the plan and subsequently took no action against the captain. Perhaps too much dirt had piled up on the floor around him which could not all be swept under the carpet and hence he had to make these admissions; perhaps he was a poor liar; or maybe was a mixture of both. According to Boland:

> This was a junior army officer talking to the Minister for Defence in the Minister's office. How did the officer happen to be there discussing such a matter with the Minister? Could it possibly have happened unless it was a mutual undertaking? The officer was now being tried for conspiring to attempt to import these arms illegally. Could even the most naive juror be expected to believe that an army officer engaged in such a subversive activity would apply for an audience with the Minister for Defence and go to his office to discuss the ups and downs of his subversive efforts? And the Minister who now maintained that this activity was subversive admitted he didn't tell him to stop it.[16]

Capt. Kelly wanted to return to the Continent but his proposed trip clashed with his regimental duties. He alerted Col Hefferon who asked Gibbons to have him excused and the Minister duly obliged.[17] This enabled the captain to travel to the Continent on 1 April. Albert Luykx, the Belgian who was acting as his interpreter, accompanied him. Luykx was a friend of at least three ministers: Lenihan, Hillery and Blaney. Among his business interests, he ran a restaurant at which they and other ministers such as George Colley dined. The captain and Luykx made it to Antwerp and from there to Hamburg where they met Otto Schlueter who informed him that there had been customs clearance difficulties in Antwerp.

Dramatic developments took place during Capt. Kelly's absence.

14

THE NIGHT OF THE EMERGENCY CONVOY

While the captain was away, the sectarian cauldron boiled over and threatened to spill out across Northern Ireland. The flashpoint was Ballymurphy, a nationalist council estate in West Belfast, approximately a mile off the Falls Road. Built as part of a slum clearance after the Second World War, it was plagued by unemployment: forty per cent compared to a nine per cent average elsewhere in Northern Ireland. The Provisional IRA was trying to establish a stronghold inside it and was becoming increasingly infuriated with gangs of local youths who were chafing against the British Army, provoking them to encroach upon the estate.

On Tuesday 31 March, a number of Junior Orange bands from the neighbouring New Barnsley estate began rehearsing the inflammatory *The Sash My Father Wore* and other tunes for an outing to Bangor contrary to an agreement that they would remain silent before they set off. In anticipation of trouble upon their return, seventy soldiers from the Scots Guards were sent into Ballymurphy to keep the peace. When the Orangemen returned, they were assailed by bottles and bricks, signalling the start of a two-hour riot which the soldiers dealt with ineffectually.

On the evening of Easter Wednesday, 1 April, a full battalion escorted by a squadron of armoured cars was deployed. They were armed with CS gas cannisters and launchers and engaged with the nationalist rioters. It took them until the next day to drive them back into Ballymurphy estate and when they did, militant loyalists followed hot on their heels, some of whom managed to tear down a Tricolour which was flying in the estate. To many nationalists, it looked as if the British Army was acting as a battering ram for the loyalists. The Provisional IRA made no appearance. Jim Sullivan, the CDC leader who was also an Official IRA leader, tried to calm things down. One of the orders he issued was to confiscate milk bottles so they could not be used to make petrol bombs.

John Kelly and another republican, Hugh McAteer, had made their way to Dublin by Thursday 2 April where they met Blaney and made a plea for guns. Blaney agreed to do what he could to secure their release. At the time Jack Lynch was on holiday in West Cork and, according to Gibbons, 'it was impossible to contact him other than by putting someone in a car to go and see him', something he understood was done but Lynch did not make contact.[1] Instead, Gibbons rang Lt Gen. MacEoin from Fianna Fáil's HQ in Naas and spoke to him in Irish. A G2 report reveals that Gibbons 'indicated that he had received information from Mr Blaney that attacks on the minority were planned and that British Security Forces would be withdrawn and accordingly would not afford protection for the minority.[2] The Minister felt that material stored in Dublin should be moved forward'.[3]

MacEoin authorised a number of trucks stationed at McKee Barracks, Cabra, to proceed to Dundalk barracks, close to the Border, with rifles. The G2 report added that on 'the night of 2 April 1970, the following items were stored in Dundalk military barracks 500 rifles 80,000 rounds of ammunition and 3,000 respirators. Military intelligence subsequently ascertained that the information given to the minister regarding reported attacks on the minority and the withdrawal of the British Security Forces were without foundation.'

Neil Blaney believed that they 'had been loaded for some weeks in preparation and Gibbons showed no reluctance to send them on their way.' However, while vehicles may very well have been earmarked for an emergency deployment, they had not yet been loaded with rifles.

It was dark by the time the officer in command (OC) of the trucks from McKee arrived at Clancy Barracks, Islandbridge, to collect arms from them. He spoke to an officer of the Engineer Corps who agreed to release the weapons under his control but first he demanded sight of the OC's orders. Upon being provided with them, he stated he wanted to retain them. When he was told he could not, he refused to release the rifles.

Following on this the OC went to Cathal Brugha Barracks, Portobello, where he encountered a captain who had been 'promoted from the ranks', an older man, who agreed to release his supply and did not demand to retain the written orders.[4]

The convoy that left Dublin consisted of 500 Lee Enfield 303 rifles, 80,000 rounds of ammunition and 3,000 respirators. The trucks criss-crossed back roads at great speed. Some of the respirators fell from the vehicles, which were picked up by children the following morning on their way to school. They were handed in to garda stations. There was some minor reporting of this in the newspapers but no significant headlines.

There is an element of confusion as to precisely where the arms were loaded. Capt. Kelly believes they were put on the trucks at Clancy Barracks, not Cathal Brugha Barracks. While it would be satisfying to be authoritative about the location, it does not distract from a more significant point, namely that written orders were supplied to the OC of the trucks, a fact that was misrepresented by Lynch loyalists in later years.

News of the convoy spread within military circles. One senior officer in a motorised division felt that the matter was of such significance that President de Valera, as head of state, should be advised about it. The officer in question contacted a friend of his, Thomas McNamara, who was the aide-de-camp to the president, and relayed the information to him. Assuming it was passed on, de Valera would have become aware of these events in early April.[5]

Col Hefferon confirmed at the Arms Trial that the rifles were transported to Dundalk for a possible distribution to the CDCs. '… I was very worried about this shipment of rifles and ammunition, and that the meaning I took out of this sudden order to send rifles and ammunition and gas masks, I think, to Dundalk was that a very bad situation was about to break out in the North and that the possibility that these rifles, or some part of them, might require to be distributed in this event could not be ruled out'.[6] He felt the captain's return to Ireland was crucial 'because he knew the people' across the border whom G2 had vetted for the receipt of weapons in an emergency. He rang Mrs Kelly and requested of her that when 'she was in touch with her husband, to tell him that it was my wish that he should return – in regard to a situation much more important than anything he would be doing abroad.'[7] Capt. Kelly and Albert Luykx, who was acting as his translator, had arrived in Antwerp, and were having dinner at their hotel when Mrs Kelly reached her husband:

> She told me that Colonel Hefferon had issued instructions that I should come home immediately because of the situation in the North – it was feared that the serious rioting in Ballymurphy in Belfast might escalate. She further informed me that weapons were being sent to Dundalk for possible distribution in the North and that I would be the person likely to supervise their distribution. I asked her if Mr Gibbons was available in his office. She told me that she did not know but that she knew Neil Blaney was at home. Accordingly I booked a call to Blaney's home.
>
> When I got through to Mr Blaney he told me that the situation in Belfast had improved. I therefore suggested that it was not necessary for me to rush back to Dublin immediately, and after some discussion agreed with Mr Blaney that I would complete my mission [to purchase arms] on the Continent. I requested him to inform Colonel Hefferon of this decision.

Capt. Kelly did not return to Ireland until 4 April.

***

The inclusion of respirators in the convoy that sped to Dundalk was significant. Gibbons would deny their presence while in the witness box. This was because respirators were designed to protect the wearer from the effects of CS gas and, in this instance, they demonstrated a connection between the trucks and the upheaval in Ballymurphy where CS gas had drenched the estate. Kevin Boland wrote in his book, *We Won't Stand (Idly) By* that:

> Gibbons admitted [at the *Arms Trial*] that in the case of the Ballymurphy incident five hundred rifles were moved to the Border in the middle of the night. He concealed the fact that there were also three thousand respirators in the convoy, but, even if there were only rifles involved, any army man will know the operation could not have been carried out at a moment's notice in the middle of the night unless the plans had been made in advance.
>
> Common sense is all that is necessary to know that, if there was a Contingency Plan for the Irish Army to assist in a 'Doomsday' situation – and Gibbons says there was – it included as a first consideration the provision of arms to those who would be under attack in such a situation.[8]

Unfortunately for him, Gibbons was positioned like a boulder in the path of the truth. He turned out to be one which was rather easily rolled aside. He at least admitted at the Arms Trial that a convoy had been sent speeding to Dundalk in the middle of the night:

> I was on my way home to Kilkenny through Naas. I was stopped by the police and asked to ring Neil Blaney, who said he had information of the direst kind and had been in touch with Mr Haughey and at that time somebody was being sent to find the Taoiseach in order to acquaint him of the position and I was requested by Neil Blaney to send certain arms to Dundalk. I rang the Chief of Staff and speaking in Irish, told him … that I had this request from Mr Blaney and it might be better to comply with it and ensure that all the strictest security was observed at all stages. I think I recall saying that 'If I don't do this, he may do something rash himself'.

One of the low points of Gibbons' testimony was when he alleged the rifles might have been sent to Dundalk yet distributed on the south side of the Border to repel an invasion from Northern Ireland:

> If, for instance, the boot was on the other foot, if the attack was from the other side of the Border as it might well be. And, in fact, incursions had been made in the recent past: there were many men such as myself, with rudimentary military training, who could, in the state of national emergency, be called upon to take those weapons in their hands and do what they could on the matter of defence of this particular area. We are talking about a hypothetical situation.

Gibbons was unable to provide an explanation for the hurried nature of the night convoy which linked it to the on-going upheaval in Ballymurphy. Overall, he had an unpleasant spell in the witness box, as appears from his cross-examination by Thomas Finlay SC, who took up the cudgels on behalf of Capt. Kelly. As the exacting cross-examination proceeded, the vines of Gibbons' increasingly implausible claims began to tighten around him and trip him up:

> **Finlay**: 'What was the purpose of sending five hundred rifles without men attached, even against the dire situation which you really did not believe would break out; what were they going to be used for?'
>
> **Gibbons**: 'Rifles! Certainly the function of rifles in our Defence Forces is for defensive purposes.'
>
> **Finlay**: 'Ah, Mr. Gibbons, you understand my question. On 2nd April 1970, to meet a dire situation which might break out, what was the purpose of moving five hundred rifles without men to Dundalk? What were they going to be used for?'

Gibbons: 'If the Doomsday situation of which we are all afraid.'

Finlay: 'What would you do with the rifles?'

Gibbons: '... broke upon us, it would be much more logical to have the rifles in Dundalk rather than elsewhere.'

Finlay: 'What were you going to do with them?'

Gibbons: 'We had no immediate plans for their distribution.'

Finlay: 'Why not move blankets or anything else, why move rifles?'

Gibbons: 'Because blankets are a rather inefficient method of defending one's life.'

Finlay: 'Isn't the truth of the matter, Mr. Gibbons, that you moved the rifles to Dundalk, while you did not think it was going to arise, against the outside possibility that you would have to distribute arms to the people in Northern Ireland?'

Gibbons: 'The eventual reason probably was ... we were dealing with a hypothetical situation which could take many, many forms. It could take the form of assault on the Nationalist, Catholic areas. It could take the form of total breakdown of law and order. It could take the form of the full occupation of the British security forces in other areas, with outside areas totally unprotected.'

Finlay: 'Yes?'

Gibbons: 'There were a great many conceivable forms which this situation might give rise to, anything in the matter of the protection of life.'

Finlay: 'Is it not correct to say that the only way five hundred rifles

> without five hundred men fitted into that picture was that they were to be distributed to civilians in Northern Ireland?'
>
> **Gibbons**: 'No, this is not a reasonable deduction at all.'

Capt. Kelly was also adamant that he and Gibbons had had a discussion about the distribution of the rifles. Finlay held his feet to the fire over the issue too:

> **Finlay**: 'I must put it to you in fairness, it will be part of Captain Kelly's evidence that he particularly pointed out to you at that time that the distribution of Irish army rifles to Northern Ireland would be a crazy operation, as every Irish Army rifle has a serial number on it and is entirely traceable, do you understand the question?'
>
> **Gibbons**: 'Yes.'
>
> **Finlay**: 'Do you remember Capt. Kelly saying that?'
>
> **Gibbons**: 'I have not the slightest recollection.'
>
> **Finlay**: 'And I suggest to you that he discussed the urgent necessity of untraceable arms if this event was ever to occur?'
>
> **Gibbons**: 'No, I have no recollection of that.'

Pádraig Faulkner was a staunch supporter of Lynch, most particularly in his denials of involvement in the quest for arms. Despite the crystal-clear acknowledgement Gibbons made in the Four Courts that the Irish Army owned the rifles which had been sent to Dundalk, Faulkner tried to cast doubt on this in his 2005 memoirs, stating this was something which had merely been 'claimed'.[9]

Faulkner then argued that the cabinet would not have countenanced the 'indiscriminate distribution' of 500 rifles.[10] This ignored the evidence of Col Hefferon who had contacted Capt. Kelly to bring him home because he was the point man who had vetted people involved with the CDC for any distribution of arms. Had the distribution proceeded, Jim Sullivan would have become one of the main recipients. Sullivan was a committed opponent of the Provisional IRA who had remained loyal to the Marxist Goulding. Moreover, ministers Hillery, Lenihan, Blaney, Haughey, Boland, Gibbons and possibly other ministers had told CDC delegations they would receive arms in a 'Doomsday' situation. Indeed, the CDCs also believed that Lynch had made promises to them, though this was probably more wishful thinking than a certainty, especially with someone as skilful as Lynch at moving without leaving a discernible trail in his wake.

There are other problems with Faulkner's account: he claimed there was 'no official documentation' with the rifles and that the convoy was merely allowed into the barracks for investigation.[11] Since written orders had been produced to secure the release of the weapons in Dublin, it is difficult to envisage any scenario whereby they would not equally have been produced in Dundalk.

The problems with Faulkner's account do not end here: he next endeavoured to give the impression that it was Lynch who had intervened to take charge of an event which had spun out of control. According to Faulkner, Lynch learned about it when he received a report from the officers in Dundalk and 'ordered the lorries to remain there all night and return to Dublin the following day'... Yet, Lynch was nowhere to be found on the night of the convoy.

By far the most serious error Faulkner made was where he gave the impression that all of the rifles went back to Dublin. Significantly, only 350 of them made the return journey. The balance along with the 80,000 rounds of ammunition remained in Dundalk and were not moved until the Arms Crisis had begun. Perforce, this means that someone in authority must have chosen precisely how many were to stay and how many to go; issued orders to this effect; sought clarification about where they would be kept, and established that reliable personnel were available to stand guard over them or dispatched a security contingent from elsewhere to attend to the latter task. None of this could have happened behind the back of Gibbons who is by far the most obvious choice for having made these arrangements. Is it likely he did this behind Lynch's back? If he did not, it means that both he and the taoiseach were complicit in storing 150 rifles and ammunition in a military barracks adjacent to the border. Leaving the smaller contingent behind has all the hallmarks of a stopgap measure pending the overdue arrival of the arms purchased from Otto Schlueter.

According to a military report, 'On 4 April 70, 350 rifles were returned to the stores in Dublin because of storage problems in Dundalk … Following intelligence reports of the possibility of a raid by a subversive organisation on Dundalk military barracks, the balance of 150 rifles and 80,000 rounds of ammunition stored in Dundalk were returned to stores in Dublin on Friday, 1 May 1970'.[12]

Faulkner was also in error in claiming that Lynch had ordered the trucks to remain in Dundalk overnight. In reality, and as previously stated, Lynch could not be found that night, and hence could not have issued any orders.

Despite all his distance and caution, Lynch was about to be hurled into the middle of the greatest political scandal in the history of the state, one that could have been avoided if the special branch and Peter Berry had not fallen for the most audacious lie yet fed to them by The Deceiver.

15

A FAREWELL TO ARMS. THE DECEIVER PULLS THE TRIGGER

The Provisional IRA was still very much in its start-up phase in April 1970. The auguries were not particularly bright for it. British military intelligence had reported the previous January that 'the majority of Catholics in the North have little or no sympathy with the IRA type of attack'. The reason for this, they believed, was because NICRA, had 'paved the way for the reforms which are now working their way through Parliament', and, as a result there was 'no point whatsoever in jeopardising the gains already made by senseless acts of violence'. While nationalists were prepared to accept IRA protection from loyalist mobs, and conceal weapons for them, the report added, there was 'no real affection for the IRA and the IRA themselves are aware of it'.[1] This report was drafted before the Provisional/Official split had become apparent to the British and applied equally to both factions.

Meanwhile, the promise of weapons from Dublin relayed by Hillery, Lenihan, Blaney, Haughey, Boland, Gibbons and others such as Capt. Kelly was keeping the spirit of the CDCs afloat, even if any arms that might materialise were destined to be kept under lock and key in the Republic.

As the events described up to this point demonstrate, The Deceiver was aware through his network of spies close to Irish military Intelligence, G2, of Capt. Kelly's on-going efforts to import arms. In April he learned that Capt. Kelly was on the verge of securing a supply of weapons from Europe. He now had a choice of telling Philip McMahon about it or not.

The arms cargo on board the *MV City of Dublin* the previous March had been thwarted due to export technicalities, although it is possible MI6 had pulled tripwires in the background. The Deceiver had not warned McMahon about it as he had hoped to hijack the consignment for the Provisionals. He must have ruminated on what had gone wrong at the port. He undoubtedly knew about the Markham-Randall fiasco – most likely from the fourth man in the Dublin Port hijack unit – and was sufficiently wily to have considered the likelihood that MI6 had thwarted the *MV City of Dublin* shipment too. Hence, there was every possibility MI6 might alert Dublin about the forthcoming arms flight and his credibility might be called into question if he did not alert McMahon to its imminent arrival.

That same month – April 1970 – the Provisionals received a substantial shipment of arms from the US with the promise of a steady supply of more to come in the future. Almost overnight, hijacking the CDC guns was not as enticing as it had seemed before. Also, the prospect of alerting McMahon provided him with a golden opportunity to create havoc for the Irish government, its military and the CDCs. Having weighed up his options, The Deceiver decided to inform McMahon about the forthcoming flight. The plan for the weapons, which were in Vienna, was that they were to be taken to Frankfurt Airport and thereafter flown to Dublin.

Soon afterwards, all political hell broke loose and engulfed Fianna Fáil, the Irish Army and the CDCs.

Capt. Kelly had returned to Ireland on 4 April and had engaged in a further discussion with Gibbons in his office in Leinster House sometime during the following fortnight. On 10 April, he was excused duties by Col Delaney, the new director of G2, who took over on 9 April. This enabled him to return to the Continent, on Friday 17 April. As before, he brought Albert Luykx with him as translator. They travelled to Frankfurt and onwards to Vienna where he examined the arms. While his 'precise feeling was that they were not the most suitable type of weapons', he agreed to take them. 'Herr Schlueter, however, was not licensed to handle such items as sub-machine guns in Austria and only the pistols and about one-third of the ammunition were in Vienna. We made arrangements to collect the missing part of the cargo *en route* to Dublin. As it was Saturday the arrangements could not be finalised until the following Monday, but as we sat down to a meal that evening it seemed that all the problems were sorted out ...'[2]

Ever the expert at using the truth to tell a lie, The Deceiver tipped off McMahon that an attempt to import arms for the IRA was about to take place. He undoubtedly indicated that the intended beneficiary was Goulding's Official IRA as all of his previous misinformation had been targeted at the Marxists he so hated.

In his memoirs, Des O'Malley wrote about a 'tip-off' that the gardaí received: 'Those involved had planned to bring arms through Customs without the consignment being examined; but the Gardaí had received a tip-off about the plot, as well as intelligence that Haughey, as Minister for Finance, had authorised passage through Customs.'[3]

Lynch gave the Dáil a different account, however, alleging the plot had unravelled as a result of questions raised by officials at Dublin Airport. It is not clear if Lynch was misled by Berry or knew the truth and was protecting the informant. What is abundantly clear is that McMahon, Fleming and Berry knew Lynch misled the Dáil, yet none of them ever corrected the record.

Berry and the garda top brass deployed special branch officers to Dublin Airport on Friday 17 April where – to use Peter Berry's phrase – they placed a 'ring of steel' around it. In reality, it was nothing of the sort. One airport employee who was present when they pulled up in their unmarked vehicles has described how 'they stuck out like men in the ladies toilets' with their unfashionably short haircuts.[4] At the time nearly 200 people worked in the cargo terminal, most of whom were wondering why they were hanging around outside it.

At 'about 1.30 p.m.' on the following Saturday, Fleming paid a call on a Mr Kilty, director of customs and excise, at his home. Before visiting him, he had consulted with the garda commissioner, Michael Wymes. According to Fleming's report, he informed Kilty that:

> a shipment of arms and ammunition was likely to arrive at Dublin Airport within the next few days, and I requested his assistance in having this shipment inspected by Customs Official on arrival. I told him … that Kelly's story of having Government sanction for the operation was a pack of lies. Mr Kilty agreed to help in every possible way …[5]

All told, five airports and a series of seaports were placed under surveillance.

***

Some special branch officers later concluded that The Deceiver perceived himself as being in a power struggle with John Kelly, not to mention the CDCs of which Kelly was national organiser. What is clear is that The Deceiver's tip-off about the Vienna flight ultimately led to Kelly's prosecution for gunrunning.

Kelly's links with G2 were also an anathema to The Deceiver. Moreover, Kelly's ambiguous relationship with Goulding must have rendered The Deceiver even more wary of him. John Kelly, was, according to himself, 'reporting to Goulding and keeping Billy McMillen [another Official] involved … from '69 into '70'.

Conor Cruise O'Brien provided an insight into how the Ó Brádaigh faction, of which The Deceiver was a senior member, viewed the young Belfastman. In his 1970 diary O'Brien describes how he went to lunch with Ó Brádaigh at the National Gallery on 2 July 1970, the same day John Kelly, Haughey and their co-defendants were returned for trial. According to O'Brien, 'Earlier [Ó Brádaigh] had agreed in deploring' a press release that Kelly had made.[6] Unfortunately O'Brien did not elaborate on what they found deplorable about the press statement. What is significant, however, is that the comment revealed a level of hostility on the part of Ó Brádaigh towards John Kelly.

There were others – inside the state security apparatus – who were just as hostile toward Kelly. They also had Gibbons,

Blaney and Haughey in their sights and were prepared to break the law to bring them down.

16

THE CIVIL SERVANT WHO WAS A LAW UNTO HIMSELF

At the Arms Trial, Peter Berry conceded to one of Charles Haughey's barristers, that 'it was a fair statement to say he was a person who liked to control his department as much as he could and act on his own initiative'.[1] Although An Garda Síochána was an independent organisation, this mattered little to Berry, who ran the special branch from the department of justice as if he were its chief.

Acting in harmony with this trait, Berry went behind his government's back to consult President de Valera in respect of what he had learned about the arms importation on Saturday 18 April, i.e., before he spoke to Lynch. 'Analysing my motives afterwards', he wrote, '... I could only suppose that sub-consciously I retained lingering doubts about the Taoiseach and that by consulting the President, and telling the Taoiseach that I had consulted the President, I would be pushing the Taoiseach towards an enforcement of the rule of law. I had not forgotten that the Taoiseach had taken no effective steps to curb the activities of Capt. Kelly of Military Intelligence about whom I had given him very definite information on 17th October '69 in Mount Carmel Hospital'.[2]

The revelation cannot have come as a complete surprise to de Valera as he had been advised by his aide-de-camp, Thomas McNamara, a little over two weeks earlier about the convoy of trucks carrying rifles which been dispatched to Dundalk, and had taken no steps to intervene.

Berry told the president, 'I am afraid that if I follow the normal course [i.e. report to Ó Moráin] the information might not reach Government. Does my duty end with informing my Minister or am I responsible to Government by whom I was appointed?' Having obtained an assurance that Berry 'was absolutely' sure about his facts, the president told him he had a 'clear duty to Government, you should speak to the Taoiseach'.[3]

Meanwhile, Customs Superintendent Tom Tobin made an effort to explain to Fleming of the special branch that the cargo due to arrive at Dublin Airport was one which he had been ordered by the Department of Finance to allow pass through customs without inspection but Fleming refused to talk to him. Tobin then sent a message to the department of finance that the special branch wanted to seize the cargo. Capt. Kelly recalls how on Saturday 18 April 'when I eventually got through to my wife [on the phone], I was given very disturbing news. "There is something wrong," she said. "Colonel Hefferon called. No one seems to know what is going on at this end, but the Special Branch have got the wrong end of the stick. They are waiting to seize the goods and arrest you".' She told him to stay where he was and that John Kelly would fly out to meet him in the morning.

According to the captain, it was Brian Lenihan, the minister for transport and power, 'who informed Colonel Hefferon that the airport was surrounded and the cargo would be seized. He suggested that the importation should be postponed until the matter was sorted out'.[4]

Haughey was advised of the message sent by Tobin and on Saturday 18 April, he called Berry who he knew from his days as minister for justice. Berry was in his bedroom about to enter an adjacent sauna when Haughey reached him. During their conversation, Berry told Haughey that the Special Branch had placed 'a ring of steel' around the airport and would seize any arms that might land. Crucially, Berry indicated that Ó Moráin not only knew about the surveillance operation *but had ordered that the arms were to be seized*. Ó Moráin would dispute Berry's claim later when he gave his evidence.[5] Ó Moráin was quite clear that he had not known about the plan to seize the cargo until the afternoon of Saturday 18 April, i.e. after it had been put in place. According to Ó Moráin, his orders had been to watch but not seize the cargo.[6] If Ó Moráin was correct, Berry had not only acted beyond the scope of his authority, but in disobedience to his minister and was now compounding matters by lying to Haughey. All of this had the potential to end his career if the truth was ever to emerge.

According to Berry, Haughey suggested that the Special Branch might let the consignment through on condition it went straight to Northern Ireland.

Haughey's account was that he had contacted Berry after he had learned about the development at the airport, and had raised a series of questions about the consignment which he knew was intended for the military. He would say that although he did not know what it contained, he had a 'shrewd' idea it was arms.[7] There are many reasons to believe he was fully aware arms were involved.

Considering that Haughey in the first place made the call indicates that he was oblivious to the fact the gardaí believed the arms were earmarked for the IRA and had been purchased with misappropriated government funds. It is inconceivable that if this was what was afoot, he would have called Berry for any sort of a discussion. Likewise it is eminently arguable he had no inkling that Garda Commissioner Michael Wymes had reached the conclusion the operation was one of 'foul treachery to the Government'.[8] Similarly, he was oblivious to the blizzard of lies The Deceiver had been feeding the gardaí about him since August 1969.

If we accept at face value Berry's version of his discussion with Haughey – that Haughey suggested that the arms be let through if they went to Northern Ireland – it confirms that the plan was initially to store the arms somewhere in the Republic. The 'ring of steel' at the airport had done no more than jolt Haughey into an improvisation i.e. his suggestion that the weapons go straight to Northern Ireland. According to Berry, Haughey swiftly changed his mind, acknowledging that his suggestion was foolish, and that it would be better to cancel the importation altogether, which is what happened. None of the arms ever landed in Dublin.

***

On Sunday 19 April, Capt. Kelly phoned Fagan at his home from Vienna to elicit further instructions from Haughey. As Seamus McKenna SC put it during his cross-examination of the captain: 'You asked [Fagan] to ask the boss man [i.e. Haughey] what the instructions were. Now there can be no doubt about this: you were asking Mr Fagan to ascertain from

Mr Haughey what the riding orders for you were, is that not right?' Capt. Kelly responded: 'correct yes', adding, 'as far as I was concerned this was a Government plan and I had no reason to think otherwise, and as far as I was concerned any member of the Cabinet could give me the instructions, and Mr Fagan, as far as I was concerned, could, if he thought necessary, ring Mr Gibbons."[9] One reason he did not call Gibbons directly was because he did not have his home number.

After the cancellation, John Kelly flew out to Europe where he joined the captain and Luykx but was unable to add much to what Capt. Kelly's wife had told him on the phone the previous night. 'We were both mystified. Neither of us could understand what was happening in Ireland. Mr Schlueter and Mr Luykx departed and John and I stayed overnight in Vienna'.[10]

The next morning, Capt. Kelly contacted the agent in Vienna and informed him that the operation was cancelled 'for the time being at least'.

Peter Berry's Saturday sauna was further delayed – if not wholly abandoned – because Patrick Malone, the head of C3, rang him shortly after Haughey's telephone conversation. He told Berry that Fagan had left a message with the gardaí that Fleming was to ring either Haughey or himself. Again, Haughey's attempt to contact Fleming via Fagan was hardly the action of a man involved in a treacherous and illegal attempt to import arms for the IRA with misappropriated funds.

Berry secured an appointment to see Lynch 'shortly after noon' on Monday 20 April.[11] His 'discussion with the Taoiseach that morning was restricted as the British Ambassador was waiting to see him'. Lynch would make the audacious claim that this was the first he learnt of the importation attempt. This would mean that Gibbons had not reached him by phone or in person over the weekend or earlier that day to let him know what had been happening. As Michael Heney has pointed out, Gibbons and Haughey had had a discussion earlier that day about what had transpired at the airport.[12] It is difficult to suspect that Gibbons had failed to approach the taoiseach before Berry spoke to him that afternoon.

Indeed, it is quite possible that Lynch and Ambassador Peck were discussing the development while Berry was waiting for his meeting with Lynch.

When Lynch admitted him, Berry handed him the 'police report to read and gave him a full account of the events of Friday, Saturday, and Sunday'. Berry also told Lynch about his conversation with Haughey around the cargo which had been due to land at Dublin Airport. If we are to believe Lynch, this was the first indication he received that there had been an attempt to import arms. 'He instructed me,' Berry continued, 'to have the matter fully investigated and to report to him at 9.30 the following morning'.[13]

On Tuesday 21 April, Berry told Lynch why he had gone over Ó Moráin's head to talk to him, saying he had had 'qualms about approaching him, as I might be intruding on a secret Government mission. I said that in my dilemma I had spoken to the President who, without being told the nature of the subject, advised me that it was my duty to speak to the Taoiseach. The Taoiseach made no comment.'[14]

On Wednesday 29 April, Lynch let loose on Berry 'suddenly' telling him that when he had said that he had 'thought the

Government might be secretly involved I saw *red*: I was not able to speak to you I was so furious.' How much of Lynch's 'red' mist was a performance and how much real, is a secret Lynch took with him to the grave. Since Berry had stumbled upon a secret government mission – something Lynch knew full well – he can hardly have been annoyed at Berry for suspecting the truth. His anger must have sprung from the fact Berry was now meddling with the mission and had created a severe political headache for his administration.

***

In his retirement Berry perpetuated a series of myths about the Arms Crisis. In one passage of his 'diaries' he included four inaccuracies. First, that the weapons were destined for the IRA; second, that Ó Moráin – not he – had ordered their seizure; third, that he had informed Ó Moráin about the surveillance that engulfed the airport *before* it had been put in place; and fourth, that the shipment had come to official attention because it had stumbled in the face of international bureaucratic red tape.[15]

On 29 April, Lynch told Berry that he was about to 'confront Mr Blaney and Mr Haughey'. Lynch was apparently 'very troubled, walking up and down the room, muttering to himself. I heard him say "What will I do, what will I do" and, thinking that he was addressing me, I said: "Well, if I were you I'd sack the pair of them and I would tell the British immediately, making a virtue of necessity, as the British are bound to know, anyway, all that is going on".' At that Lynch 'rounded' on him and 'abused' him 'for giving him advice. I apologised and said that I thought that he had asked for advice. He went back to muttering. He suddenly made up his mind to go.'[16]

On 30 April, Lynch again sent for Berry and told him he had spoken to Haughey and Blaney both of whom had assured him there would be no further attempt to bring in weapons and that the matter was closed. 'I asked incredulously: "Does this mean that Mr Haughey remains Minister for Finance? What will my position be? He knows that I have told you of his conversation with me on 18th April and of the earlier police information." The taoiseach replied: "I will protect you". I felt a very sorry man returning to my department where I told the tale to my usual colleagues.' Andrew Ward, his deputy, was undoubtedly one of his colleagues.

This passage may be one of the most instructive of the entire Arms Crisis as it provides a motive for the litany of dirty tricks Berry would perpetrate in the lead up to, and during, the two Arms Trials: Berry not only wanted to preserve his career but was fearful of Blaney and Haughey's wrath should they return to power. Berry may also have been nursing a grudge against Haughey. During a conversation with Charlie Murray of the Department of Finance on 20 May 1970, he said, 'On one occasion when my then Minister [i.e. Haughey], who became your Minister for Finance, tried to do something he blew me out of the room but if he blew me out of the room I still refuse to do so – to do something irregular.'[17]

At this juncture, if one tries to reconcile what Lynch said about his showdown with Blaney and Haughey to various parties with different interests and agendas, confusion will reign supreme. If instead, one looks at Lynch as a desperate politician trying to keep a series of political plates spinning in the air and there is no common thread of truth to be found, the confusion recedes.

Lynch's first account is that just described to Berry, namely that the ministers admitted the importation and would not attempt to do so again and that the matter was closed. A second version emerges from Lynch's Dáil speech, 'I had said to both of them … that the information that I had would justify my asking for their resignations … the Minister for Agriculture … asked for some *time to consider the position*' [my emphasis].

Boland provided a third version. He wrote that at the cabinet meeting on Friday 1 May, Lynch 'informed the government of the matter. He said he had got this information, had put it to the two Ministers and that *they had both denied being involved* in an illegal attempt to import arms. He said he had decided to accept their denials, the matter was now closed and warned the members in general that any specific action in relation to the Six Counties should be brought to the Government for sanction'.[18]

Unfortunately, Pádraig Faulkner's memoirs are riven with blunders. Bearing this *caveat* in mind, however on this issue he confirms Boland's recollection. He described a Cabinet meeting at which Lynch 'said that he had discussed the matter with [Haughey and Blaney] and both had vehemently denied the allegations'.[19]

Boland unravelled what had probably happened: Lynch had sought the ministers' resignations privately but he had been rebuffed. In *Up Dev*, Boland recounts how on Friday 1 May Haughey was 'still in fairly bad shape [after a horse-riding accident on 22 April] and the position was that his resignation had been requested. After the Government meeting I said to Blaney "I think I should go to the Mater [Hospital] and set Haughey's mind at rest" [as he was not going to be dismissed involuntarily]. Blaney said "No. I don't trust him [Lynch]". I replied, "He has told the Government the matter is over and done with. Surely he's not going to go back on that?" I, accordingly, went straight to the Mater Hospital and told Haughey what had transpired …'[20]

Faulkner was particularly struck by the fact that Blaney seemed unperturbed. 'Nobody made any comment and we then turned to an item on agriculture. I can still clearly recall Neil Blaney, Minister for Agriculture, vigorously arguing a point on the subject. It was if the Taoiseach had said nothing of any significance. I was deeply shocked by the revelations, and in view of the allegations made, whether they were true or false, I was amazed that Blaney could apparently ignore them. Perhaps this attitude may have been to show contempt for Jack Lynch. In any case, this, to me, extraordinary display by Neil Blaney underpins my memory of that day.'

Blaney and Haughey simply knew too much for Lynch to force them out against their will. It is inconceivable that Gibbons – with whom they had worked hand in glove – had not told them that Lynch had given him the green light to take over the arms quest in January 1970. And even if that factor is removed from consideration, Blaney and Haughey had been present when northern delegations had visited Dublin to meet the taoiseach, Hillery, Lenihan, Gibbons and others and they knew arms had been promised to them. Moreover, if Lynch had known about the London/Dublin Airport arms shipment of September

1969, as Boland implies, he could hardly have forced the two ministers out without repercussions for himself, not to mention other ministers, should they decide to reveal it. Then there was the meeting with Seán Keenan and Billy Kelly – two members of the Provisional IRA – at his office earlier in 1970 (most likely February) – when he had considered arming them with surplus Irish Army rifles overnight, ultimately deciding against this. Indeed, that meeting indicates that Lynch's ministers were not keeping him in the dark about their desire to arm the CDCs.

While the ministers may have had some leverage over Lynch, there was little the taoiseach could do to restrain Peter Berry and the special branch who now had the smell of blood in their nostrils. The new director of military intelligence, Col Delaney, now joined this hunting pack.

17

'A PAWN IN A VERY STRANGE GAME'

By 1 May the ice underneath Lynch's feet was beginning to crack. While he was assuring his cabinet that the matter was 'closed', Capt. Kelly was in custody, having been arrested that very morning by Fleming and a colleague. Lynch was not only aware of this, he was about to interview the captain personally in his office at government buildings.

It had taken the gardaí a while to arrest the captain. He, John Kelly and Albert Luykx had flown back to Dublin on Tuesday 21 April. The omens were not auspicious: their passports were inspected on arrival, something Capt. Kelly felt was an 'unusual procedure'.

Unfortunately for the captain and his colleagues, the new Director of G2, Col 'Bud' Delaney, who had taken charge of G2 on 8 April, did not know about the importation operation. According to a G2 report, for two months before Col Hefferon retired 'Colonel Delaney had been in the Intelligence Section to familiarise himself with its operations'. However, Col Hefferon had not told him 'of Captain's Kelly's activities because it was a matter of great secrecy, in which some Government Ministers and in my mind acting for the Government were involved'. Col Hefferon believed that if anyone should have informed his successor, it should have been 'the Minister for Defence'.[1]

On 22 April, Gibbons received a verbal briefing from Col Delaney about Capt. Kelly's efforts to import arms. Col

Delaney clearly still had no idea that Gibbons and the captain had been working hand in glove with each other. Gibbons did not put him straight. Instead, Gibbons donned a mask and let Col Delaney describe what he must have believed was sensational and shocking information: an attempt had been made to import arms for subversive groups on both sides of the border.

The new director also maintained that from November 1969 Capt. Kelly had allegedly 'ceased to have any contact with the Security Sub-Section and no reports from him are on record in the Intelligence Security Sub-Section'.[2] This was a curious allegation as the captain's handwritten report on the Bailieboro meeting was not only preserved but released by the National Archives decades later. Persisting in the mistaken belief that the arms were destined for the IRA, the colonel argued that the purchase of arms 'had grave implications for military and state security. Weapons should be purchased only for the forces of the state NOT for illegal groups.' Such weapons, he continued, could be used not only against the British, 'but against our own forces'. He feared that if any of the weapons were to be captured, it would be 'possible to trace their origin'. He also warned that it:

> must be accepted that British intelligence, now operating in a big way in Northern Ireland, will get onto it. They have their own international links with European security agencies and with the CIA, so the likelihood of these activities going undetected is small. As well as the intelligence implications there is the political reaction of the British government to be considered.[3]

Gibbons did not let his mask slip and pretended to share his concerns. This is apparent from the memo the colonel wrote up later in which he stated that Gibbons 'agrees that (a) arms could be turned against us (b) untrained people in NI should not get arms (c) British Intelligence and CIA could know.'

The next day Capt. Kelly attended a meeting in Leinster House with Blaney. At the captain's suggestion, Col Hefferon, now in retirement, was invited to join them and did so a while later. A few minutes after Col Hefferon arrived, Gibbons came by. 'The two Ministers did most of the talking; both seemed to be puzzled as to why the Special Branch should have mounted the weekend operation to seize the expected arms,' Capt. Kelly said at his trial. According to him, the 'sense of the meeting was one of puzzlement as to why investigations were taking place, and how this could be explained, or how various people could be contacted so that it could be sorted out, this error or mistake which was being made by someone who did not know what was going on'.[4]

To the captain's dismay at 'one point, Mr Gibbons suggested to me that I was 'in the hot seat' – the first intimation I got that he was going to deny authorising the arms importation. I reacted somewhat aggressively to this but the matter could not be clarified there and then, because both Ministers were scheduled to attend a ceremony in Rathfarnham, County Dublin, where St Enda's, the school founded and run by Patrick Pearse, the executed 1916 leader, was being handed over to the nation'.

The captain explained during his trial that it was not until this meeting had taken place that it had begun to 'dawn on me that Mr Gibbons was – all I can say is that he was changing colour or backing out; for it was then [Gibbons] made his remark to me: "You are in the hot seat", and this immediately annoyed me very much. I said: "What do you mean, I'm in no hot seat", and it was then he used the phrase: "You're a brazen bastard". It was then it dawned on me that Mr Gibbons was playing some game.' As the ministers 'rushed to their waiting cars it was decided that the meeting should reconvene later in the day. It did not do so and I was left wondering what exactly Mr Gibbons meant by telling me I was in the hot seat'.[5]

***

The next day, 23 April, Albert Luykx sent a letter to Gibbons. Significantly, it was addressed to 'the Minister, Department of Defence, Infirmary Road, Dublin 7'. By sending it to the Department, it was certain it would be opened and read by Gibbons' civil servants. This fact and the content of the letter indicate that it was hardly sent by someone who believed he was involved in an illegal operation to import arms. Luykx advised Gibbons that 'Otto Schlueter GmbH., licensed arms – and ammunition – dealers, in Hamburg' was due to 'arrive in Ireland on the 3th [*sic*] of May next'. What Luykx described as the 'ultimate purpose of his visit is to lay-on a demonstration of various military and ancillary equipment for your department on Monday 4th May. On this occasion Messrs Schlueter do not visualise a large-scale demonstration, Rather [*sic*] they would appreciate the opportunity of meeting some of your purchasing officers for a general discussion, with emphasis on the use of the latest equipment and riot control. Hoping that the suggested meeting will be arranged. It can only be to our mutual advantage'.[6]

Capt. Kelly met Gibbons again on the night of Monday 27 April at Leinster House when Gibbons 'indicated that the arms could still be imported provided secrecy were maintained'.[7] Capt. Kelly felt that 'his attitude at the earlier meeting must have been an aberration'.

Gibbons also told him that he was organising to have him transferred from Intelligence to 'an undemanding position in Dublin' from where he could carry on his work and 'report directly to him'. He was taking these steps 'to maintain secrecy'.[8]

Col Delaney was still labouring in the dark on 28 April when he issued a clear and unambiguous order to Capt. Kelly to have no more contact with his Northern Ireland contacts and transferred him to the Command Training Depot of the Eastern Command at Cathal Brugha Barracks where he was told to occupy himself with more routine military duties.[9] That same day 'I was virtually arrested by two comrades from Intelligence and placed under a definite form of restraint'.[10] Still, he was optimistic, '... Mr Gibbons had assured me that his successor, Colonel Delaney, knew nothing about the arms importation. I felt, therefore, that there had simply been a breakdown in communications and made an appointment to see Mr Gibbons that night.'[11] When he met Gibbons, he told him about his orders to break off contact with his contacts. 'You must keep your Northern contacts,' Gibbons replied. When the captain told him that he could be court-martialled for disobeying Col Delaney, Gibbons insisted he should still maintain his contacts.

The captain also informed Gibbons that certain people

from Northern Ireland would be coming down to see members of the government and asked if the meetings would still go ahead. Gibbons assured him they would.[12]

He left the minister's office that evening 'convinced that I was to be a pawn in a very strange game'. He now feared the worst: 'I was certain that the Minister was changing his stated policy vis-a-vis the Northern situation and that he was attempting to place me in a compromising position with the army authorities, in a position where I could be court-martialled for disobeying a lawful order. But even if I did not walk into the rather obvious court martial trap, my position as an army officer was still virtually impossible. I was already under partial restraint and it would have been easy to hold me completely incommunicado, debarred by military law from giving my interpretation of events.' He felt he had no choice but to 'retire and retire quickly' to protect his position. That night he and his wife 'sat up for hours discussing the advisability of retiring. We have five children; I had been in the army all my working life ... but I really had no choice, the decision was inevitable'[13] The following morning, he applied to retire.

He met with Mr Gibbons again on Wednesday 29 April. His retirement documents were on the table. The minister wanted him to stay but he had made up his mind to go. Gibbons asked if he wanted him to sign the documents. Capt. Kelly told him he did. He returned to the barracks the following morning and waited until official word came through that his retirement papers had been signed. Hence, when he was arrested by the gardaí on Friday 1 May, he was no longer subject to military command.

Kelly's move turned out to be the right one for him: certain gardaí had – or were about to – leak the news of the arms operation to the Opposition. They claimed the weapons had been intended for the IRA and that Gibbons was involved. Pointing a finger at Gibbons created yet another headache for Lynch who would sink or swim with him.

18

SECRET BRIEFINGS FOR THE OPPOSITION

The joke immortalised by the celebrated BBC comedy *Yes Prime Minister*, that the Ship of State is the only vessel that leaks from the top, rang true during the Arms Crisis.

On 5 May 1970, Jack Lynch informed the Dáil that Mícheál Ó Moráin, the minister for justice, had resigned on grounds of ill health. When Liam Cosgrave asked him whether this would be the only ministerial resignation the House could expect, Lynch replied, 'I don't know what the Deputy is referring to', to which Cosgrave responded, 'Is it only the tip of the iceberg?' Cosgrave was then invited by Lynch to enlarge on what was on his mind but declined. What was clear, however, was that Cosgrave had learned about the arms importation operation. As Garret FitzGerald recalls in his memoirs, on the evening of 5 May:

> I went into Cosgrave's office shortly before 8 o'clock to find a number of members of the front bench talking with him in grave tones. The discussion was clearly confidential; I left them to it. Much later I learned that Cosgrave had been consulting the people present about *two separate reports* [author's emphasis] he had received of a plot to import arms for the IRA, which allegedly involved Government Ministers. Fearing that these reports might have been a trap, he hesitated to take action, but Mark Clinton said he should present the information to the Taoiseach. He agreed, returning an hour later to tell his colleagues, 'It's all true'.[1]

One of the reports was an anonymous note Cosgrave had received from someone who described himself on it simply as 'Garda' and who had dropped it into his house. Significantly, it identified the role played by Gibbons and Col Hefferon. Intriguingly, Cosgrave omitted both of their names from the Opposition onslaught on the government when the full-blown crisis erupted a short while later.

The anonymous 'Garda' note disclosed:

> A plot to bring in arms from Germany worth £80,000 for the North under the guise of the Dept of Defence has been discovered. Those involved are – Captain James Kelly, I.O, Col Hefferon X Director of Intelligence (both held over the weekend in the Bridewell) Gibbons, Haughey, Blaney, and the Jones Brothers of Rathmines Road and Rosapena Hotel, Donega [*sic*]
>
> SEE THAT THIS SCANDAL IS NOT HUSHED UP.
>
> GARDA

Armed with the note and the information from his second source, Cosgrave confronted Lynch at 8 p.m. on 5 May. According to research conducted by Stephen Collins, the second source was *The Deceiver*'s handler Philip McMahon.[2] Cosgrave told Lynch that it had come to his attention that Gibbons and the others were involved in a plot to bring in arms for Northern Ireland. It is clear that Lynch saw the note and that it contained Gibbons' name. When Lynch came to describe it as part of his narrative in the Dáil, he outlined how Cosgrave 'showed me a document but I will not even tell the House what that document was like because there has been some comment as to whether the information was on headed paper. I will leave it to Deputy

Cosgrave, if he feels like it, to do so. At any rate, he was kind enough to show me a document on which was a cryptic message'. This coyness spared Gibbons' his blushes for the moment.

When Fleming gave evidence in the Four Courts Seamus Sorohan, SC for John Kelly, asked him if the Branch had investigated the leak of information to Cosgrave. Fleming replied, 'My branch did not investigate any leak of security'. Without missing a beat, he deflected the question by adding: 'I think, my Lord, that Mr Sorohan is making an accusation against the Special Branch on this. I would like to state on oath that I definitely did not leak any information'.[3] Fleming, however, must have had a shrewd idea – if not explicit knowledge – that McMahon was Cosgrave's source. Who else possessed such information?

Lynch did not decide to dismiss Blaney and Haughey until after his confrontation with Cosgrave on 5 May. Thereafter, he strove to give the impression that dismissal had been his intention all along. 'When I came back to my office on Monday [4 May], I got some further evidence which was not very conclusive but nevertheless it was evidence' he told the Dáil on 8 May. According to Kevin Boland, Lynch behaved as if:

> his second request for the Ministers' resignations came before Deputy Cosgrave's visit to him with his anonymous letters. This was untrue. Deputy Cosgrave gave the time of his visit to the Taoiseach as 8 p.m. [on Tuesday 5 May] and this has not been contradicted. Blaney was sent for at 9:45 p.m.[4]

Boland knew the precise sequence of events because he had been present at a meeting of the Organisation Committee of Fianna

Fáil which Blaney was chairing. He was there at 9.45 p.m. when a note requesting Blaney to go to the taoiseach's office was passed to him. Blaney guessed what was about to happen. 'What did I tell you? This is it. Will you take the Chair?' he requested of Boland. By the time the meeting ended at 10 p.m. Blaney had returned and informed Boland and Paudge Brennan that Lynch had demanded his resignation. He revealed that he had said he would furnish his response the following morning. To this, Lynch had responded that he 'could' not wait and would have go to the president and secure his dismissal instead.[5]

Having dealt with Blaney, Lynch rang Haughey at his home in Kinsealy. Neither Lynch nor Haughey have ever revealed what transpired during this discussion or any additional one they may have had subsequent to it, whether directly or through intermediaries. Can we deduce anything about the call from the approach Lynch took after it? On 7 May, he attended a dinner hosted by Fianna Fáil in Laois, at which he referred to Blaney and Haughey as 'able, brilliant and dedicated men'. If he genuinely believed they had tried to purchase arms illegally with misappropriated government funds for the benefit of the IRA, he was hardly likely to have been so fulsome in his praise of them.

Blaney and Haughey clearly had a lot of cards to play against Lynch in what had become a game of high-stakes political poker. Balanced against this was the imperative of avoiding a diplomatic clash with the UK, not to mention the very real danger of unleashing lethal loyalist violence against the nationalist minority. All of this had the potential to happen if the Dublin government was to acknowledge that it had been involved in a conspiracy to import arms even if only to store them in a monastery for possible distribution to the CDCs in the unlikely event of a Doomsday scenario. Both Lynch and Haughey were sophisticated, experienced and seasoned practitioners of the complex art of politics and sufficiently astute to have reached an accommodation whereby events could play out without destroying both of them or unleashing havoc. Haughey must have appreciated that Cosgrave had forced Lynch's hand but – crucially – before the thumb screws had been applied, Lynch had been content to let him remain in his cabinet and cover-up the affair.

The reaching of an accommodation of some sort – whether on 5 May or shortly thereafter – would not only account for Lynch's comments in Laois but also those he would utter on 8 May in the Dáil when he told the chamber sometime close to midnight of the 'heartbreak of my decision' to dismiss his ministers, adding that:

> I knew the effect it was likely to have on the political future of able and brilliant men. Deputy Haughey has, in a statement issued yesterday, said he regarded his political future as less important than the future of Fianna Fáil. But his political future was and I hope could yet be particularly bright.

Lynch was also conciliatory towards Blaney, describing how they had received their seals of office on the same day thirteen years previously and had 'grown to political maturity together'. Lynch could hardly have considered defrauding the exchequer of funds to illegally arm a secret army that was opposed to the state as an act of 'political maturity'. Lynch would also tell Ambassador Peck that he hoped 'Charlie' would be acquitted.[6]

Haughey may have despised the role he was assigned, but was caught in a vice. He would never have been forgiven by the grass roots of Fianna Fáil, let alone the wider public, if he had acted out of pique and brought the government crashing down around him by revealing what he knew about Lynch's knowledge of the affair. In addition, he had a great number of cousins across the border with whom he had spent many happy summer holidays. He knew just how vulnerable they were and was under no desire to endanger them. He had once even witnessed a violent riot on his way out of a cinema during one of these holidays.

In private Haughey was caustic in his criticism of Lynch, whom he loathed, accusing him of having 'hung him out to dry' over the Arms Crisis and criticised how Lynch exploited his 'saintly demeanour'. John Kelly has described how Haughey 'hated Lynch with a passion'.[7]

***

Following the call to Haughey on the night of 5 May, Lynch went home. Shortly after midnight, Eoin Neeson, the head of the Government Information Services, contacted various newspaper offices, asking them how long could they wait before going to print because Lynch would be issuing an important announcement. After this, Lynch dictated the words of a statement over the phone from his house to Neeson and it was released close to 3 a.m. It read, 'I have requested the resignations as members of the Government of Mr Neil T. Blaney, Minister for Agriculture and Fisheries, and Mr Charles J. Haughey, Minister for Finance, because I am satisfied that they do not subscribe fully to Government policy in relation to the present situation in the Six Counties, as stated by me at the Fianna Fáil Ard-Fheis in January last'.

Boland resigned voluntarily at about 10 p.m. in protest at what Lynch was doing. Garret FitzGerald was a witness to his departure from Lynch's office. At 'about 10 o'clock, unaware of what was playing out behind closed doors, I walked into the Ministers' corridor in search of a member of the Government to whom I wished to speak ... The door from the Taoiseach's office at the end of the corridor opened. A glowering Kevin Boland – Minister for Local Government – came along the corridor, too preoccupied to notice me'.[8]

'Last night at approximately 8p.m.,' Cosgrave told the Dáil the following day, 'I considered it my duty in the national interest to inform the Taoiseach of information I had received and which indicated a situation of such gravity for the Nation that it is without parallel in this country since the foundation of the State.' Cosgrave paraphrased from the garda note thus: 'A plot to bring in arms from the continent worth £80,000 under the guise of the Department of Defence has been discovered. Those involved are a Captain Kelly, the former Minister for Finance – the former Minister for Agriculture and two associates of the Ministers.'

Why did Cosgrave omit the names of Gibbons and Col Hefferon? The strongest possibility is that Lynch had assured him that they had not been involved and Cosgrave had taken him at his word.

Kevin Boland and his parliamentary secretary Paudge Brennan resigned in protest at the sackings.[9]

In the marathon Dáil debate that commenced on 6 May,

Blaney told his colleagues that he wanted 'straightaway to deal with the allegations of gun-running that have been made so freely, made in so many places during these last few days and to say here before the house that I have run no guns, I have procured no guns, and I have paid for no guns, I have provided no money to buy guns and anybody who says otherwise is not telling the truth.' A very narrow parsing of these words would show that Blaney was technically correct for he had *attempted* to import guns with government funds but had not 'procured' any.

Haughey's medical condition – he had suffered a fall from a horse – precluded him from speaking in the debate but he issued a statement in which he denied involvement in the *illegal* importation of arms. His statement included the following passage:

> So far as I have been able to gather, the Taoiseach received information of a nature which in his opinion cast some suspicion on me. I have not had the opportunity to examine or test such information or the quality of its source or sources. In the meantime, however, I now categorically state that at no time have I taken part in any illegal importation or attempted importation of arms into this country.[10]

Haughey now entered the political wilderness. Lynch remained taoiseach until February 1973 while Haughey languished on the backbenches. However, Haughey was appointed to the Opposition Front Bench in 1975 and became a cabinet minister in the summer of 1977 when Lynch swept back into power. His rehabilitation reinforces the idea he had made an arrangement with Lynch in 1970.[11]

Another indication that Fianna Fáil was putting on a show for the public is illustrated by a story told by Gerry Jones, a businessman from Bandon who was a friend of Blaney. It implicates Gibbons in playing a charade. According to Jones, 'Right throughout the whole thing you had perfidy and double-standards. I remember Neil Blaney and I were sitting in the Parliamentary Secretaries' den one evening and Jim Gibbons came over and said "Neil – we're all in this together".'[12]

Haughey came to harbour a deep loathing for Lynch but masked it well most of the time. Faulkner provided a glimpse at the 'vitriolic' nature of their relationship after Haughey had returned to the Fianna Fáil Opposition front bench in 1975:

> Generally speaking affairs ran relatively smoothly except on one occasion when a clash of views between Jack Lynch and Charlie Haughey at a meeting resulted in Haughey leaving the room. I met him later in the corridor and, as I was returning to the meeting, I suggested that he should return with me. On the way back we called in at another meeting, where Haughey launched into a vitriolic attack on Jack Lynch. This embarrassed many of those present, including myself. The bad feeling on Haughey's part was suspected, but the verbal attack was so unexpected that nobody commented. It was a clear sign that despite Haughey's return to the front bench little had changed in their relationship, at least so far as Charlie Haughey was concerned.[13]

Haughey's reaction to the mention of Lynch's name in the sanctuary of his home, Abbeville, could result in a 'knowing look or a frown'. Such a frown would crease his face when Lynch might be mentioned in connection with a 'newspaper report featuring him' or something similar. His family recall no other person for whom Haughey reserved such a deep and abiding resentment.[14] His wife Maureen shared the emotion. She was the daughter of the former taoiseach Seán Lemass. While she and her husband followed the example her parents had set not to mention politics in their home, she could be disparaging about Lynch from time to time inside domestic quarters.

What was the source of Haughey's antipathy? One plausible explanation is that in May 1970 neither Haughey nor Lynch anticipated that the former would actually have to endure the crucible of two trials, but rather a quick rehabilitation. After all, in 1970, the government controlled criminal prosecutions which were brought in the name of the attorney-general. The independent office of the Director of Prosecutions was not introduced until 1974. Yet, prosecutions followed. The moving force behind them was a combination of Berry and George Colley, not Lynch. The bottom line now was that Lynch would have to get Gibbons to lie on an industrial scale about his recent activities.[15]

19

THE GANG THAT COULDN'T SHOOT STRAIGHT

When Jack Lynch realised the cat was well and truly out of the bag, he instructed James Gibbons to conceal their discussions and the efforts he – Gibbons – had taken to procure untraceable arms for storage in the Republic. For Gibbons, this must have felt like being strapped to the mast of a ship and thrust into the turmoil of an oncoming storm. Inevitably, Lynch's instruction also meant that Capt. Kelly would have to be thrown to the circling sharks.

According to Ben Briscoe TD, Gibbons 'died a broken man because of this; because of Jack Lynch'.[1] Gibbons came to loath Lynch too, making snide remarks about how he was 'not a man' because Lynch had no children whereas he had nine.[2]

Frank Dunlop, Lynch's press secretary, described mutual contempt between the parties in his memoirs:

> At first I imagined that because of the events of 1970, Lynch and Gibbons would be close friends, or at least something approaching political allies. In fact the opposite was the case, and I was amazed on one or two occasions to discover that their attitude to one another was distinctly chilly, even glacial. Underneath Gibbons's antipathy to Haughey there lay an animus, bordering on contempt, against Lynch. Again, it clearly went back to the events of the Arms Crisis. Gibbons did not trust him and was downright dismissive of him in many of the conversations I had with him. This seems extraordinary in circumstances where Lynch,

> to all intents and purposes, stood by Gibbons in the white heat of the controversy. Sometimes Gibbons could show chilling disdain for his colleagues and Lynch did not escape his sharp tongue.[3]

The cover-up instruction from Lynch to Gibbons may have been issued at Lynch's Rathgar home on the evening of 30 April when they were joined by Fleming, the attorney-general and Col Delaney, the new director of G2, for what transpired to be a most bizarre conference. Berry was not invited. Fleming visited Berry's home at 9.30 that night and reported that he had not been asked any questions, nor had Col Delaney. Berry's version of events is worth quoting extensively at this point:

> [Fleming] said that he was bewildered as to why he was summoned to the Taoiseach's house as he had not been asked any questions or for an opinion. He told me that the Attorney General and the Minister for Defence, Mr Gibbons, were present, as was Col Delaney, Director of Military Intelligence (only since 9th April, i.e. for three weeks) who was not asked any questions either – not, said the Chief that he could contribute anything. He said that the Taoiseach and the Attorney General did most of the talking to one another with an occasional remark from the Minister for Defence but it was inconsequential kind of talk which did not clarify any matter that he could see.
>
> When the Chief Superintendent was speaking to me the phone rang and I answered: it was the Taoiseach. He said: 'I have had a conference with … including Col Delaney and Chief Supt. Fleming and I now have a better understanding of the position.'
>
> I said: 'Mr Fleming called to my home after he left your house and he told me that he was bewildered as to why he was present as he was not asked any question and his opinion was not sought; he also told me that Col Delaney was not questioned. I think that

> you should know this as the Chief Superintendent will be making a report on these lines tomorrow to the Commissioner.'
>
> There was an appreciable pause and then the Taoiseach said: 'why did he not ask questions if he was in doubt about anything'. I said that nobody had told him for what purpose he had been summoned to the Taoiseach's house.
>
> Initially the Taoiseach's voice was angry.
>
> Chief Supt. Fleming and I conjectured as to the purpose of the exercise and did not become apparent that the Taoiseach was bridge building until he delivered himself of the following in the Dáil on 9th May: Col. 246 No. 7 cols 1331/2/3.
>
> '… I had consultation jointly with Officers of the Special Branch of the Garda and the Army Intelligence service and the Attorney General and the Minister for defence were also present at these consultations. The Minister for Justice, who would have been the other appropriate Minister, was not present because he had entered hospital some days previously. The purpose of that meeting was to coordinate as well as I could the evidence that was available from both of the special source [*sic*] and also to receive guidance from the Attorney General …'
>
> As a result of the misstatement already recorded, with more to follow, I lost respect for the Taoiseach's credibility.[4]

Lynch and Gibbons did not manage to co-author a neat and co-ordinated cover-up story at these early stages in the crisis, whether at the meeting in Lynch's house in Rathgar or on another occasion. Instead, they sailed in different directions.

The Gibbons' camp was first out of the traps with a spin on what had happened. Tony Gallagher, a reporter with *This Week* magazine, published an article entitled 'The Arms Deal That Split A Cabinet' on 8 May 1970. It was based on an interview with a 'minister' who fed Gallagher some rather unsavoury lies.

Before publication, Gallagher approached Capt. Kelly at his home in Terenure. The captain described later how:

> Mr Gallagher had the real Gibbons story, he told me. He knew of my involvement and his suggestion was that if I told him my story it would be published alongside the Gibbons story. He intimated that in this way I could clear my name. His attitude did not appeal to me. He sounded too 'know-all' and, anyhow, I did not feel I had to clear my name.
>
> 'Who gave you my name in the first place?' I asked.
>
> 'A Minister of Government.'
>
> 'Which Minister?'
>
> He would not give me the name of the Minister, claiming that it was against journalistic ethics to do so. I declined to give my story and Tony Gallagher left, leaving me to ponder the identity of the communicative Minister. I assumed it was George Colley, Minister for Industry and Commerce, soon to be appointed to Finance in place of Haughey in the reshuffle on May 8. He was known to be a friend and mentor of Gibbons.[5]

According to Gallagher's article, Blaney and Haughey had been acting in league with the IRA Army Council and 'coming up to the end of [1969]' Lynch had received 'a bombshell' when he was 'consulted privately by James Gibbons, the quiet, unflappable Kilkenny-born Minister for Defence, who had some very disturbing information'.[6] According to the minister who was whispering lies into Gallagher's ear, 'Gibbons had reports from army sources that the connection between the IRA Army Council and the two Cabinet ministers was still being continued. The reports were vague; there were no times, places or hard-and-fast details to back them up'. The so-called 'army sources' Gallagher referred to can only have been to Col Hefferon of G2 and his colleagues, none of whom ever made such reports. This underlines the unscrupulous deceit of the minister who misled Gallagher. Col Hefferon's account at the Four Courts and at the Public Accounts Committee was at 100 per cent variance with what Gallagher was told.

The reference to the Army Council in the *This Week* report is Machiavellian. It echoes what The Deceiver had been telling the gardaí for months. At some stage Ó Moráin must have asked Gibbons about the reports he was receiving from Fleming concerning the ministers and the Army Council. While Gibbons would have dismissed them as nonsense at the time, at this juncture he and his advisers must have appreciated their potential as gold dust for him: Gibbons could exploit the information in the reports and, if it later became necessary to buttress his *This Week* version of events, details about the reports – however inaccurate – could be leaked.

The reference to the meeting at the end of 1969 is also of particular interest: Gibbons had indeed gone to Lynch at the end of 1969 but had received no direction from him. After he had expressed his concerns to Colley, the latter had told him to go back to Lynch, something he did in early January 1970. In the wake of the January discussion, Gibbons had taken over the arms quest with the assistance of G2. However, the spin put on this now – as reported by Gallagher – was that Lynch had somehow tried to shut the mission down after the December meeting. 'Unverified, the information [Gibbons] brought could not be acted upon immediately. Lynch was left in a lonely dilemma of doubt, which he had no clear way of resolving.'

More 'concrete evidence was not too long emerging, however. Within the last two months, hints, rumours – and a lot more factual material – snowballed,' Gallagher added. This was all balderdash.

Was Capt. Kelly's assumption that Colley was Gallagher's ministerial source a reasonable one? Clearly, neither Haughey, Blaney nor Boland were responsible for it.[7] Nor was Brian Lenihan, who had acted to protect the operation on 17 April. Moreover, there is no indication that Lenihan was aware of the Gibbons-Lynch meeting of December 1969.

Faulkner and Brennan were not close to what was happening as they had abandoned their roles on the cabinet Northern Ireland Sub-Committee and hardly knew about the Gibbons-Lynch meeting either.

It is difficult to see what motive Ó Moráin could have had to concoct a story that contained a mixture of falsehoods and truth and focused on saving Gibbons' neck from the political chop at the expense of Haughey and Blaney with whom he was friendly.

Hillery had every reason to let sleeping dogs lie. He had met CDC delegations and had surely learned about what had happened in London during the Markham-Randall fiasco from 'Con' at the Irish embassy in the city. Again, there is no indication that he was aware of the Gibbons-Lynch meeting.

Tánaiste Erskine Childers hardly knew what was afoot. For a start, he was known to loathe the Irish Army and for that reason alone would have been kept out of the loop of a covert military operation. Born in London in December 1905, he had grown up in Britain. Educated at the University of Cambridge, he did not become an Irish citizen until 1938 yet rose to become tánaiste in July of 1969. His hatred of the army was a longstanding trait: when he was sixteen in November 1922, the army had executed his father for possessing a gun Michael Collins had given him while his appeal against his death sentence was pending. This resentment endured throughout his life. When he became president in 1973, he attempted to keep the military off his staff. In addition, he was married to a woman who had worked at the British embassy until 1952, something that must have made Gibbons, Blaney and Haughey even less likely to confide in him. Finally, Haughey was far from friendly with him.[8]

There is no indication that the remaining cabinet ministers were kept in the loop. This leaves only Gibbons and Colley, both of whom knew about the December meeting, a fact which puts them squarely in the frame.

The *This Week* article can only have heaped the pressure on Lynch to arrange another 'ring of steel', this one around Gibbons because it exposed one menacing albeit distorted fact: that Lynch and Gibbons had discussed the arms plot at the end of 1969. When Lynch read it, he must have realised just how dangerous it would be for him to bring the hammer down on Gibbons.

Within weeks of Blaney and Haughey's dismissals, rumours were flying around the country about the active role Gibbons had played in the drama. Colley came out to bat for him publicly. He spoke at a Fianna Fáil dinner in Carlow on 19 June 1970, telling his audience, 'I know that a concentrated effort for base tactical reasons is being made to denigrate Mr

Jim Gibbons. Because of his legal position his hands are tied. In due course he will tell people of this country the whole story. I tell you, do not believe one word you hear denigrating Jim Gibbons.'[9]

Meanwhile, the taoiseach opted for a simple denial of any knowledge of the arms plot before his 20 April meeting with Berry. During the marathon Arms Crisis debate, Lynch said that at 'no time had I any reason to suspect that Deputy Gibbons was engaged in any activity that did not befit his office. Allegations made following the opening of this debate have been thoroughly examined. As a result, I am satisfied that Deputy Gibbons was not involved in the importation of arms. If I were not so satisfied I would not now be asking the House to approve of his nomination as minister for agriculture and fisheries'.

There were many who did not believe Lynch's assertions about Gibbons' non-involvement. Foremost among these was John Fleming of the special branch who was leading the inquiries into the affair.

20

'TOO LATE TO HAVE THE AFFAIR SWEPT UNDER THE CARPET'

Jack Lynch had the authority to seize control of the garda inquiry into the arms affair and did so. While he undoubtedly acted with the intention of covering-up the role he and Gibbons had played in it, it was – to use his own words – too late to have the affair 'swept under the carpet'.[1] One person over whom he tried to exercise some control was Berry. On 23 April he criticised him for haranguing witnesses from the Revenue Commissioners from whom he wanted statements and whom he believed were dragging their feet. Berry described how he had expected to have been 'praised, not blamed' by Lynch for his zeal.[2]

Another problem facing Lynch was that Fleming, who was in command of inquiries at ground level, was already suspicious of his involvement but Lynch found a way of outfoxing him.

Capt. Kelly was arrested and taken to the Bridewell Garda Station where he was interviewed on the morning of 1 May. He refused to make a statement but told Fleming and his colleague Insp. Doocey that he would talk to Gibbons. Fleming put a call through to Berry who rang Lynch and it was arranged that the captain would be conveyed to Fleming's nearby office at Dublin Castle where Gibbons would then join them. Berry instructed Fleming to prevent the captain from talking privately to the minister. Berry had no authority to issue such a command as the gardaí were independent of the Department of Justice but they invariably jumped to his command.

When Gibbons reached Dublin Castle, he was still in cover-up mode. 'Treat Capt. Kelly well, Superintendent. He was a very good and competent officer', he declared. 'He got caught up in the changeover of Directors of Intelligence'.[3] When the captain asked for an opportunity to talk to Gibbons privately, he was told he could not. Instead, with Fleming hovering over them, Gibbons told him that he should provide an account of all he knew. The captain asked him if he was sure about this. Gibbons had no choice but to confirm what he had just said. He then took his leave of them.

Capt. Kelly felt 'undertones of deceit darkened the sunshine as the door closed behind the departing Mr Gibbons. The 'sneering brazen bastard' comment [Gibbons had made] a few days earlier in Blaney's office came to mind and I wondered why the Minister had not told the Taoiseach that he knew all about the matter; that he had authorised the operation. Why was I in custody? If Mr Gibbons was playing it straight and not acting to some hidden agenda I should not have been arrested. It was Gibbons who should be making the statements.'[4]

The captain decided to divulge nothing of substance to Fleming but said he would talk to the taoiseach. Hence, Lynch received a call shortly before four o'clock to inform him of this development. Lynch agreed to see him. Before the meeting, Lynch had told his cabinet that Haughey and Blaney had denied gunrunning and that the matter was closed. Clearly, he was in full cover-up mode and had no intention of launching a rigorous interrogation of the captain. When they met, the soldier was struck by how 'pale, powdery pale, gentle voiced and uncertain' the taoiseach looked as he rose from behind his corner desk:

> 'Is this Kelly?' [Lynch said] in a murmur to the Superintendent, and it seemed strange to have dropped one's rank. He hesitated slightly before he took my automatically offered hand.

Lynch asked if Capt. Kelly wished to speak to him in private or if he would prefer to have the superintendent present? He said he didn't mind:

> The Taoiseach had ordered the investigation and consequent decisions were his also. But I was under arrest and the Taoiseach seemed in some doubt as to the propriety of speaking to me alone in such circumstances. But was it doubt, or was it gamesmanship? He checked with the Superintendent. Mr Fleming might know if he, the Taoiseach, was permitted to speak to me in private? The Superintendent demurred. What did I think? The Taoiseach deferred to me again. 'It's your privilege, Taoiseach.' The Superintendent departed. The Taoiseach had his secretary standing by.
>
> If I was making a statement, there was a witness needed, he said. 'But I'm not making a statement, Taoiseach.'[5]

The captain parried with Lynch, telling him he felt the issue was 'a question for the Cabinet, a matter between you and your Cabinet colleagues.' Lynch replied by saying, 'Yes ... well now ... memory, memory is a funny thing. One does not remember everything one hears. A lot goes into one ear and out the other. One only remembers what is relevant, what applies to a particular situation, what is necessary to achieve a particular objective.' There was a pause. 'I understand perfectly,' the captain interjected.

Lynch next raised the threat posed to Anglo-Irish relations by the events they were discussing. 'A serious situation with international implications; the Taoiseach suggested':

> I did not get his point.
>
> 'Too many people know about it, Departments of State, various individual functionaries, it cannot be swept under the carpet,' he said.
>
> 'Possibly not but ...'
>
> 'Members of the Cabinet involved?' he queried softly.
>
> 'Possibly.'
>
> 'Two members?'
>
> 'Yes, possibly.'
>
> 'Names.'
>
> 'No, it's not my business to name people in this situation.' He knew them anyhow, the Taoiseach indicated.
>
> 'Then I think you should approach them yourself, Taoiseach.'
>
> 'But I have approached them, they won't talk to me.'[6]

Obviously, Blaney and Haughey were the 'two members' of the cabinet at issue here. However, this account of their behaviour is at odds with the version of events which Berry provided in his diaries where he claimed Lynch had told him Blaney and Haughey had acknowledged their involvement in the arms plot and had undertaken not to attempt to import weapons again. The fog of deception is so dense here it is best not to try to figure out who was lying, Lynch or Berry, or both.

Capt. Kelly asked to be let go, but this was not acceptable to Lynch who wanted 'names'. The captain protested that he was 'only at the practical end and there is ... there is another end.' Lynch knew exactly what he meant. 'The policy end,' he filled in and asked the captain again for names. In a reference to Haughey he suggested: 'One of them is sick.' In reference to Blaney: 'The other one, is he near here, could you get to him easily?' The captain replied: 'If I'm allowed to go free I could talk to various people.'

Lynch now focused on the possibility of violence in Northern Ireland. 'Not talking really, but thinking out loud, the Taoiseach was murmuring something about violence. Uncertainty seemed to be dominant', Capt. Kelly recalled. Was Lynch testing the soldier, trying to establish if he might be prepared to go along with a cover-up to avoid inter-communal violence in the Northern Ireland?

After the meeting ended, Capt. Kelly spoke to Fleming who told him that he was 'probably right not to make a statement' and that 'Anyhow, he knew who was involved … and named three Ministers, Haughey, Blaney and Gibbons'. He indicated he was suspicious about the taoiseach too. 'What do you think, did [the taoiseach] know all along?' Capt. Kelly said he did not know 'but in view of my arrest it would seem as if he didn't unless … Well, he certainly knew about the Bailieboro meeting and ...' At that Fleming cut in saying 'I believe he knew'. To this, Kelly replied, 'Then it's time you let me go'.[7]

Fleming had ample ground for his suspicion of Gibbons and Lynch. Yet, to his dying day, he never aired them, at least not in public.[8]

By the time Lynch rose to speak to the Dáil on 8 May 1970, he had to explain why he had spoken to Capt. Kelly. The self-portrait he presented was one of a statesman who had diligently tried to get to the bottom of a mystery despite encountering a lack of co-operation on all sides. He stated that Gibbons had told Capt. Kelly:

> that he should tell everything he knew and made some reference about his competence as an officer. I believe the Minister felt rather sorry for the plight in which Captain Kelly found himself. However, the Minister then left and, at about 4 o'clock or shortly before it, I had another telephone call to say that Captain Kelly had begun to make a statement but after the usual preliminaries, date of birth, occupation, address, decided to say no more. He said that if he was brought to me – and this is the message I got – he would name names. I readily agreed to see Captain Kelly and perhaps, within 20 minutes or so, he and Chief Superintendent Fleming arrived at my office … [Capt. Kelly] objected to the Secretary of the Department coming in so I agreed to his telling me what he wanted to say. He refused to tell me anything.
>
> I said to him: 'You asked the Minister for Defence to go face to face with you in Dublin Castle and that you would make a statement then, and you refused. You asked permission to come to me and said you would name names and make a statement and again you refuse.' He said: 'Well, that is the position.' I kept him for some minutes talking around the subject but he refused to give me any information whatever.[9]

Lynch made no reference to his comment that 'too many people' knew about the importation to have it 'swept under the carpet', nor about his concerns about the 'international implications' it posed.

There were others who were less concerned than Lynch about the 'international implications' of the affair and were determined to expose its entrails to the public, even if they had to do so by breaching the provisions of the Official Secrets Act, a criminal offence in its own right.

21

THE GARDAÍ WHO BREACHED THE OFFICIAL SECRETS ACT

Despite the taoiseach's best efforts to keep the Arms Crisis genie in the bottle, someone or a covert group inside the state was working diligently in the shadows to bring the affair to public knowledge.

On Thursday 30 April 1970, Ned Murphy, the political correspondent of the *Sunday Independent*, handed a story to his editor, Hector Legge, for publication the following weekend. During his career, Murphy had written many stories based on information provided by the gardaí. While this one was riddled with mistakes, overall, it was more accurate than the story fed to Tony Gallagher of *This Week*. It began by asking what had 'happened to the consignment of automatic weapons shipped to this country by air from Vienna on April 17th?' This was a mistake as Schlueter's consignment had not actually reached Ireland. More accurately, he asked, 'Who gave permission for their entry to this country and why? Why was that permission cancelled after the advice notes had been received in Dublin? Who are the two gentlemen, very closely connected in Cabinet circles, who organised the gun running?

'Who was the departmental secretary who went to the highest authority in the land to ensure that the guns would not be landed?' Murphy asked in obvious reference to Berry's phone call to De Valera.

The article reported that London was aware of at least parts of the saga. 'Why,' Murphy asked 'were previous warnings to the Government by Britain's M.I.5 about the previous activities of the organisers ignored?'

'These are questions,' Murphy added, 'that must be answered if a certain story circulating only in the highest Government and official circles last week is to be proved untrue. A formal denial from the Government Information Bureau will not be enough. Evidence must be produced that a certain charter pilot had to be persuaded to take the weapons aboard in Vienna; that permission was given for their landing in Dublin; that the fact became known to the highest officers in the Garda and that it was only then that preventive action was taken to stop the landing.' This was another mistake since no 'charter pilot' had had 'to be persuaded to take the weapons abroad in Vienna'.

Hector Legge decided to suppress the story to avoid a diplomatic rumpus between Dublin and London and violence in Northern Ireland.

On 8 May, Lynch admitted that he had realised what Cosgrave was hinting at three days earlier after he had asked if Ó Moráin's was 'the only Ministerial resignation' that was going to take place. He now said that if Cosgrave had 'given me any indication as to his knowing something I might have said that I had something in mind'.[1]

The opposition had also inquired if Ó Moráin's resignation had been requested; in other words, had he been forced out or not. Lynch stated, 'I said at the start of my opening statement, and I repeat it now, that his resignation was tendered to me on grounds of ill-health'.

As Boland described it, Lynch 'had not denied the truth in so many words but he certainly deliberately gave the Dáil the impression that the resignation was tendered without a request by him. I don't think this is very important except as another example of a typical Lynchism'.[2]

On 8 May Lynch was probed about Ó Moráin's resignation more forcefully and in circumstances where he had to be more forthcoming:

> **The Taoiseach**: 'I announced the resignation of the Minister to the Dáil the following day. After I had made the announcement Deputy Murphy asked me if the resignation was asked for. I replied that it was tendered. Some point is being made out of this to the effect that I was not truthful but I never said that I did not ask for the resignation.'
>
> **Deputies**: 'Oh.'
>
> **The Taoiseach**: 'I wish to say quite candidly that to my knowledge Deputy [Ó Moráin] was not involved in the importation of arms. I did not wish him in any way to be associated with the action that I felt was imminent in the case of two other Ministers. I was conscious, too, of his physical condition and, frankly, I did suggest to him that he should resign because of that condition and mainly because of the length of time that he was likely to remain under medical treatment.'
>
> **Mr. Cosgrave**: 'It does not tally with the earlier story the Taoiseach has given.'[3]

By now, Cosgrave had become convinced that the arms G2 had tried to import had been for an 'illegal organisation', i.e. the IRA, and he would say as much during his contribution to the extended Dáil debate.

***

What is clear is that the ministerial dismissals caused political consternation. In the south, there was speculation about a general election. However, any dissension in the ranks was quashed during a fifty-minute meeting of the parliamentary party. There would be no election for nearly three years.

The reaction in Northern Ireland was more visceral. Conor Cruise O'Brien visited Belfast on 7 May to appear on Ulster TV. He found 'the atmosphere which previously had been tense and ominous, had become electric. I have never seen so many frightened people in so short a time. Deputy Garret FitzGerald who was with me will bear that out. In the television studio we saw the tension and alarm of the producers and the controllers; we heard the hostile telephone calls; we saw a little, rather pathetic Paisleyite mob in the street, including small children whose faces were contorted with hatred and fear. The hatred and fear are being carried along by people like Mr Paisley in the North and Deputy Boland and Deputy Blaney here – the Deputies who still sit on the benches in this House as honoured members of the Fianna Fáil party.'[4]

James Callaghan described how 'the great gun-running scandal ... of course, led to increased tension in Belfast and renewed outbreaks of violence'.[5]

22

THE IRA STEPS INTO THE BREACH

Paddy Doherty concluded later that Jack Lynch 'created a vacuum which the Provisional IRA was only too willing to fill'.[1]

Kevin Boland reached a similar determination. 'Prior to this people had placed their faith in the broadly-based Citizens' Defence Committees. These in turn placed their faith in the promises of the Dublin government. When these promises were so dramatically and publicly reneged the Defence Committees were discredited and the threatened people turned to the IRA for defence …'[2]

The despair of the CDCs was displayed to the world at a press conference held on Friday, 8 May, at the Gresham Hotel, Dublin. It was organised by Seamus Brady at the request of John Kelly. Brady introduced Kelly in his capacity as organiser for the Citizens' Defence Committees of Belfast, along with his brother James, who was the chairman of St Patrick's Parish Citizens' Defence Committee of Belfast. The speakers described how the CDCs felt shocked and betrayed by the events of that week; that they had been promised help in the face of further attacks, but now 'there was only despair for the Northern minority'. According to Brady, the delegation 'cut a sorry picture. They were dismayed and aghast at the sudden turn of events. They were instinctively offering their support to the dismissed Haughey and Blaney, the two members of Jack Lynch's government who had openly given moral assistance to the minority in the North.

But they were at this time powerless, removed from the scene of effective action and quite without influence.'[3]

Matters were further exacerbated when John Kelly was arrested on 20 May, along with Blaney, Haughey, Capt. Kelly and Albert Luykx.

***

The relationship between the British Army and nationalists in Derry had remained on an even keel in the months after the Battle of the Bogside. Eamonn McCann recalls that during the six months that followed the 'Military police patrolled the area. They were very friendly and fairly popular. People accepted them, chatted to them, invited them in for a cup of tea. And as the barricades tumbled the politicians re-emerged, blinking in the sunlight'.[4]

There were, however, dangers on the road which were about to present themselves. Bernadette Devlin MP had been handed a six-month prison sentence for her involvement in the Battle of the Bogside but had appealed against it. On Monday 22 June 1970, her appeal was dismissed. The following Friday, 26 June, she was stopped and arrested at a road-block by the police, something which sparked widespread rioting in Derry. In response, the soldiers deployed CS gas to quell the unrest. Michael Canavan, who had been the Derry CDC's principal negotiator with the British Army, tried to quell the fermenting upheaval:

> All day Saturday through Sunday afternoon the 1969 scenario with the army in the RUC role, was acted out, the fighting surging back and forth around the mouth of Rossville Street. On mid-afternoon

> on Sunday, supporters of Mr [John] Hume called a meeting of 'prominent people' in one of Michael Canavan's bookmakers shops to try and find a peace formula. It was suggested that a deputation should go to the military authorities and ask them to withdraw the soldiers from around the area. Seán Keenan, the best-known figure in the embryo Provisional organisation, refused to be part of the delegation. Seán said that what we had to do was to prepare to defend ourselves. 'Against whom?' he was asked. Against the British army. Most of those present were incredulous. 'But the army is here to defend us.'[5]

Meanwhile, 6,000 beleaguered nationalists were hemmed into Short Strand in Belfast, a 'Catholic island' surrounded by 60,000 loyalists, many of whom worked in the shipyards of Harland and Wolff and the Shorts Aircraft factory. An Orange Order parade took place annually on 26 June and was known as the 'Mini 12th'. On this occasion, the planned route was to take it along streets which had been burned out the previous August by loyalists. When the Orangemen paraded down the Crumlin Road that Friday, they passed the nationalist Ardoyne where they hurled insults at nationalists, something that provoked a hail of bottles and stones followed by rioting.

The following Saturday, another Orange Order parade was due to march by the Ardoyne, and then along the Crumlin Road and onto Hooker Street. Orange lodges from the Shankill, the Bone, Cliftonville and Oldpark, along with other groups, were assembling for a show of strength. No one was in any doubt that they would provoke rioting, yet it was given the green light by the Joint Security Committee (JSC) which sat at Stormont. The JSC was made up of Stormont ministers, the RUC Chief Constable and the British Army GOC and was the vehicle which was enabling the Stormont government to gain increasing control of the British Army. Oliver Wright, the UKREP at the time, felt that the decision to let the parade go ahead was 'the greatest single miscalculation I have ever seen made in the course of my whole life.'[6]

Inevitably, rioting spread across the city. The most vulnerable nationalists were those in the Short Strand. Several thousand loyalists massed at the top of Seaforde Street and Newtownards Road readying to invade it. A provocative Tricolour was hoisted on the roof of a shop at the top of Seaforde Street to test to see if the loyalists had guns. The answer was quick in coming: a bullet tore through the flag.

A delegation was despatched to Mountpottinger RUC Barracks where Inspector Hamill was warned about what was happening but said he could offer no help because his resources were over-stretched. Instead, the Provisionals stepped into the breach. The Short Strand formed part of their Third Battalion area, which was under the command of Billy Kelly from Unity Flats. Tom O'Donnell, the newly appointed finance officer of the Provisional's brigade staff, came from the Short Strand. He was issued an order to uplift weapons from the organisation's arms dumps. Twelve Provos assembled in Lowry Street, just off Seaforde Street, close to an adjoining school and church grounds. They, along with members of the CDC, prepared for the inevitable clash. Crucially, it was the IRA who armed the CDC volunteers because the latter had little or no weaponry of their own, nor any prospect of obtaining any elsewhere. The men were deployed to various points across the urban battlefield.

Jim Gibney, a local resident, and later a Sinn Féin leader, recalled how he saw 'neighbours, people I knew, coming down the street carrying rifles. I was just dumb struck by this experience. I'd never seen such a thing before. They were much older than me, of course. I watched them take up position on the corner and fire up the street that I lived in. I was 15 going on 16 and it was incredible to witness this at first hand. On one level it was exciting of course, because of what you were witnessing. It was something that you only see on the television or in films. The gun battle lasted right through into the early hours of the following morning. I think the defence of the district was a mixture of IRA activists and the local Citizen's Defence Committee. I think they occupied all the key places including the church that night to defend it against the loyalist gunmen'.[7]

The British Army was conspicuous by its absence. The British journalist Peter Taylor has written how, as 'the night drew on the attacks intensified but the [British] soldiers still declined to intervene and separate the two sides, either because they felt they were not numerically strong enough or did not wish to get caught in the middle of a sectarian fight, in the darkness, with shots being fired by both sides'.[8]

'We went over to see what could be done', Billy McKee, commanding officer of the Provisional IRA in Belfast, said later, 'and we realized that it was getting more serious as time went on. So, we sent up to [IRA] Headquarters and asked them to send what weapons they could'. Six M1 Carbines along with five full magazines were soon en route from the Falls.

McKee made it to Ballymacarrett at around 10 p.m. where O'Donnell warned him that the situation was going to deteriorate further. By now, loyalists had climbed onto the roofs of buildings opposite St Matthew's and had struck a house with petrol bombs setting it ablaze. McKee's men swept the roofs with gunfire and drove them back onto the streets near the church pursuing them with a hail of gunfire.

While British soldiers were eventually deployed on the Lower Newtownards Road, there were too few of them to disperse the loyalist crowds. The soldiers decided to hem the loyalist mobs in where they were, initially by blocking Queens Bridge and later the Albert Bridge, but this did not curtail the threat to the Short Strand.

The fighting continued after midnight. Early on Sunday morning, McKee asked Paddy Kennedy, MP, to go to Mountpottinger Barracks to see if he could find a way to convince the authorities to send British soldiers to their aid. Kennedy was told troops would be deployed at 1.05 a.m. In reality, the troops earmarked for deployment were only being given their orders to fly out from bases in England. In the meantime, a platoon of British soldiers pitched up, but soon came under attack from loyalist petrol bombers and withdrew.

Provisional IRA men, along with CDC volunteers and others, had taken up positions inside the grounds of the church from where they were sniping at the loyalist petrol bombers. At about 2 a.m. on Sunday morning, McKee was badly injured while one of those who was fighting alongside him, Henry McIlhone, from Sheriff Street, was killed by a bullet which struck his back and drove up into his neck.

As the night wore on, the fighting shifted to the Albertbridge Road end of the Short Strand. While some buildings and public houses were set ablaze, the homes of the locals were not damaged. Had the loyalists smashed their way through to them, groups of men were waiting to push them back. The battle ended at about 5 a.m. Shortly afterwards, British Army lorries with fresh troops descended on the district and lined up along Bryson Street. As Dr Thomas Hennessy has noted, the Provisionals 'had emerged from their first major engagement victorious, defending Catholics from Protestant mobs'.[9]

According to Richard English, 'McKee and his comrades defended the church in an epic encounter which has subsequently acquired legendary standing in republican memory, and which has been used to testify to the necessity and efficacy of the Provisionals.'[10]

As Kevin Kelley noted in his book, *The Longest War*, 'The honeymoon between Catholics and British ended when the troops failed to repel the loyalist mob which was menacing the Short Strand. At the same time, the Provos now came to be looked upon as rough and ready defenders of imperilled communities. At last, thought many Catholics, the IRA was doing what it should have done last summer – shooting at people only understanding of the bullet. The Provisionals' status as heroes was officially certified in late July 1970 when leaders of the central citizens' defence committee, including a few priests, invited a PIRA contingent to tea and thanked the lads for saving St Matthew's from desecration.'[11]

Jim Gibney felt that the battle 'added to the rebirth of the IRA and fitted in with the emergence of the IRA as a defensive force in nationalist Belfast. That's its significance. Had the IRA and the Citizens' Defence Committees not been on the streets, then I believe Short Strand would have been razed that night. I'm firmly convinced of that, such was the intensity of gunfire and petrol bombing taking place around the fringes of the district. But the people who defended the street stood their ground. The following morning there was just sheer elation and relief that the IRA were there to deal with that situation.'[12]

Whatever kudos the CDC fighters earned, soon faded. The future belonged to the Provisional IRA.

Martin Meehan, a Provisional IRA leader, claimed later that the IRA 'had proved what they said they were going to do, they had done. The date – 27th of June 1970 – is more significant for that than anything else. As a result, the whole broad spectrum of the nationalist people actually supported what the IRA was doing. Everybody, man, woman and child came out and supported us in any way possible. I never saw support like that in my life. It was unbelievable'.[13]

All told, two loyalists died during the battle at St Matthew's; another three elsewhere. 200 people were injured and ten soldiers received hospital treatment. The morning after the fighting, militant loyalists expelled approximately 500 nationalist workers from Harland & Wolff.

On 1 July Reginald Maudling, the new Conservative home secretary made his first visit to Northern Ireland. He was assailed on all sides by conflicting demands and perspectives. 'For God's sake bring me a large scotch. What a bloody awful country!' he said when he boarded his flight to London.[14] Had he known what was afoot in the south, he might well have demanded a second.

23

LYNCH LAW

Jack Lynch proved adept at muddying the waters of truth in a way that aided his cover-up. During the lengthy Dáil debate of May 1970, he referred to inquiries he had made about the purchase of the arms and the type of price involved. The anonymous garda note furnished to Cosgrave had mentioned the figure of '£80,000'. According to Lynch, he had made 'specific inquiries as to whether any Exchequer moneys would cover, roughly, a transaction of this size. I am told that the probable cost would be of the order of £30,000, not £80,000.[1] I had the usual sources from which one might expect these things could be paid for, checked. The Secret Service Funds amounted to £11,500 and had to be spread over the Departments which draw on these funds. Therefore, there was no question of the Secret Service funds being used. As well as that, it was established for me that all moneys expended by the Department of Defence were expended as voted by this House. Therefore, I do not know where the moneys came from that paid for these goods, if they were paid for.'[2] Yet, Lynch knew full well that the cabinet had sanctioned a Fund for the Relief of Distress in Northern Ireland. It was the source of funding for the arms.

By 19 May, Berry was spreading the word that criminal proceedings against Blaney, Haughey and others was on the cards. That day he spoke on the telephone to Charlie Murray at the Department of Finance and told him:

> At this very moment – when I say this very moment I mean – in the consultations between the Attorney-General and the Minister and a high-ranking Garda Officer last night, the contemplation of criminal proceedings against certain persons was involved.[3]

Later, Brian Lenihan spoke to his son about the prosecutions. 'It is not clear at this point why Jack Lynch opted to put those involved on trial in the courts. My father always said that the main person pushing for prosecution was George Colley. In all of the discussions around the issue with his ministerial colleagues my father said it was Colley more than anyone else that wanted people put on trial. The fact of the matter is that this was both a legal and political call. My father told me that the lawyers around the cabinet table argued against the policy of prosecution. There were solid political as well as legal reasons why a prosecution of those involved might not work and in fact rebound on the government.'[4]

Capt. Kelly, Blaney, Haughey, John Kelly and Albert Luykx were arrested and charged between 27 and 29 May for conspiring to import arms and ammunition into the state between 1 March and 24 April 1970.

Haughey was arrested at his house while a judge of the Supreme Court, Brian Walsh, was present. Walsh had been part of Haughey's social circle for many years. He and his wife Noreen lived nearby on the Howth Road. On this occasion he had come to Abbeville alone to advise Haughey about what might lay ahead.[5]

Gibbons was not troubled by the gardaí. Crucially, the arrests were ordered before Fleming and his colleagues had managed to complete their inquiries. Hence, in the absence of evidence, he was allowed to slip off the hook.

The first strike went to the defendants. Liam Hamilton, who later became chief justice, spearheaded Blaney's defence. On 2 July, he argued that the state's book of evidence was actually a 'book of no evidence'. District Justice Donal Kearney, to whom the argument was made, agreed. 'I am returning the other four men for trial and I'm refusing information against Mr Blaney', he ruled.[6] In 1970 the attorney-general had the authority to overrule a district judge and direct the reinstatement of charges in circumstances like this. The attorney-general was certainly coming under pressure from the prosecution team to have Blaney charged as it was felt some of his more extreme republican utterances could be used to good effect in the prosecution of the case. The attorney-general decided to consult the cabinet. A 'Secret Cabinet' conclave took place to deliberate on the matter. By now the surviving members of cabinet and their new colleagues had reconciled themselves to the fact that a trial was going to take place. The 'Secret Cabinet' resolved not to reinstate the charges against Blaney because he had made a momentous contribution to Fianna Fáil's June 1969 general election victory, was admired by the rank and file of the party and, unlike Haughey who was regarded as an arriviste in the party, had deep roots within it. Moreover, a move against Blaney had the potential to split the party. On the other hand, Haughey did not have the political weight among the rank and file to generate this level of disquiet.[7]

A slew of dirty tricks were deployed against the remaining defendants. Col Delaney had made a statement to Fleming on 26

May 1970 which was subsequently amended. A second version was found decades later. It denigrated Capt. Kelly's abilities, motives and loyalty alleging that he had 'openly consorted with subversive groups', the seriousness of which could 'not be over-emphasised'. Furthermore, that his 'emotional reactions to events in Northern Ireland pointed to his having lost that cool behaviour so necessary in an Intelligence Officer'.[8]

Col Hefferon made his statement on 30 May. Sixteen sections were deleted from it too by a mysterious censor. The lines revealed that the captain had acted with his authority and that of Gibbons. Notes written on it indicate it was seen by Berry on 31 May. The deleted passages were those noted by Berry.

The directive issued by Gibbons on 6 February 1970 allegedly disappeared in the days preceding the opening of the prosecution. This was most mysterious as Col Hefferon had contacted one of his still serving colleagues, Col John O'Donovan at GHQ regarding it a few days before it allegedly disappeared. The colonel obliged by consulting the directive and reverting to Col Hefferon confirming the accuracy of the latter's recollection of what was contained within it.

The directive's importance can be gauged from the fact that during the first trial, Justice Aindrias Ó Cuiv described it as having the potential to provide the 'best evidence' in the case. Seamus McKenna, SC, told him he did not know where to get it.[9] The odds are that it was stolen and a forgery was manufactured to replace it. A perturbed Patrick Murphy, an assistant secretary, and later secretary of the Department of Defence, was present at a meeting at Army HQ while the forgery was being written. Murphy knew Boland from the latter's tenure as minister for defence and warned him about what was afoot. In *Up Dev,* Boland revealed that:

> During the second trial Mr Gibbons himself volunteered the information that [the Directive] had now turned up. For a time it appeared as if the defence were now being challenged to repeat their request for it to be produced. In fact, it had been re-written in the meantime in the office of Mr Gibbons' successor with the assistance of phone calls to the Taoiseach. Apparently it was felt that this 'reproduction' could safely be produced in court but, when the matter was further considered wiser counsel prevailed ... After the existence of this document had been made known in court I received information and was able to make one of the Defence counsel aware of the re-writing of the document, of the people present when it was done, of the name of the Army Officer, who actually wrote it down, and of the phone calls to the Taoiseach ...[10]

Capt. Kelly was also tipped off. A week or so after the first trial collapsed, he was contacted by phone by a friend attached to G2 at GHQ, a man he had known and trusted for many years who told him:[11]

> that it was a matter of extreme urgency that he speak to me. He suggested that we meet in a supermarket car park in Dublin's southside. In the car park, he was at the door of my car before I could open it.
>
> 'Sit where you are,' he told me. 'Listen carefully, I'll be fast'.
>
> It seemed that he had overheard or had been a party to a conversation in the Director of Intelligence's office in GHQ [i.e. Col Delaney's office], which indicated that I would be discredited in the second arms trial. My claim of authorisation [by the Government for the importation] would be counteracted

> in a most positive fashion, as would Colonel Hefferon's evidence. There was talk of an amended document or record. My defence of authorisation, supported by the Colonel, would crumble when it was produced, was the belief.[12]

But the defendants avoided the trap by not seeking the Directive.

Jerry Cronin was the new minister for defence who had been present during the creation of the replacement. Capt. Kelly met him 'years later' in the Dáil where:

> He greeted me warmly. In the course of our conversation, I mentioned the changing of the Directive and his part in it. Far from denying it, he accepted what happened and excused his part in the affair on the basis that he was new to the office; and that he [had] accepted the good faith of the Taoiseach, Jack Lynch, in the matter.
>
> 'Jack was the boss. I trusted him,' he explained.[13]

The essential difference between the original and the forgery was the former was an order to the military to prepare for incursions into Northern Ireland whereas the counterfeit had merely instructed it to prepare *to train* forces for such incursions. The original had also ordered the Army to set aside surplus arms and ammunition for the incursions whereas the forgery had indicated that weapons and ammunition were to be made available for the training.[14]

The forged directive was only the tip of an iceberg of deceit. In his biography of Brian Lenihan, James Downey, who knew his subject well, described how, after the Arms Crisis had erupted, ministers had been placed under surveillance. 'For the

Lenihan family', Downey wrote, 'this was a terrible time. Anyone associated with Haughey and Blaney came under suspicion … Telephones were tapped …' Downey's source was a 'senior official of the Department of Justice' who informed him that the Special Branch had 'filled an entire room in Dublin Castle with tapes of tapped conversations, mostly involving ministers.' According to Downey, 'Men, presumably from the intelligence services, lurked outside Lenihan's house. He was "shadowed" on his way to work and social functions.'[15]

Des O'Malley was informed by Berry that Haughey's home was under surveillance in the run up to the first trial. Lynch told the Dáil, 'I want to say before I proceed that I did not at any time have Ministers' homes watched during this investigation.'[16] This was not quite the same thing as saying surveillance was not taking place, nor that somebody else could have issued a surveillance order.

Lynch also told the Dáil that in 'answer to another allegation by Deputy [Garret] FitzGerald that no attempt was made to prevent the ministers taking their private papers from the office. I said that I was not convicting them of any crime on what amounted to legal proof. There was no attempt to search their houses and I do not think there should have been in the circumstances'. In reality, a far more intrusive activity was taking place. In 1984 Vincent Browne described in *The Tribune Sunday* how Haughey's home had been bugged in 1970 by the gardaí.[17] Haughey was in Cork at the time of the revelation and responded to it by describing how Abbeville was an 'open' house with family members and their friends coming and going all the time, something he feared made the property extremely difficult to monitor, and rendered it vulnerable to those who might want to plant a surveillance device. He added that he could not rule out the possibility that it had been bugged because 'as you know, these days electronic devices are so sophisticated that it would be a very difficult thing to prevent something like that happening'.[18]

There is also a firm possibility that the offices of the solicitors acting for the defendants were burglarised by the state. Capt. Kelly recalled how his first solicitor had called to the bridewell on the night of his arrest. He instructed him that in the event of his non-release the following day, he:

> was to take whatever legal action was possible. It was Monday evening when I eventually got down to his office. His office had been broken into over the weekend, he told me, but it was no ordinary burglary. Only the files had been disturbed and, in particular, one relating to a Captain James Kelly, a seaman.[19] Nothing taken, however. Obviously, Fleming's men had been out and about over the weekend, and not too worried about the legality of their operations, it seemed … So much for the police respect for the confidentiality between solicitor and client.[20]

In *Orders for the Captain*, he describes how he and his solicitor had considered that the break-in might have been 'coincidence' but they 'did not think so'.[21]

A break-in at the office of a solicitor by the gardaí was far from the most egregious of the state sponsored dirty tricks that were being prepared behind closed doors.

24

'I AM NOT GOING TO COMMIT PERJURY'

The first Arms Trial opened in the Central Criminal Court in the Four Courts in Dublin on 22 September 1970. The president of the High Court, Aindrias Ó Cuiv, presided although he had been 'reluctant to take this case' as he had served as attorney-general in a cabinet which had included Haughey. The case collapsed on 29 September after counsel for Albert Luykx accused him of unfairness. Mr Justice Seamus Henchy presided over the second trial which commenced on 6 October and concluded on 23 October 1970.

On the morning of the opening day of the first trial, 22 September, Col Hefferon sent a message to Frank Fitzpatrick, the solicitor now acting for Capt. Kelly that he wished to meet him. According to Fitzpatrick, 'I met him in the Main Hall of the Court. A tall dignified person who said to me that "I spent two hours in the church this morning" – and I think he mentioned the evening of yesterday morning – "and I am not going to commit perjury. I have to tell you that your client is telling the truth".'[1]

Unfortunately, he did not specify if it was an individual or the opening address by the prosecution – which outlined what he was expected to say – that was the source of pressure to commit perjury. In any event, he severely undermined the prosecution at the first trial. A decision was taken not to call him at the second trial. He was, however, called after much legal wrangling but as a 'bench witness' by the judge. The legal consequence of this was that the state could cross-examine him although he had originally been their witness.

Over the course of the two trials, Col Hefferon explained that Capt. Kelly had developed nationalist contacts in Belfast and Derry and had reported directly to him. He was not his only agent and he was in receipt of 'intelligence from many sources. [Capt. Kelly] was only one of them. He was working with the Defence Committees, but I was getting intelligence and information from many sources'.[2]

At the end of September or early in October 1969, the colonel had ordered him to remain inside the Republic. After that, the captain had maintained his contacts by meeting them in the Republic. He had attended the meeting in Bailieboro with what the colonel described as 'members of defence committees'. Following on from that, the captain had reported to him what they were saying, what their intentions were, and what requests they were making of the Irish government. Col Hefferon then confirmed he had made a full report to Gibbons shortly afterwards. 'The Minister would have known about the [Bailieboro] meeting and what went on about the middle or more towards the end of October [1969]. I should say that I don't know whether he knew about Capt. Kelly by name at that stage. I am not quite certain, but at a later stage he did.'[3]

The colonel agreed with Thomas Finlay, SC for Capt. Kelly, that the Northern Ireland delegates 'were pointing out the necessity for arms for purely defensive purposes'; they also wanted 'training facilities'.[4]

Col Hefferon explained that other G2 officers had communicated requests from the CDCs for arms and training to him. He explained that Gibbons was aware that the captain had been asked for assistance by the CDCs to procure arms and that Gibbons had taken over the operation.[5]

When Seamus McKenna, SC for the state, asked the colonel if he could recall Capt. Kelly suggesting or alleging that any minister had promised support to the defence committees by way of arms, he replied, 'Yes, I believe that Mr Gibbons had'.

When McKenna asked him if Capt. Kelly had alleged that any other minister had promised arms, he was told that 'Mr Blaney' had done so. McKenna also wanted to know, 'Was there anybody else?' Col Hefferon told him, 'I don't think that there was anyone else so specific in promising support. They were sympathetic, a number of other ministers.'[6]

He spoke about how Capt. Kelly had eventually become 'a direct link between the Minister for Defence and other ministers and the northern committees' and how Gibbons had been willing to ensure that the captain was excused from regimental duty so he could assist them.[7]

The failed shipment from Antwerp also featured in the evidence. He explained how he had informed Gibbons that Capt. Kelly was going to the Continent in February to vet arms under the cover of a visit to his sister in Frankfurt and that Gibbons had not objected.[8] Capt. Kelly had gone to the appropriate minister – Haughey – and had obtained clearance for the cargo he was hoping to import.[9]

Another feature of his testimony was that he had contacted Capt. Kelly's wife after the Ballymurphy riots while he was on the Continent since the captain knew the 'right people' in Northern Ireland to whom any distribution might be made.

When McKenna asked if Capt. Kelly had undergone an emotional involvement which had led to a change of allegiance, he replied, 'Everybody at that particular time was feeling worked up about this thing ... He did not appear to be any more worked up than anybody else'.[10]

The colonel was not the only prosecution witness to cause the state a headache. Michael Ó Moráin inflicted one too.

Brainse Fhionnglaise
Finglas Library
Tel: (01) 834 4906

25

AN INCONVENIENT WITNESS

Michael Ó Moráin testified on 28 September. In preparation for his appearance, he contacted Berry on 21 September at 12.50 p.m. to tell him he intended to visit the Department of Justice that afternoon to review the reports he had read as minister. The conversation was secretly recorded by Berry who kicked for touch, saying that he would have to consult with his new minister, Des O'Malley, who was 'someplace in Glenbeigh'. He advised Ó Moráin to phone back. After the call Berry noted, 'I spoke to Mr Quigley of the Attorney General's office who advised that Mr Ó Moráin had no legal entitlement to see official papers, and that I would be in breach of the Official Secrets Act if I were to communicate official papers without my Minister's direction'.[1]

Ó Moráin rang back at 4.50 p.m. and was told he could not see his old files. When he testified, Ó Moráin told the court, 'I cannot be sure about the dates. I think I can save time if I say here and now: these events with which the Court is concerned took place six months ago or more. I applied last Friday to see the documents with which I was concerned and in some of which I made notes and I was refused permission to see them by the present Minister for Justice and the Attorney General.' He then explained how he was under 'great disabilities' with regards to the dates.[2]

Unwelcome as he was, the state had no choice but to call Ó Moráin. Apart from Gibbons, he was the only other minister who had the authority to import arms. The state needed both men to testify that they had not sanctioned the defendants to import weapons.

Once counsel for the state established that Ó Moráin had not authorised the importation – something that took about a minute – Seamus Sorohan, SC, appearing for John Kelly, rose to his feet. One of his objectives was to demonstrate the lack of communication between the gardaí and G2, such that the military would not have told the police about their involvement in a secret government-backed operation to import arms. Sorohan probed Ó Moráin to establish if the special branch had been investigating rumours and reports of suspected attempts to import arms from the autumn of 1969. Ó Moráin confirmed they had. Sorohan followed this up by asking if it had come to his knowledge that there was 'something going on under the umbrella of Army Intelligence in relation of arms; did you get some hint or whisper about that as Minister?' Ó Moráin recollected 'some information about Captain Kelly and arms. This would be very little'.[3]

Sorohan developed the idea that the G2 operation had been a secret one and that the special branch had been kept at arms' length. Had 'military intelligence [been] working in a comparatively watertight or hermetically sealed-off compartment from the police force in this matter?' Sorohan inquired. Ó Moráin replied that there had been 'a grave lack of co-operation between the two bodies; that one crowd did not seem to know what the other was doing and they tried to do something about this'. He agreed with Sorohan that 'military intelligence was reluctant to part with more than a minimum of information to the police force and particularly to the Special Branch'. He had tried to rectify the matter 'in the few months before April' 1970 by suggesting that 'a Cabinet sub-committee be set up for the purpose of co-ordinating these matters among other things. I made that suggestion to Mr Gibbons and to the Taoiseach ... That there be a Cabinet sub-committee to deal with Northern matters, including this intelligence'. His suggestion was not put before the cabinet and, 'Nothing was done about it'.

He then proceeded to explain that special branch officers had eventually gone to Northern Ireland. 'They were not going up to watch Capt. Kelly. They were going up to give an objective report to me or to the Government on matters up there. At this stage there were very conflicting reports from the North and we felt it would be better to get an objective report on matters up there and that was their main purpose.'[4]

One of Haughey's barristers, Peter Maguire, SC, raised the existence of the government's NI Contingency Plan. 'Now were you aware, Mr Ó Moráin, of the Government's desire that the Army would prepare contingency plans to meet any development in the North of Ireland during the period we are dealing with?' Ó Moráin confirmed he was aware of the plans. Maguire inquired next if it was 'correct to say that the Minister for Finance, Mr Haughey at that time, was authorised to make moneys available to the Army in connection with these contingency plans?' Ó Moráin's answer was: 'Yes, he was given authority, himself and Mr Gibbons to do anything, get anything that was required.' To dispense with any doubt, Maguire followed up with: 'And that included getting arms?'

'Oh, yes, as far as I understood it', Ó Moráin replied.[5]

At the second trial, much of this terrain was revisited. In answer to Niall McCarthy, SC, who was Haughey's lead counsel, Ó Moráin testified:

> Ó Moráin: '… I think it was around the end of September or the beginning of October. Again, I cannot trust my recollection of this, without seeing the papers, but I do remember this decision. I remember the matter being left to the Minister for Finance and the Minister for Defence to get together. There were different propositions discussed and it was left to these two ministers, Mr Haughey to give the Minister for Defence what he needed to deal with the Northern situation.'
>
> **McCarthy**: 'Can you recall any specific matters that were gone into with regard to what these contingency plans might involve?'
>
> 'Ó Moráin: There were different plans, including what I think they called limited incursions by the Army into the North, and there was some discussion of these, and we did not know at that time what might transpire, what might happen. There were discussions on different alternatives depending on events which were rapidly changing and expecting to rapidly change from day to day.'[6]

However, there was one witness the state could rely upon to keep to the script that had been prepared for the trial: the man who wrote it, Peter Berry.

26

BERRY BOXES CLEVER

Peter Berry furnished a document to the state's prosecution team in which he alleged it had never entered his 'mind that the arms were being imported' for the 'purpose of giving means of self-defence to ordinary people in Northern Ireland' and that he had 'never heard of the notion until after the public disclosures in relation to [Blaney and Haughey's] participation in the attempted importation of arms. Ordinary men have no wish to handle firearms'.[1] Instead, he had always believed the arms were 'for the IRA'.

He duly stepped into the witness box on 29 September. In the run-up to the trial, he had given a great deal of thought as to how he could draw a curtain of guile around the fact that he – not Ó Moráin – had issued the order to seal off the airport; moreover, that he had initiated this behind his former minister's back. During his conversation with Haughey on 18 April, Berry had told him that the special branch had placed 'a ring of steel' around the airport and would seize any arms that might land. As previously highlighted, Berry had claimed that Ó Moráin not only knew about the surveillance operation *but had ordered the seizure*. Berry wrote to Declan Quigley at the office of the attorney-general making suggestions about the questions that might be put to him on the issue. He explained that he did 'not intend to seek to volunteer any additional comment designed to stress that the Minister had had a discussion the previous day and that he had given directions'.[2] In simple terms, he wanted to deflect and be vague about the issue.[3] Suffice it to say, few plans survive engagement with the enemy and the one Berry prepared for the trial fared little better than most. Ó Moráin, who testified before Berry, had explained that he had not ordered the seizure of any cargo that might arrive. His orders had been to watch but not seize it.[4]

Berry denied that special branch officers had been sent on cross-border missions.[5] This made Ó Moráin look like a liar or a fantasist, at least for a while. When cross-examined by Seamus Sorohan for John Kelly, the following exchange took place:

> **Sorohan**: 'So, I take it as a result of that, were Special Branch officers sent to the North?'
>
> **Berry**: 'No.'
>
> **Sorohan**: 'It was for some other reason they were sent?'
>
> **Berry**: 'No, there were no Special Branch officers sent to the North, if you are speaking of 1969.'
>
> **Sorohan**: 'Yes, from August 1969 to the spring of this year.'
>
> **Berry**: 'I state categorically there were no Special Branch officers sent to the North in 1969.'[6]

Berry added that none had been sent in the spring or early part of 1970 either. Fleming joined Berry in this deceitful quickstep when he testified.[7]

The issue was resolved when Assistant Garda Commissioner John Lincoln was called to the witness box and stated that Ó Moráin had told him to send experienced, mature officers across the border to make on the spot observations and to report back to Dublin.[8] Where possible, Ó Moráin said, the officers were to have a Northern Ireland background, but there was no question of it being a special branch operation and no special branch men were sent. He explained that Berry had been present when he received his instructions from the minister and that when reports came back they were transmitted through Berry to the minister whence they eventually went to cabinet.[9]

In *Up Dev*, Boland confirmed that Ó Moráin had 'informed the Government that two detectives had been sent to the Six Counties for the purpose [of gathering intelligence]. I don't know if he said they were members of the Special Branch but, obviously, he, like the rest of us, naturally assumed that they were ... It appeared to me that the idea was to represent the former Minister for Justice either as giving false evidence or as having a peculiarly unreliable memory'. Boland believes that the cabinet discussion about garda spies had taken place in the wake of the CDC convention at Bailieboro in early October 1969.[10]

As Boland emphasised, 'Surely, the correct thing for witnesses wanting to help the Court would have been to say that detectives were sent but they were not members of the Special Branch. That would be my interpretation of "the whole truth", but, then, I'm a layman.'[11]

An overarching threat to Berry was his powerlessness to influence the questions the defence lawyers might put to him. On 12 October, he was cross-examined by Sorohan who forced him to be precise about the surveillance at the airport:

> **Sorohan**: 'Having become appraised of the fact, I take it that you gave all the necessary, directions in the matter.'
>
> **Berry**: 'No, the Minister gave the directions to me in the presence of the deputy secretary [Andrew Ward].'
>
> **Sorohan**: 'And you passed them on to the proper quarter, like an efficient civil servant?'
>
> **Berry:** 'That is right.'[12]

Berry tried to stack the cards against Haughey too. A memorandum he furnished to the prosecution before the trial contained The Deceiver's fictitious account of the meeting between Haughey and Goulding in August 1969 at which a deal had allegedly been struck. Berry's memorandum reads as follows:

> It is a question for the Attorney General whether I should, under pressure of cross-examination, or on the initiative of State Counsel, reveal, in deciding as I did to inform the Taoiseach of the situation, that Mr Haughey had been reported on earlier occasions by the 'S' Branch of having a secret meeting with a high-ranking member of the IRA and of the 'deal' that they were alleged to have concluded (the burning and destruction of the property of aliens by the IRA ceased after that meeting – whether by design (as the gardaí reported) or by sheer coincidence.[13]

The state did not pursue this line of inquiry during the trial for the rather obvious reason they had no witness to testify about what had transpired at the encounter. Presumably, they also had the wit to appreciate the rather obvious reason why the sporadic arson campaign had petered out: had the tiny handful of IRA volunteers involved in it persisted, they would have brought the wrath of the entire spectrum of republican support down upon their heads because the rank-and-file wanted whatever meagre resources the IRA had to be deployed to aid the imperilled nationalists.

To buttress the accuracy of his memory against the anticipated evidence of Haughey, Berry told the court that he had made contemporaneous notes of what had transpired during the telephone discussion he had conducted with him on 18 April. According to Berry, he had received a call from Haughey during which he told him the special branch had placed a 'ring of steel' around the airport and were lying in wait to seize the arms. Berry told the court he had consulted his notes and felt there was an important distinction between what counsel for the prosecution had outlined in his opening statement and what he – Berry – had written down. Berry gave the impression that his notes were so precise, he could be extraordinarily accurate about the exact words Haughey had uttered. Yet, decades later when these notes were released from the National Archives, it transpired they were rather threadbare. Yet in the witness box, Berry had claimed, 'My Lord, I think I should say here that in Counsel's opening statement in describing my conversation as of paramount importance, [Counsel] used the expression [attributed to Haughey that]: "I had better call it off", that is, as reported in the newspapers. The expression used by Mr Haughey was: "I had better have it called off". I made notes there and then in my personal diary as to what Mr Haughey had said'.

The first sentence quoted above implies that Haughey was in effective control of the endeavour; so much so that he could call it off on his own volition. The second version implies that others were involved and that Haughey would have to secure their approval for the cancellation. The second version – which Berry emphasised as accurate – was consistent with a wider, high-level conspiracy, one that justified the ill-fated decision to prosecute Blaney. For those who followed these events closely, the nuanced difference in language was important as the latter version was consistent with Blaney's guilt in the affair. Since the charges against Blaney had been dismissed at an early stage, there was a strong possibility that he might yet return to cabinet or perhaps one day even become taoiseach. What Berry was implying had the potential to shut Blaney out in the cold for the foreseeable, if not long-term, future if the trial verdict went his way and public opinion followed suit.

The judge appreciated the point Berry was making and stated that he felt, 'It is very important that that should be rectified' to which Berry replied: 'I made notes there and then in my personal diary as to what Mr Haughey said. Furthermore, on going to the Department of Justice on Monday morning I made similar notes.' Unfortunately, his note simply read as follows:

> C.J.; knew about cargo into D. Airport/Can it be let through on a guarantee goes direct to North/bad decision. 'Man from Mayo'/ what happens when cargo arrives/call off.

Worse still, a letter in my possession reveals that on 18 September 1970, Berry wrote to Declan Quigley in an attempt to choreograph his evidence – and in which he referred to himself in the third person – he addressed this issue in it, stating that:

> In giving evidence of the final part of the telephone conversation, the Secretary does not propose to wait to be asked if he is quite sure of the accuracy of everything in his account of the conversation. Instead, when it comes to the relevant part, he proposes to say-
>
> I am not completely certain of the exact words used by Mr. Haughey then. To the best of my recollection, and I'm nearly certain of this, what he said was:
>
> *I had better have it called off.*
>
> But there is a slight possibility that his words may have been:
>
> *'I had better call it off'.*
>
> If he is asked – as he might be by counsel for a defendant – what distinction he sees between these two versions, he proposes to say that he is not suggesting (not that he does not think – because in fact he does] that there is any distinction and that he merely wants to state the facts as accurately as possible. If pressed further, on the lines that he must be seeking to suggest that there is some distinction, he would say something like this:
>
> 'I am not making any suggestion. The reason I have mentioned both versions is that it seemed to me that the Court or the jury might see a distinction and might regard the matter as having some significance'.

Berry even suggested how he should be questioned and the answer that could be expected by way of reply as follows:

> Question: But what distinction could they possibly see?
>
> Answer: *Possibly, a person might think that 'I had better call it off' implies that the speaker was in immediate and sole control of the operation himself whereas 'I had better have it called off' might imply*

> *that he would be acting in consultation with some other person or persons'.*

If Berry was the author of the prosecution script, the weakest role he wrote was the one for Gibbons who, at times, appeared as if he was opening his mouth in the witness box only to change his feet.

27

THE MINISTER WHO KNEW NOTHING

James Gibbons testified at both trials. Implausibly, he even went as far as to deny that he had ever been asked for arms by the Northern Ireland delegations. Thomas Finlay, SC for Capt. Kelly, cross-examined him on that particular assertion as follows:

> **Finlay:** 'Are you suggesting that you were unaware of any request or requests by the representatives of these [defence] committees in the North for arms to be supplied to them by the Irish Government?'
>
> **Gibbons**: 'I have no recollection of the remotest kind.'[1]

When Finlay's questioning turned to the FCA training at Fort Dunree, he suggested it implied a willingness on the government's part to supply guns. 'What was the point of training them in the use of guns if they were not going to get guns?'[2] Gibbons' reply was that his 'chief motivation in this gesture would be to convey to them that their dire straits were perceived by us and were sympathized with by us.'[3] He said nothing about the training at Finner Camp.

When asked if the training had been halted because of newspaper publicity, he answered: 'The Taoiseach was on leave. I sanctioned it on my own initiative. On his return, I acquainted him of the fact. The Taoiseach considered the matter and advised that it be discontinued, and it was.' This was misleading as Col Hefferon had halted it on his own volition and then informed Gibbons after the event.[4]

In the marathon debate the previous May, Richie Ryan Fine Gael TD, had raised the training at Fort Dunree by saying that instruction had been 'given in at least one military camp to civilians in the use of arms'. Gibbons had interrupted: 'That is not true'. That interruption now came back to haunt him. His explanation in the witness box was that the Derrymen had been sworn into the FCA before their training had commenced and hence, they were technically not 'civilians'. When asked if that did not 'mean that this was a device to enable the Army to train them for the defence of the Bogside?' he replied: 'I admit that this was a device to enable Derrymen to join the FCA and obtain training'. Counsel's follow up was to ask him if he thought his 'reply to Deputy Ryan was not something of a half-truth?' In response he argued, 'I am suggesting that what Deputy Ryan said was inaccurate.' Counsel continued to press him: 'Would you accept that in this instance you had not told the truth but only half the truth?' He replied: 'This is a Dáil debate in which Deputy Ryan and his colleagues are seeking to demolish the Government and the Government party', was his response.[5]

Another pitfall for Gibbons was the CDC Convention at Bailieboro. Boland was adamant that he, Gibbons and every other member of the government were aware of the Bailieboro meeting.[6] Yet, Gibbons now denied any knowledge of it.[7] This flew in the face of the evidence that Berry had not only learned about it, but had raised it with the Taoiseach who had asked him – Gibbons – for further information about it. Gibbons had then obtained an account of the meeting from Col Hefferon. When the colonel gave evidence, he flatly contradicted Gibbons' account.[8]

Gibbons acknowledged that 500 surplus Army rifles had been brought to Dundalk but denied this was done for a possible distribution to the CDCs because of the eruption of violence in Ballymurphy. Instead, he now suggested one possibility they had been moved could have been to have them available for distribution on the south side of the border to repel an invasion from Northern Ireland, presumably by armed loyalists.

Nothing was disclosed about the 150 rifles which had originally formed part of the consignment of 500 which had been rushed to Dundalk but had not been brought back to Dublin.

When Eamonn Walsh questioned him about his first meeting with Capt. Kelly for the state, he claimed it had not happened until mid March 1970 but Capt. Kelly said that they had met for the first time the previous month. The discrepancy in dates was designed to distance Gibbons from the far closer relationship that Capt. Kelly maintained had existed between them.[9]

With regard to the meeting with the CDC delegation at Leinster House that same month, he claimed that he was not sure who the delegates were and denied he had promised to procure arms for them. On 25 September he told Finlay, '... I was not quite clear that they represented anyone, except citizens of Belfast. I was not quite clear as to whether they were defence committees or not.'[10]

When Gibbons first provided a statement to the gardaí, he informed them that he had known about the *MV City of Dublin* importation attempt:

> When Captain Kelly told me about the consignment expected at Dublin docks and its failure to be dispatched, I said 'I suppose that is the end of that' or words to that effect. He said 'No, it will be all right' or something like that. This conversation took place, I think, on Captain Kelly's second visit to me which took place at Mr Blaney's request probably in early April [1970].

This passage was excised from his statement before it went into the book of evidence. Nonetheless, the issue was raised when he was cross-examined on 24 September:

> **Gibbons**: 'I cannot be absolutely precise about the date, but I would, from my recollection, say it would be possibly the last days of March, and on that occasion Capt. Kelly, at the request of another member of the Government came to my office in Leinster House and he informed me of a visit that had taken place at Dublin docks in the recent past and the story was to this effect:
>
> 'That they or we, meaning the people who conspired to take in the guns, expected them to come into Dublin docks and when they went there to meet them that the Irish Army was present there in strength, taking delivery of a regular Army shipment of weapons, and at that stage I said to Captain Kelly – I presume at that stage – to disappear into the shadows, and from my recollection again he seemed to assent to this.
>
> 'I said, "Well I presume that's the end of that lot anyway" and Capt. Kelly said "No, it isn't", and he indicated that by some means or other it will be possible to retrieve them.

> 'I seem to have a recollection of Capt. Kelly mentioning the possibility of having them shipped through a port on the Adriatic, for I suggested to him that port would possibly be Trieste and his reply was rather vague and I don't recall it.'[11]

Gibbons also had to explain why he had allowed the captain go to the Continent:

> **Finlay**: 'Isn't it correct to say that at the time the official information available to you was that [Capt. Kelly] was going in connection with these affairs to the Continent, to Germany, and that the ostensible reason being given out as a cover for that was that it was to visit his sister in Frankfurt?'
>
> **Gibbons**: 'The Director of Intelligence told me that [Capt. Kelly] had applied for permission to visit his sister.'
>
> **Finlay**: 'Didn't the Director of Intelligence say that the real reason was … to visit it for arms?'
>
> **Gibbons**: '[The Director] dealt with it in a rather equivocal way. He said: "I have an idea that the real reason may be to vet arms". That was the expression used.'
>
> **Finlay**: So, the Director of Intelligence told you, this would have been sometime around the middle of February, that Capt. Kelly, he believed, was going to vet arms and that he was giving as a cover, or ostensible reason, for that leave, to visit his sister in Frankfurt?
>
> **Gibbons**: 'Yes. I asked if he had a sister in Frankfurt and I understood him to say that he had. That was my knowledge of the situation at that stage. To me it appeared to be a somewhat unreasonable assumption.'
>
> **Finlay**: 'I must suggest to you that subsequently, when you met

> Capt. Kelly, certainly on March 4, possibly on other occasions, he referred to the visits he had made to the Continent?'
>
> **Gibbons**: 'This is not so.'[12]

In Gibbons' defence, his predicament was that he had been painted into a corner by Lynch and left there on his own with little choice but to plod across a floor of wet paint and create an unholy mess *en route*.

It was now time for the defendants to have their say.

28

HAUGHEY AIMS CAREFULLY

Peter Sutherland acted as Capt. Kelly's junior counsel. Before his client climbed into the box, Sutherland urged upon him: 'Don't worry, Jim. When you're battling from the truth, you can't go wrong.'[1] These words worked their magic. When the captain took to the witness box it was with all guns blazing. His account has been covered in earlier chapters and will not be repeated here.

When Charles Haughey climbed into the same witness box on 19 October, he testified that Gibbons had been given 'a general instruction from the Government' to prepare 'contingency plans' and that the government had decided that the Army was to be prepared for any possible emergency that might arise; moreover, that he had been given instructions to make available whatever additional moneys might be required to Gibbons 'to procure any sort of special equipment, or anything else that we might need, so that the Army might be in a position to meet any contingency that might arise … we might by UN decision, have been asked to send troops into certain areas to patrol these areas. It is possible that if there was a completely chaotic situation, the British Army or the British Government would agree to our patrolling certain areas, where we would be acceptable. There was also the question of complete breakdown, there was the possibility that the Army here might go inside the Six Counties on rescue operations.'[2]

This passage from Haughey's testimony mirrors the records which have since emerged from the army's secret archives but were not disclosed to the defence lawyers in 1970. No doubt, the state believed they were privileged. Irrespective, justice and the guarantee of a fair trial would then have required that the prosecution be abandoned rather than allow crucial evidence be withheld. In February of 1973 John Wyman, an acknowledged MI6 agent, was put on trial in Dublin for allegedly trying to obtain secret garda files from Patrick Crinnion of C3. The charges in respect of the confidential documents were withdrawn because they were too sensitive to produce in court, even one sitting *in camera* (closed to the press and public).

Haughey added that the government had 'realised that in order to prepare for [these contingencies] we would have to supply the Army with special equipment [it might] be gas masks, it might be anti-riot equipment, it might be a special type of arms. The Army was to work this out and I was to make the money available for the supply of these items'.

Haughey also described how Ó Moráin had indeed been 'instructed by the Government to send Garda officers, and I at that time thought they were to be Special Branch officers, into the Six Counties to be able to give us a first-hand account of everything that was happening within the Six Counties ... A number of reports were read by the Minister for Justice to Government meetings'.[3]

When asked by his barrister if there had been 'any individual or person not in the Cabinet who was concerned with creating a link between you and your fellow members and the people in the North?' he told him that Capt. Kelly had fulfilled that role. He also described how the captain had introduced him to John Kelly as part of a delegation from Northern Ireland.[4]

On 19 or 20 March, Haughey recounted, Anthony Fagan had informed him that G2 had asked him to bring in the consignment 'without having it subject' to the usual clearance. 'I said if I had the power to do it, I would do it. He assured me that I had the power and I said, "OK, go ahead". May I add that at that time, on the 19th or 20th Captain Kelly came to Mr Fagan as an official approach. Both Mr Fagan and myself had no doubt that this was an official approach from Army Intelligence through official channels.'

Niall McCarthy, SC, who also acted for Haughey, asked his client, 'If you had known, first, that the consignment contained arms, ammunition and bullet proof vests, would that have made any difference?' He replied: 'Not the slightest, no. The contingency plans naturally envisaged items of that nature ...'

'If you had known that they were intended for possible ultimate distribution to civilians in the North would that have made any difference?' Haughey replied: "No, not really, provided, of course, that a Government decision intervened. I would have regarded it as a very normal part of Army preparations in pursuance of the contingency plans that they would provide themselves with, and store here on this side of the Border, arms which might ultimately, if the government said so, be distributed to other persons.'

Haughey confirmed that he had called Berry on Saturday 18 April and provided the following account under cross-examination to Eamonn Walsh, SC for the state:

Walsh: 'So, there was a conversation then, relating to certain cargo ... Was there any reference to what the consignment consisted of?'

Haughey: 'No, none. And, as far as I can recall, Mr Berry did not say what it consisted of.'

Walsh: 'Your conversation with Mr Berry ended with your telling him, "It had better be called off, whatever it is"?'

Haughey: 'Yes. That is my recollection.'

Walsh: 'Did it occur to you to ask Mr Berry at any stage what the consignment was?'

Haughey: 'No, for – I just recall – the first thing Mr Berry asked me was, had I a scrambler, and he was very conscious of the need not to be talking in any careless terms on the telephone.'

Walsh: 'I gather from what you say that Mr Berry was totally and absolutely wrong when he says you asked, if a guarantee was got that it would go direct to the North, could it come through?'

Haughey: 'I could not have had that kind of discussion. I would have it with the Minister for Justice. The question of guarantee could not arise, I can only say that Mr Berry must be mistaken in his recollection of the particular word "guarantee".'

Walsh: 'Was the North mentioned?'

Haughey: 'No. As I said, we spoke about the consignment as such, not where it was going or what it was or anything of that sort.'

Walsh: 'Did you even question what was in the consignment?'

Haughey: 'I certainly had a very shrewd idea that it was something that Army Intelligence was bringing in in pursuance of their plans.'

Walsh: 'You did not know for certain but you had a very shrewd idea that this was a consignment of arms and ammunition?'

Haughey: 'That is quite correct. I did not know for certain, but I did not exclude the possibility that it was arms and ammunition.'[5]

Haughey also testified that after he had spoken to Berry, he had telephoned Fagan at his home and told him that he had consulted Berry 'about this and that the consignment, whatever it was, had to be called off.'[6]

Charles Haughey was the last witness to testify.

29

VERDICT AND FALL OUT

In terms of establishing the truth, the marathon Dáil debate of May and the Arms Trials of September and October were poor vehicles of delivery.

The existence of the arms flight from London in September 1969, about which a large number of cabinet members had known, did not emerge.

Lt Col E.S. Barry, Comdt. Gerry O'Sullivan and Comdt. Kevin P. Kelly, authors of the report by the Planning Board on NI Operations, did not testify.

The evidence of the men who underwent training at Fort Dunree in September 1969 and at Finner Camp went unheard.

During their evidence at the Four Courts Berry and Fleming concealed the fact Berry had spoken to Jack Lynch at Mount Carmel hospital.

The experience of 'Con', the official from the Department of External affairs who met John Kelly, Gerry Fitt and Jock Haughey in London during the Capt. Markham-Randall spy fiasco, remained a secret.

The discussions Gibbons and Lynch exchanged in December 1969 and January 1970, and the fact Lynch later ordered Gibbons to conceal them became one of the deepest secrets of the entire affair.

Since Lynch did not testify, the juries in both trials heard nothing about his meetings with Seán Keenan and Billy Kelly about the possible provision of the surplus Irish Army rifles.

The addendum of 10 February 1970 was suppressed, i.e. the one which recited that the 'Taoiseach and other Ministers have met delegations from the North. At these meetings urgent demands were made for respirators, weapons and ammunition the provision of which the Government agreed. Accordingly truckloads of these items will be put at readiness so that they may be available in a matter of hours'.[1]

Gibbons had ordered the transport of 500 rifles to Dundalk on the basis Blaney had told him that 'attacks on the minority were planned and that British Security Forces would be withdrawn and accordingly would not afford protection for the minority'.[2] He was not cross-examined on the contradiction between these comments and the excuses he provided in the witness box for the transport.

The fact 150 rifles had been left behind in Dundalk; the identity of those who had arranged this; and their motive for the division of the cargo was not explored.

Undoubtedly, the best-kept secret was that the gardaí had learned about the proposed arms flight from an informer and that the Dáil and the public had been hoodwinked into believing the pending flight had come to light because of inquiries by customs officials.

***

After Haughey's evidence there were closing speeches by the prosecution and the defence after which the judge charged the jury and pointed out that there was a clear conflict between the sworn testimony of Gibbons and Haughey, which could not be accounted for by failure in recollection. Many commentators have framed the judge's remarks about the clash as a stark choice between a man who told the truth and one who perjured himself. It is probably more accurate to say that both men failed to tell the full truth. Gibbons' deceit was produced on an industrial scale and designed to preserve his reputation and that of Lynch, even if it meant sending men like Capt. Kelly to jail whereas Haughey's deviations were designed to keep him and his co-defendants out of prison in circumstances where a litany of dirty tricks had been deployed against them to twist the truth and create a fictitious narrative about their activities.

The jury retired to consider its verdict at 3.28 p.m. on Friday 23 October 1970. They returned at 5.40. Tom Mac Intyre, author of *Through the Bridewell Gate, A Diary of the Dublin Arms Trial*, described what happened:

> Counsel rise – the gathering sits tight – to ask the Trial Judge for clarification of certain questions touched on his charge to the jury. At 4:30 the jury is recalled, and the Trial Judge clarifies as requested; nothing major. The court empties, as best it can, into the lobby – which is packed. Dare a man rush off for a drink? No. Chance it. But few chance it. How long? Could be hours, could be twenty minutes. Roar of talk, argument, prognostication. Slop. What? The jury are coming back. Christ, get in there. Mad drive for the court-room. The jury file in. Not a breath in the place, the foreman rises, the place spasms – but, no verdict, the man has a question: did Colonel Hefferon say that the Directive involved the provision of arms against the contingency of possible distribution to civilians in Northern Ireland? Yes. The jury depart, no indication about them, Yea or Nay, but – back to the lobby – an interesting question, a pointer, maybe. No room to move in the

> lobby but no one will move from it. Everyone's here. You meet men you haven't met in twenty years, and hope to Jesus you'll meet again. Several false alarms, they're back, no, they're not, they are – and then a definite summons. Back in there, the court-room jammed, blaze in the eyes and necks rigid. All assembled but for the jury. No, wait, the door, their door, opens, and – wonderful – two cranin' women enter, and – did they bring those chairs with them? – settle themselves like Duchesses to watch the finish. Still waiting. A mob something owns Court No. 1 now, unmistakably, wait, Yes, the jury – and the court rises to the jury, a blind craven salute but no time to ponder it, the foreman, no-nonsense the cut of him, hands the verdicts to the clerk of court, pause, a silence now would split rock, and he reads, Not Guilty, Not Guilty, Not Guilty, Not – the place flies asunder to a brute roar, timber, bodies, spin of faces, that roar, it dips, renews itself – but a cleaner poetry, abruptly, through the fury, beyond it, where, on a span of wall between Bench and jury-box, the sealed windowless weeks are in procession through two open doors.[3]

Conor Cruise O'Brien was undoubtedly accurate in his assessment that:

> … No one in Dublin with whom I discussed the case – and I discussed it with many people of widely different views – had any hesitation in believing Captain Kelly and Colonel Hefferon.[4]

After his acquittal, Haughey laid down a challenge to the leadership of Lynch using coded political language. Lynch was in New York at the time. Haughey threw a celebration party at his house that night. One of those who attended was Muiris Mac Conghail, the then editor of *7 Days*, RTÉ's current affairs programme. He has described how he was 'staggered' by what he saw there: senior members of the judiciary; senior gardaí; senior civil servants; heads of semi-state bodies and even Jack Lynch's aide-de-camp, Jack O'Brien, who was related to Haughey through marriage. 'Anyone who was anybody in public life was present'.[5]

Lynch addressed the twenty-fifth anniversary commemorative session of the United Nations in New York on the general theme of 'peace, justice and progress'. On the Saturday morning, he called a press conference and opined there was 'no doubt' that an 'attempt to smuggle arms' had taken place and that those dismissed had been involved. In support of this he added, 'Members of the Government know how arms can be imported on behalf of the Army and Gardaí and they know that it can only be by means of a duly signed certificate'. This was in fact legally inaccurate.[6]

Any momentum behind the heave Haughey had initiated collapsed after the taoiseach received a welcome from the members of his parliamentary party at Dublin Airport upon his return. Following on from this, on 4 November he sought and won a vote of no confidence in the Dáil, 74 to 67, with even Haughey and Blaney voting for him. Boland, however, failed to join the chorus. 'I was drinking my last cup of tea in Leinster House with my wife and a few friends downstairs in the restaurant when the vote was taken, with Blaney and Haughey in the government lobby.'[7]

The Deceiver must have watched these events with a deep sense of satisfaction, not to mention amusement. He would not be slow to exploit a series of opportunities which now presented themselves to advance the rise of the Provisional IRA.

30

THE BENEFICIARIES OF THE ARMS CRISIS

The Provisional IRA was one of the few winners to emerge from the rubble of the Arms Crisis. John Kelly attributed this to Lynch and his supporters. 'What I'm saying is that they created the conditions on the ground for the formation of the Provisional IRA by their abandonment of Northern Nationalism. There was no IRA existing in 1969. What happened on the ground was that Northern Nationalism, withdrawing in on itself to defend itself, was the breeding ground for, if you like, the paramilitary approach. That is what gave the water, in which the IRA could swim.'[1]

A string of calamitous mistakes followed, which created an atmosphere even more favourable to the Provisionals. In 1978 James Glover, who later became head of the Defence Intelligence Service (DIS), produced a report, *Northern Ireland: Future Terrorist Trends*. It provided an insight into the British Army's analysis of the re-emergence of IRA in the shape of the Provisionals. According to Glover, they gained momentum after 1969 against a background of decades of loyalist oppression. 'Republican fears of a Protestant ascendancy being re-established would enable the PIRA to pose as defenders of the minority interest'.[2] Glover reasoned that the 'fear of a possible return to Protestant repression will underpin this kind of support for the Provisionals for many years to come.'[3] He also cautioned that an 'isolated incident, such as "Bloody Sunday", could radically alter support for violence.'[4]

Bloody Sunday was far from the only incident to generate 'support for violence'. The Falls Road curfew, which took place less than two months after the eruption of the Arms Crisis, was an earlier precipitating factor in that development.[5] The Official IRA had established arms caches in Belfast. One of them was in a house on Balkan Street off the Falls Road. After an informer pinpointed it for the British Army, a detachment raided it on Friday, 3 July 1970, and seized nineteen illegal weapons.

Paddy Devlin noted that it was 'a most remarkable situation for the military to raid for arms at 4 p.m. on a Friday afternoon. All arms raids took place discreetly at 4 a.m. never in daylight or at a time when some local males would be fired up, drinking in the pubs'. Soon news of the attack spread and 'hundreds of youths quickly gathered around Balkan Street. Predictably, stones were thrown from both ends of the street, as the captured guns were removed from the house in full public view. I arrived on the scene with a number of clergy from the adjacent Catholic church and together we persuaded the stone-throwers to stop, although they remained in the vicinity. Unknown to us, however, there was a major force of troops mustered on the corner of nearby Durham Street and Divis Street. Hundreds of men were deployed in lines of lorries and armoured vehicles. It was clear the arms raid was only the trigger for a major, well-planned confrontation.'

Devlin was only too well aware that the Lower Falls area 'was an acknowledged stronghold of the Official IRA and I calculated that this was clearly a punitive raid on the entire district'. He believed this was so because Jim Sullivan had recently criticised Lt-Gen. Freeland. Indeed, he had issued a warning a fortnight earlier stating that Freeland was 'not to come onto his patch' without his approval. The army also believed that arms caches were hidden in the district and that in the wake of the violence of the previous weeks 'a deliberate confrontation with these challengers was called for.' Devlin's efforts at calming the situation achieved nothing. Instead, the violence intensified with up to 3,000 CS gas canisters being deployed by the Army. 'A helicopter, with an underslung loudspeaker, descended to virtual roof level and a voice announced that the area was under curfew and anyone on the street after the warning would be shot.'

Devlin decided to head to the CDC HQ to establish a 'contact post, where some journalists joined me'. He felt that the Officials were afraid of losing the 'little face they had left' and would become vulnerable to future attack from the Provisionals or loyalists if they did not put up a fight. As he put it, the 'shooting increased in tempo as darkness fell. The high-pitched whine of the armoured cars as they manoeuvred around the narrow streets and the occasional burst of heavy calibre fire filled me with dread.' The fighting stopped at dawn. Devlin went to the CDC headquarters on the Falls Road, which lay on the boundary of the curfewed zone where he and others spent the night listening to the shooting, 'fortified by tea, coffee and soup laid in for just such an emergency'.[6]

There was to be no let-up in the morning. 'Daylight brought the follow-up search by the military. They axed doors down that could easily have been opened, ripped up floorboards, broke furniture unnecessarily and tipped the contents of drawers and cupboards all over the place. Residents later complained bitterly about the Black Watch, a Scottish regiment, which seemed to give most of its attention to breaking religious objects and symbols of the Glasgow Celtic football club, which enjoyed huge support among Belfast Catholics.'[7] Residents would also claim that the soldiers stole from them.

During the curfew five people were killed, two of whom were snipers. Sixty-five were injured of which fifteen were soldiers. An accurate tally of those wounded never took place because many of the victims were scared to attend hospital where soldiers lay in wait to arrest them. Raids on the fifty or so streets uncovered approximately 100 arms, 100 home-made bombs, 250 lbs of explosives, 1,000 rounds of ammunition and eight two-way radio sets. They were piled up and put on display at Springfield Road barracks, for newspaper and television reporters to see.

The upheaval provided the Provisionals with a propaganda windfall. Hundreds of people, including journalists, had been arrested and brought to court, but the charges were later dropped when it was declared that the curfew had been imposed illegally. Devlin was one of those arrested during the turmoil although he was soon released. Gerry Fitt rang Devlin to arrange an immediate visit to Westminster, which fell into place on 6 July. Fitt arranged to see Lord Carrington, the new minister for defence, and Reginald Maudling, the new home secretary who was responsible for Northern Ireland. When they got to London, Devlin recalls that 'Maudling would not allow me in, but later we pushed Carrington for an independent enquiry into the army's extreme behaviour. I gave him a detailed account of incidents which I had witnessed and other reports we had received.'[8]

On 23 July the Stormont government banned all public processions until January 1971.

According to Paddy Devlin, the impact of the Falls Road curfew was that, 'Overnight the population turned from neutral to even support for the military to outright hatred of everything related to the security forces.'[9]

The relationship between the CDCs and the British Army went from bad to worse. According to a CDC pamphlet *Law (?) And Orders* which was published in 1970 after the events of July, the Army planted false evidence at the Central CDC's premises at Cyprus Street.

The point of no return had not yet been reached. As Eamonn McCann recalls, the events of July did not 'totally alienate the Catholics from the army. There were many who believed that, despite all, the presence of the army was still some sort of defence against extremist Protestant attack. It was said that the army had been misled by unionist politicians, that this did not really represent army policy, that only a Scottish regiment had been involved, English regiments were different. People believed what they wanted'.[10]

There were other glimmers of hope for a lessening of tension. On 18 August 1970 *The Irish News* reported that the army:

> had reached its best popularity rating in Belfast since it was welcomed with open arms by the Catholics almost a year ago. The troops' weekend flood rescue work could well pave the way for a new relationship between Belfast and the Army. People, who on

> Saturday swore and spat at soldiers, yesterday offered cups of tea and food and paid warm tribute to them. Women from Hutchinson Street, which lay between Grosvenor Road and the Lower Falls Area, could not speak too highly of the unselfish manner in which The Coldstream Guards went about their work in helping the victims of flooding. One man spoke of a soldier up to his neck in water rescuing three greyhounds from the rear of a heavily flooded house. Others spoke of the army getting food to people. As members of the Guards used dinghies, while others waded shoulder height, to rescue families and elderly people trapped in the upstairs of their Falls homes by floods, Paddy Devlin paid tribute to their work. The St Paul's Citizen defence committee expressed its gratitude, particularly to Lieutenant Michael Willoughby, the soldiers' OC, as they 'got down on their knees and cleaned the floors of the flooded houses'. Forty-five soldiers from The Green Howards had 'drinks on the house' in a club in west Belfast as Catholic and Protestant joined in the tributes.[11]

That same month nationalists who did not want to support the Provisionals were provided with a new political alternative, the Socialist and Democratic Labour Party, or SDLP. Paddy Devlin was one of those to join. However, violence was about to become an ever present feature of the Irish condition.

On 11 August 1970, Const. Samuel Donaldson, age twenty-three, and Const. Robert Millar, aged twenty-six, were killed by the IRA, the start of the campaign that continued for decades. The pair had been attempting to tow away a Ford Cortina car left on the Lisseraw Road off the main Crossmaglen to Dundalk Road. Fifteen pounds of gelignite had been placed under the bonnet of the vehicle and wired to a light inside the passenger compartment. Millar pulled the door open slowly. As he did, the light switch triggered the bomb. His arm was torn off and mangled by the heat and pressure of the gas. Both he and Donaldson were thrown into a shallow ditch, still alive but the pair died shortly afterwards.

In February of the following year, the Provisionals shot dead a young married British soldier, Robert Curtis, aged twenty, in Belfast; he was the first of many such fatalities. In May 1971, the Officials shot Corp. Robert Bankier.

Indisputably, these or similar killings would have occurred despite the outbreak of the Arms Crisis and the demise of the CDC that followed on its heels. Nonetheless, it is conceivable that had the CDCs retained their status, some of those who deserted them to join the Provisional and Official IRA, might have remained with the former. Looking to the future, some of those who enrolled with the IRA would have had an alternative had they merely wanted to protect their communities rather than participate in a campaign to end partition.

From a British perspective, Dublin was now a hot bed of intrigue rather than a sleepy backwater. British Intelligence and the diplomat-spy-black propagandists running the British embassy in Dublin were redoubling their intelligence gathering operations. A lot of the information presented to them was bunkum and can only have been detrimental to Anglo-Irish affairs.

31

DIPLOMAT-SPY AND BLACK PROPAGANDA MAESTRO

Ambassador Gilchrist left Dublin in early 1970, sometime around March, although there appears to have been an overlap with his successor John Peck, who arrived in January 1970. During the overlap, Gilchrist handed over some of his contacts to Peck. One of these was the Tánaiste Erskine Childers. As Gilchrist recorded:

> The three Irishmen with whom I can talk most freely and frankly about Irish politics are moderate men, and they know very well what side they are on. They are General Collins-Powell, Mr David Nelligan, & Mr Erskine Childers.[1]

Childers enjoyed a warm relationship with the British embassy and the ambassadors who ran it by virtue of his English background and his second marriage to Rita Dudley who had been employed at the British Representative Office in Dublin during the Second World War in a number of secretarial positions.[2] Her work had drawn the attention of Sir John Maffey who ran the office. She became the assistant press attaché in 1942.[3] Impressed, Maffey recommended her for a position at the Irish Desk in the Ministry of Information in London in 1943 which she took up. From there, she moved to the Foreign Office for a while. During her spell in London, she was permitted sight of classified files about the Holocaust which troubled her greatly. She returned to Dublin in 1942 to resume her role as assistant press attaché. The press attaché at the time was John Betjeman who conducted intelligence gathering and propaganda operations in the Republic.[4] He drew the attention of the IRA, some of whose members plotted to assassinate him. Amazingly, the operation was denied a green light because of Betjeman's skill as a poet.[5]

Rita Dudley met Erskine Childers in 1952 while he was minister for posts and telegraphs. They married later that year. De Valera had not been happy that she was an employee of the British embassy and she had been obliged to resign from her post.

When the Troubles erupted, Childers relied on her insights into what she perceived the British establishment was thinking.[6]

Ambassador Peck was no ordinary diplomat; rather, he was the former head of the Information Research Department (IRD), a suitably Orwellian euphemism for the Foreign Office's propaganda machine that worked hand in glove with the various branches of British Intelligence. More than most, he knew how to spin a good yarn. If we are to believe him, the British embassy knew nothing of the endeavours of Haughey, Gibbons, Blaney *et al* until they became public knowledge in May. In his book, *Dublin from Downing Street,* Peck described how, on 6 May, he had been awoken by Peter Evans, his 'Information Secretary' at 7.15 a.m. to be told the allegedly shocking news that Haughey and Blaney had not only been dismissed by Jack Lynch, but had 'actually been arrested on charges of illegally financing and trafficking in arms ... The British government naturally had to be told what was going on and what was likely to happen, particularly as the arms, if any, were presumably destined for the Catholic minority in Northern Ireland'.[7] It is far more likely that by now Peck had learned his way around Dublin's dark political corners and had a shrewd idea about what was lurking therein. Thanks to Gilchrist, he had sources close to and inside the Irish government to help him understand 'what was going on', one of whom was the aforementioned Childers. Peck described Childers in his memoirs as 'a very remarkable man … when I knew him he was Minister of Health and a very steadfast supporter of Jack Lynch'.[7] Moreover, Peck saw him as 'a very wise and experienced man, who had always been friendly and helpful'. Childers was a regular dinner party guest at the ambassador's residence. Peck recalls that at one of the last parties he hosted 'without warning Erskine Childers rose and made a speech, very warm and simple and obviously straight from the heart, not about our guests of honour [the Canadian ambassador and his wife] but about Mariska and me and our time in Dublin. There is, of course, no text or record of it, but one of the points that he stressed went something like this: "We in the Irish government soon discovered that the British ambassador interpreted our position and our problems faithfully and fairly to his government. But we also learned that he was a lucid and outspoken ambassador, and I would like people on both sides of the water to know that when, as often happens, there were differences between us, we were never left in any doubt what the British felt and why".'[8]

Childers may or may not have realised he was playing with fire in his dealings with Peck. As an experienced diplomat-spy, Peck would have been in dereliction of his duties had he not tried to absorb as much information as he could from the tánaiste. Records which have emerged from Britain's National Archives show that Peck received at least some information from Childers – really no more than malicious gossip – after the jury at the Arms Trial acquitted Haughey and his co-defendants, which he recorded in a memorandum and dispatched to London:

> There is a Dublin businessman called Gerry Jones who is a close friend of Mr Blaney and an associate of Mr Haughey in the various property deals and other transactions in which he specialises. The Deputy Prime Minister [Erskine Childers] told me that to his certain knowledge Mr Jones had tracked down and 'got in touch with' all 12 jurors in the trial.[9]

In reality, at least some of the jury had sided with the defendants before the trial ended. After John Kelly wound up his speech from the dock, he received the applause of at least one member of the jury.

In his 2020 book, *The Arms Crisis, The Plot That Never Was*, the former RTÉ broadcaster and producer, Michael Heney, quoted two former jurors he interviewed in 2001. They had noted that Garret FitzGerald had claimed they had been intimidated. One of them described how, after Gibbons had:

> said that he was aware of the arms coming in. He had been made aware of it ... You could actually sense the reaction in the jury box, because that was a turning point for the whole thing. A complete denial on the one hand, and then an admission that he was aware of it ... There was another lad on the jury and when we both - when we went in – we were saying, 'that's a revelation', and

> another few of the jury were in the vicinity and also of the same opinion. That, that was absolutely – I suggested myself that the four lads shouldn't be up on trial, that it was Jim Gibbons should have been up for perjury.[10]

Childers' comments about interfering with the jury can only have deepened British concerns about Haughey. They came to believe that the importation had been organised by him, Gibbons and Blaney for the benefit of the IRA. No doubt Berry and Fleming fuelled these concerns in further discussions with their UK counterparts. The combination of this and, very likely, many other secret briefings from people acting on faulty information or with axes to grind, proved detrimental to Anglo-Irish relations after Haughey became taoiseach. Robin Haydon, one of Peck's successors, profiled Haughey for Peter Carrington in the run up to Anglo-Irish discussions between Haughey and Thatcher in May 1980. Haydon had access to the embassy file on Haughey. Clearly, he was labouring under the misapprehension that Blaney, Gibbons and Haughey *had tried to import arms for the IRA.* According to Haydon's profile:

> At all events in May 1970, together with two other ministers, Gibbons and Blaney, he was involved in an alleged conspiracy to import arms for the IRA in Northern Ireland.[11]

The reference to 'an alleged *conspiracy to import arms for the IRA in Northern Ireland*' involving Gibbons indicates that London did not believe Gibbons' flat denial of involvement was true. Haughey, however, was the one they most feared. Over the next decade British intelligence officers directed a campaign of vilification against him during which its various branches attempted to link him to the IRA, once even suggesting he had directed it to bomb Belfast so he could purchase property on the cheap. In the meantime, Peck and MI6 kept a close eye on what was happening in Dublin.

32

THE 'FRUITS OF A VERY DIRTY VICTORY'

Erskine Childers was not the only politician keeping Ambassador Peck abreast of developments in Dublin. After the Arms Trials, the Public Accounts Committee (PAC) decided to look at how the money provided for the relief of distress in Northern Ireland had been distributed. They were assigned the task in December 1970 and composed of deputies from a number of political parties. According to a communication from Peck to London on 18 December 1970:

> Deputy Garret FitzGerald, a member of the [Public Accounts'] Committee, told us last night that the Committee intends to question all those involved in the arms trial and to publish the proceedings in full. Evidence will be taken from people in the North, whose identities will however be protected. He said that of the £100,000 or so expended, it appeared that perhaps half had been spent on genuine relief works.
>
> It looks increasingly as if the proceedings of the committee could be a re-run of the arms trial and be awkward for Messieurs Haughey and Blaney.[1]

Lynch appointed Ben Briscoe, a close friend of Jim Gibbons, to sit on the committee.

One of those to testify at PAC was John Fleming whose evidence left Capt. Kelly aghast. The captain had met Cathal Goulding on three occasions in Dublin in September and early October 1969 with the permission of Col Hefferon. In turn, the colonel had notified both garda C3 and garda special branch about the encounters so as to avoid any misunderstanding relating to them. According to Capt. Kelly, the meetings were initiated 'by an influential member of the nationalist community in Northern Ireland, who suggested that it might be beneficial to meet Mr Goulding'. Although he did not name the individual in either of his books, it was probably someone like Seán Keenan, John Kelly or Jim Sullivan who set it up. According to the captain, there was nothing clandestine about the encounters. One of them took place in Coman's pub on Dublin's Rathgar Road and the discussions that ensued were 'friendly and straightforward'. The men talked about events in Northern Ireland. Overall, Capt. Kelly felt Goulding was 'too astute to give anything away and I expect I was equally circumspect. As regards giving him money, the issue did not arise, because quite simply, and as emerged at the Inquiry, no such money was at my disposal at the time. I reported back to Colonel Hefferon, who told the [Public Accounts] Inquiry, "out of it emerged absolutely nothing".'[2]

Capt. Kelly was infuriated by the cloud of suspicion which Fleming cast over his contact with Goulding at PAC, especially the sequence where Fleming claimed he had provided the IRA man with thousands of pounds. Kelly argued that it was 'exceedingly strange' that Fleming failed to mention his – Kelly's – authorised meetings with Goulding, which had been brought to the attention of Fleming's superiors 'while spilling out details of totally fictitious meetings'.[3]

The captain also attacked Fleming for covering up Gibbons' role in the affair. 'Similarly, when [Fleming] denied to the Inquiry that he had named Haughey, Blaney and Gibbons to me [during an interrogation after Kelly's arrest] as the three Ministers involved in the arms importations on May 2, 1970, substituting Boland for Gibbons in his evidence to the Inquiry, it seemed to me that he was under severe pressure'.[4]

The PAC inquiry was conducted with scant regard for due process and resulted in Jock Haughey taking an action against it in the courts. Haughey's action was successful. The resulting decision, known as *In re Haughey*, became a cornerstone of constitutional law and a guide for the proper conduct of such inquiries.

Ben Briscoe resigned in protest at how PAC was operating. Lynch wanted Briscoe, who he knew was one of Gibbons' closest friends, to rejoin it. Briscoe anticipated he would be questioned as to why he changed his mind and asked Lynch if he could say that he was returning because he – Lynch – had wanted him to do so. Lynch said no. 'Lynch wanted me to lie. I was not prepared to do that. I refused to go back to the committee'.[5]

PAC furnished an inconclusive report in July 1972. It proved a disappointment for those hoping to establish that Capt. Kelly and his associates had been trying to import guns for the IRA. Garret FitzGerald emerged from the process believing Lynch had been kept in the dark. In his memoirs he described how:

> we brought our Fianna Fáil colleagues on the committee to accept that if three ministers, Neil Blaney, Charles Haughey, and Jim Gibbons, had 'passed on to the Taoiseach their suspicion or knowledge of the proposed arms importation' the misappropriation of part of the money spent on the arms might have been avoided.[6]

This was not how the British embassy viewed the outcome of the inquiry. David Blatherwick, sent a confidential report to FCO in London, Frank Steele, a senior MI6 officer in Belfast, and others on 24 August 1972 stating that:

> We see no reason to change our earlier judgement that Hefferon and Gibbons were willing to go along with Capt. Kelly and his influential Ministerial supporters until the crisis point came in April/May 1970, when Kelly became the fall guy, and Gibbons, by means of lying and eventually perjury preserved his head.

Blatherwick added later that, 'the affair is now part of the past and seems likely to be treated as such in the Republic ... Mr Blaney's political career in Fianna Fail has collapsed. Mr Haughey is still doing good deeds in the political wilderness. Mr Lynch and Mr Gibbons, the villains of the piece, continue to enjoy the fruits of a very dirty victory. The Opposition has been unable to make any decisive use of the whole muck-raking exercise. And the electorate continues to vote Fianna Fail.'[7]

Meanwhile, the Foreign Office and British Intelligence were aware that another scandal was flying under the radar. It would take all the duplicity and skill of Ambassador Peck to keep it under wraps.

33

THE CAMPAIGN TO SUPPRESS CAPTAIN KELLY'S BOOK

The British embassy monitored the activities of Capt. Kelly after his acquittal. If they hoped he was about to disappear into the sinkhole of history, they were to be sorely disappointed. On the contrary, he was determined to publish a book on the crisis.

In January 1971, Ambassador Peck alerted Kelvin White, a senior diplomat at the West European Department of the FCO, about it. 'I should mention here a small point that I have not previously reported. When I saw the Taoiseach just before Christmas [1970] he mentioned casually that Captain James Kelly was trying to produce in double quick time, a book about the arms trial which, he claimed, was going to be full of damaging material about the involvement of the whole Irish government.'[1]

Belying the comment that Peck considered the development 'a small point', the British sallied forth to sabotage its publication, but the book was eventually released under the title *Orders for the Captain*. Kelly first secured a contract with the British publisher Collins who described it as the 'most explosive book for some time' in the London media. Peck provided the FCO with some thoughts about how London might exert pressure on Collins to drop it, specifically that it might be libellous. The FCO was soon advising Peck they had a contact in Collins. A. C. Thorpe of the FCO contacted a 'friend' who promised him a proof of the book. Suffice it to say, all of this was done behind the author's back.

When they read the manuscript, the FCO found something in it that confirmed their worst fears; something so alarming they intervened and successfully persuaded Collins to abandon the publication. Thorpe was well pleased with the result and commented that the author's search for a publisher would now 'have to start again from scratch.'[2]

Michael Gill, managing director of Gill and Macmillan, stepped into the breach with an offer to publish it. Plates were made up and sent to a firm called Cahills for printing. On this occasion, George Colley swooped. As Capt. Kelly put it, Cahills had some 'valuable government printing contracts and this was the soft underbelly that gave the Irish government its chance, with word coming down from George Colley's ministry of finance to halt printing or else! As far as both governments were concerned, *Orders for The Captain* was not going to see the light of day and they nearly succeeded'.[3]

Undaunted, Capt. Kelly decided to self-publish the book and approached a series of printers but, 'the word had got out' and they were 'not prepared to print in the face of official opprobrium'.[4]

Help materialised out of the shadows: the captain next received a phone call from a man who refused to identify himself but 'requested that I meet him in an office in Jervis Street in Dublin's city centre. He indicated that he might be in a position to help solve my printing problem. In Jervis Street, I climbed one or two flights of stairs in the designated building and found myself in a dark, dingy office. An apparently sturdy figure of average height sat hunched behind a small bare desk. He gestured towards the chair. Reiterating that he did not want to be identified, he requested that I should forget the meeting once it was over. To this day, I have not met the man again nor do I know who he was, but somehow or other I got the impression that he was a lawyer'.[5]

The mysterious figure told him that there was a 'small printing machine, operating on the phonographic system around the corner in Abbey Street, which I could rent. We discussed the "ins and outs" of the matter and it was agreed that I should print 2,000 copies of the book initially, sell them and then pay the rent of the machine and the wages of the operator; and carry on from there. We shook hands on the deal and I went straight to the printing shop, where I introduced myself to the young machine operator and explained what I intended doing. Obviously, he had been briefed to expect me and I arranged to bring in the plates on the following week. Without hesitation or payment, Michael Gill instructed Cahills to release the plates to me, while the printing firm, despite the official diktat not to print, agreed to collate and bind the book. On the due date, I arrived in Abbey Street; the machine was set up, and we were ready to go'.[6]

The first 2,000 sold out in days, but Kelly found himself short of copies when the 'clamour for them was at its highest'. Nevertheless, he spent a year producing and distributing the book, 'considerably relieving the impecunious position I and my family found ourselves in after the trauma of the trials'.[7]

***

One of the more unpleasant myths to emerge from the vines of dishonesty which have wrapped themselves around the Arms Crisis was a tendril which tried to manufacture a link between Capt. Kelly and Saor Éire, the paramilitary group which murdered Garda Richard Fallon on the Quays in Dublin in April 1970. Shortly after his arrest, Fleming and Inspector Doocey interviewed Capt. Kelly at the Bridewell. As he recounted in *Orders for the Captain,* the first question put to him by Doocey had been: 'What do you know about the Garda Fallon murder?' When Capt. Kelly responded with purple veined outrage, the question was withdrawn.

The reason for the question was a rumour that the captain and his associates had helped Saor Éire to procure the gun used to shoot Garda Fallon. While there was no evidence for this, the allegation clearly poisoned the attitude of the gardaí against Capt. Kelly and his associates. The name of the informer who fed this falsehood to Fleming has never emerged but was probably the ever-mischievous Deceiver.

Blaney was so incensed about rumours linking him to the group, he not only denied them but referred to the organisation in the Dáil during the Arms Crisis debate as 'that lousy outfit Saor Éire'.[8]

So, where did the murder weapon come from? According to Seán Boyne, author of *Gunrunners*, Saor Éire had been amassing weapons in the late 1960s. One of its members revealed to him that they had established a contact who worked at the British Small Arms factory in Birmingham. It 'proved' 9mm Star pistols for the Star munitions factory in Spain. The contact was able to set aside perfectly good pistols as 'rejects' and later smuggle them out of the factory. They were then sent to Ireland, passing surreptitiously through Dublin Airport.[9]

Another source of guns for Saor Éire had been a high-profile Dublin underworld figure.

Boyne discovered that the gardaí had come to believe that one of the Birmingham guns had been used to murder Garda Fallon. Berry, however, had attempted to introduce this as an issue at the Arms Trials – or at the very least – inflame the ire of the state's prosecution team. In a memorandum sent to the lawyers he stated:

> In September and October the Special Branch were receiving information from confidential sources that small consignments of arms were being imported by the I.R.A. without customs checks at Dublin Airport and at Dun Laoghaire sea-port. Their information, which was highly confidential, was that imports were timed when particular officers were on duty who would turn the blind eye. They had information that one such consignment went to the gang robbing banks who, later on, on 3 April 1970 were to shoot Garda Fallon. The importations were coupled with, *inter-alia*, the name of [redacted] and it was freely said in Special Branch circles that Mr Charles J Haughey was aware of what was going on.[10]

On 3 April, Garda Fallon was shot dead by bank robbers, one of whom had been reported some months earlier to have received guns which were imported without undergoing any customs checks, 'through general arrangements in which [redacted] was playing an active part and of which Mr Charles J. Haughey was alleged to have a general awareness'.[11]

In reality, the only captain who had a case to answer in relation to the Saor Éire murder weapon was Capt. Peter Markham-Randall. Recall that he was described by Capt. Kelly in *Orders for the Captain* as a 'small, dark-haired, goatee-bearded man'. This description bears a striking resemblance to the arms dealer that Boyne described as having helped Saor Éire. He was also a 'small man with a goatee beard' and was called 'Randall'. According to Boyne's source, Randall had made contact with a person linked to Saor Éire in the UK in the late 1960s:

> The 'arms dealer' gave his name as Randall, although other versions of the name were also reported. The Saor Éire-linked individual in the UK, in good faith, passed on this contact to his friends in the organisation back in Ireland, who were equally unsuspecting. In retrospect, the possibility opens up that British intelligence somehow detected Saor Éire activities in the UK and decided to infiltrate the subversive group by using an agent or a 'front' man, the mysterious Mr. Randall.[12]

Suffice it to say, if British Intelligence had moved to cut off the supply of weapons from Birmingham instead of exploiting it to preserve Markham-Randall's cover and develop other leads, it is possible Garda Fallon might not have been killed, or at least not by a weapon emanating from Birmingham.

Bearing all the foregoing in mind, a passage in the captain's book must have alarmed London to wit:

> The quest for arms by Northern representatives continued, and in November a suspected British agent was lured to Dublin. After three or four days' negotiation in the Gresham Hotel, the supposed arms salesman offered a bribe to one of the Northerners. Negotiations were immediately broken off and an agent, who was using the name of Peter Markham-Randall, presumably returned to England. I reported the affair to Colonel Hefferon and he initiated enquiries with Garda Headquarters.[13]

Another person the British monitored was Jock Haughey who knew about Markham-Randall from his participation in the attempt to purchase arms from him in November 1969. In October 1970 he went on a holiday to Portugal with his wife Kitty. One leg of the journey took the couple through Britain where they noticed they had picked up a tail, a British gentleman who shadowed their every move. In the mornings he would sit at the table next to them while they ate breakfast and then monitor them during the day. At night he would sit next to them again. While he had disturbed the Haugheys at the start of their holiday, they soon found his pedantic and predictable behaviour amusing, especially his habit of ordering lobster – and no other option on the menu – for his evening meal. On at least one occasion they attempted to engage him in conversation much to his embarrassment and without success. On their return to Britain, he skipped the passport control queue and went directly to talk to the officials while the other passengers were queuing up.[14]

The most plausible reason for trying to sabotage *Orders for the Captain* and the shadowing of Jock Haughey across Europe was because he and Capt. Kelly were members of a tiny group of people who knew about Markham-Randall and could provide clues linking him to the murder weapon Saor Éire might have used to kill Garda Fallon; further, that British Intelligence had not shared the information Markham-Randall had gathered about Saor Éire in the late 1960s to help shut it down. Fallon was not murdered until April of 1970. Had this connection been made, the incandescence among the rank-and-file gardaí, not to mention at middle and senior level, had the potential to set garda relations with MI5 and MI6 at nought, with little prospect of any reconciliation for years.

The roots of the British operation to suppress this information undoubtedly reached far deeper than anything described here. For a start, MI6 had clearly learned of the Hagheys' holiday plans in advance and had been able to book an agent into the same hotel they proposed to visit. To achieve this, they must have had access to the family's phone conversations. In 1970 phone tapping was carried out by making a physical connection to a phone line, something that could only be done in the vicinity of a junction near the target's phone. It is unlikely that MI6 deployed a tapping unit to Dublin in 1970. Instead, the information was probably furnished to them by a senior figure with access to the transcripts generated by special branch tappers.

A retired special branch officer familiar with Saor Éire and the two informers who were recruited by the gardaí from within it is adamant that Jock Haughey had 'nothing whatsoever – absolutely nothing – to do with Saor Éire'.[15] Yet, Jock Haughey spent the rest of his life unfairly tarnished by questions about the murder of Garda Fallon. Garret FitzGerald continued to press the issue in the Dáil over the next decade.

The gardaí did not forget their fallen colleague. In 2014 a detective superintendent attached to the Serious Crime Review Team at the National Bureau of Criminal Investigation conducted a fresh inquiry. He and his team would have been well advised to make enquiries in London about the spy who masqueraded as Capt. Peter Markham-Randall and the files MI5 and MI6 undoubtedly hold about him as well as the Saor Éire gun smuggling network he penetrated.

34

THE SHADOW OF A GUNMAN

The role of The Deceiver in the Arms Crisis has been the best kept state secret of the last half century. He is now dead. Fortunately, however, a mountain of information about him survives.

Although his mother was a Protestant with unionist roots in East Belfast, she baptised him as a Catholic and later sent him to a Catholic school. When he was seven, she told him, 'I'm Irish, therefore you're Irish. You're half Irish anyway. Don't forget it.' She died when he was ten, an only child, leaving him in the care of his father, an Englishman, who worked as a solicitor's clerk and was a heavy drinker. Father and son never managed to get along and his father's drinking blighted his childhood. At school he befriended Irish students and began to study Irish history. He joined Conradh na Gaeilge in the early 1950s and mixed socially with Irish exiles in North London becoming pro-Sinn Féin. He left school in 1944 at the age of sixteen, was conscripted into the RAF the following year, where he remained in service until 1948, rising to become a corporal. While in the RAF, he was stationed in Jamaica, which he remembered for its 'racism and poverty', both of which he perceived as the product of Britain's colonial system.

His career as an Irish republican began shortly after he left the RAF in what turned out to be a disappointing spell for him working as a volunteer with a pro-nationalist organisation in London called the United Irishmen. At this time he was employed in the building trade and later by British Rail. He soon set his sights on becoming an IRA volunteer. He and a group of like-minded young men approached the IRA in Dublin with a request that it authorise the formation of a unit in London. The young aspirants were made to kick their heels for a time before a representative of the GHQ in Dublin materialised in London to assess them. In a round table discussion they explained that they wanted to join the IRA. Failing that they wanted to come out openly in England as its political wing, Sinn Féin.[1]

His group was informed they would be left to their own devices for three months and warned that if news of their existence reached Dublin, they would be cast adrift. The Deceiver made it his mission to ensure there would be no loose talk. His efforts paid off. After the lapse of three months, his unit was absorbed into the IRA. He was appointed as its officer-in-command, London. Initially there were six members in the London unit. Their number expanded to sixteen before contracting again because of his concern that word of its existence might emerge.

As OC, The Deceiver set about educating himself to become a revolutionary by rooting out books, magazines and newspaper articles about underground armies. One of his initial insights was that while the IRA in the Republic was able to train in the countryside reasonably unmolested, that was not going to be feasible in the UK. His unit would need to adapt to a far more exacting environment. Further research led him to study guerrilla forces that had operated in urban theatres. He consumed books about the exploits of the Polish underground during the then not too distant Warsaw Rising of 1944 and its commander General Tadeusz Bor-Komorowski, as he felt there were lessons to be drawn from the Pole's experience. Another book he found useful was *The Revolt* by Menachem Begin, one of the Jewish underground leaders who had delivered a series of black eyes to the British in Palestine. The Deceiver, a tall and physically imposing man, often led his unit to the military section of Foyle's bookshop to review newly published volumes.

Guerrilla Days in Ireland by Tom Barry was another memoir into which he delved to uncover what he called 'technical points'. He concluded that while many of Barry's tactics were still valid, a general overhaul would be required to bring them up-to-date. He anticipated a campaign against heavily fortified transport vehicles, soldiers dressed in protective flak jackets, helicopters and improved radio communications. After his unit carried out parade training in London, he convened discussion groups to explore how they might further overhaul IRA tactics to reflect the modern era.

Incredible as it may seem, The Deceiver had yet to set foot on Irish soil. His first visit to Ireland was in 1949 in the company of his wife Mary, a Cork woman. The trip was something he described as a deeply 'emotional experience for me from the moment we set out from Paddington station on the boat-train for the journey to Fishguard and Wales. Even at that time of year the train was packed with Irish people returning home from holiday. The carriages were full of happiness and good humour, and it was the same on the boat. Everybody was obviously delighted to be going back, even for a visit'.[2]

Yet, he returned to London with 'very mixed feelings indeed'. The source of his malcontent was the dearth of interest in republicanism he had observed among the general population. For this he blamed 'the Dublin politicians [who] had led the people up blind alleys, doing as much as the English to maintain partition themselves'.[3] He was especially scornful of Fianna Fáil whom he blamed for sabotaging the IRA at every turn, even in England where the organisation had carried out a bombing campaign at the outbreak of the Second World War. He believed it had been betrayed by agents of Fianna Fáil who had 'succeeded in feeding information to the Irish Special Branch, who passed it onto their British counterparts. As a result, men and equipment were seized in England, in some cases as soon as they landed'.[4]

The Deceiver dutifully carried out the instructions he received from Dublin, most of which focused on the collection of information, scouting for supplies and equipment, and the recruitment of volunteers. His unit also raised money for the IRA from Irish sympathisers in London. He soon developed a fascination with intelligence work. 'I realised the value of this early on and, on my own initiative, proposed to Dublin that I should report to them on various matters. They agreed, and asked me to develop this side of our activity in England, which I did. In a revolutionary force, every member should be an intelligence agent. I encouraged my comrades to report everything of interest they might see or hear. And later on, when I was appointed Director of Intelligence for the movement, I added to that "or read". In those London days, I quickly learned how much a shrewd intelligence organisation can put together from systemic study of serious newspapers and military magazines, apart from the efforts of its own agents and contacts. There was a case in the 'thirties in which one man was able to build up the accurate order of battle of the German army just by close analysis of the German provincial press down to reports of dinners and even the engagement notices.'[5]

Counter-intelligence became his guiding star. He conducted background checks into potential recruits in London with a 'very watchful eye for possible attempts [by] British or Free State agents' to penetrate his unit. When volunteers came from Ireland, he asked GHQ in Dublin to screen 'their backgrounds thoroughly'.[6]

He visited Ireland again in June of 1951, this time to attend the annual Bodenstown commemorations. He was struck by the number of special branch detectives among the assembly, most of whom appeared to be engaged in intelligence gathering by recording what they were hearing in notebooks.

During this period The Deceiver delivered some of the first walkie-talkies that became commercially available to Dublin and encouraged his comrades to study and improve their understanding of modern communications so they could monitor police and military broadcasts.

In 1953 he was directed by Dublin to assist Goulding and Manus Canning in executing a raid on the armoury at the Officers' Training Corp School at Felsted in Essex. The operation went ahead on 25 July 1953, but proved a shambles. The Irishmen overloaded their vehicle with so many arms that when they reached the motorway its undercarriage was all but scraping off the road. Inevitably, this drew the attention of the police subsequent to which all three were arrested and later imprisoned.

The Deceiver used his time in prison to gain what was in effect a degree in counter-intelligence studies. He was detained in a number of prisons including Wormwood Scrubs where he befriended a group of EOKA prisoners, all of whom had been arrested during the revolt against the British in Cyprus. The Cypriots were fresh from engagement with Britain's then most up-to-date counter-insurgency tactics and possessed a great deal of 'insight and experience'. He took detailed notes of their 'revolutionary and guerrilla tactics'. He became a student of the type of torture techniques the British Army meted out to Cypriot prisoners. 'Our EOKA friends had their sad memories, and their defiant ones. All of them had been beaten or tortured for information ... Two of their former gymnasia lads had been put sitting on blocks of ice, which can cause frostbite in the genitals with effects that can be imagined. To cover the cruder beatings, the British had extended to twenty-eight days the time a prisoner could be held before appearing in court. This gave time for facial bruises and marks to fade somewhat before he was produced.'[7]

On 12 December 1956, the IRA launched what became known as the Border Campaign. The Deceiver was still behind bars when it commenced. It continued until February 1962 during which time six RUC officers were killed during it. Observing what was happening through newspaper reports, he experienced a profound sense of disappointment. He would have preferred a full throttled confrontation with the RUC.

Instead, he noted, none 'of the Special Branch in the North had been eliminated.'

In early 1959, just before he was to regain his freedom, an official photographic session was scheduled at Wormwood Scrubs to take an up-to-date picture of him. In an attempt to frustrate this, he and some other prisoners who were also due for release wet their faces so the resulting pictures would develop as dark and patchy thus obscuring their features. He hoped the prison authorities would not develop the negatives before he walked free. 'We were well aware of how photographs taken by British authorities appeared in special branch files in Dublin. In the opposite direction, police photographs of republicans taken in Dublin had already appeared outside RUC barracks in the North.' On this occasion his ruse was thwarted. The photographs were printed before he scarpered out the front door and he was marched back to face the cameraman, 'this time with a couple of warders keeping a close eye on us'.[8]

He took the boat to Dublin the day he was released. Ever vigilant, he 'kept a wary eye for any surveillance, and again when I reached Westland Row station [in Dublin]. But there was no interference'.

He journeyed to his wife's home in Castletownroche, Co. Cork. After a while he moved his family to Cappoquin, Co. Waterford, where he was offered a job as a garage storeman. Having spent nearly six years in prison, he now enjoyed a high-profile as a former political prisoner and the respect that accompanied it in republican circles. He was invited to speak in favour of the Border Campaign at meetings, rallies and protests throughout Cork and in other parts of Munster.

After he moved to Cork, he contacted the local republican leadership who advised him he would have to wait a while before he could resume active service. When he was readmitted, he found that the local unit in Cork City was made up of 'lads from several different walks of life and of various personal types. We had a couple of university students. We had craftsmen, artisans and labourers. Some of them, in spite of having only a little formal education, were well able to express themselves and argue their points quite articulately. Others, though very good workers and oozing with sincerity, had difficulty in communicating things they actually felt quite deeply [about]'.[9]

He was later offered a command role and immediately began to work out 'a proper training programme that would retain the interest of the volunteers'. One of his first steps was to provide an outlet for discussion, 'so that any misapprehensions could be cleared up'. This worked well and helped his unit develop a 'good, close working relationship'.

According to The Deceiver, the IRA hierarchy in Dublin supported the continuation of the Border Campaign, while Cork was desirous of bringing it to an end. In the summer of 1961, the Cork leadership was ousted and The Deceiver was given overall charge instead. At first, he found the task difficult, not least because he was denied a helping hand from his predecessors. Over time he managed to surmount this obstacle. Yet 'because of my unwavering support for HQ policy, some coolness remained.'

Financially, his time in prison had all but beggared his family. In August 1961 he took a few months' leave of absence to stabilise his financial position. A local IRA man took over during his sabbatical and he was still on leave in February 1962 when the Border Campaign was called off. He had not been consulted in advance and only learned of its demise from a radio broadcast. As republicans descended on his house to glean his assessment of the situation, he put on a brave face assuring them that 'the national leadership would not have ended the campaign if there had been a chance of carrying on with any hope of success'.[10]

Further dissension in the ranks followed and a new Cork OC was appointed. When he returned to active duty he found that 'pessimists were already saying that it would be at least 15 to 20 years before an armed struggle could be launched again'. Undeterred, he committed himself to 'build things up once more'.[11]

***

In Dublin there was also a change of guard. Goulding became the new chief of staff in 1962. The Deceiver was appointed to the IRA's Army Council and GHQ staff. Goulding appointed him as his Director of Intelligence in 1967. The Deceiver found himself less than impressed with the work of his predecessors. 'I cannot convey my amazement when the intelligence files were handed over to me. It took me about two days to go through them. My comment was, "ninety per cent rubbish, five per cent of historical interest and five per cent useful material". When I stared at the small pile of what had been worth saving, it didn't seem much of a basis for a modern intelligence branch. I had taken on a task that would tax me to the limit if it were done properly.'[12]

The Deceiver grew increasingly concerned that the military function of the movement was being run down in favour of the development of left-wing politics and complained about this to Goulding who initially failed to comment. According to Goulding's ally, Dr Roy Johnson, The Deceiver 'took this as the OK to go ahead, and he went around all the Northern units, with military intelligence as top of the agenda'.[13]

He decided he would focus on placing the intelligence wing of the IRA in Northern Ireland on a war footing. He believed that if he took a hands-on approach, 'practically living there' with his intelligence officers, he would be able to impress on them the 'urgency' of their work. Secondly, he implemented a training programme which included the production of an intelligence manual, something that had not been done for many years.[14]

Under The Deceiver, IRA intelligence officers were directed to spy on RUC Special Branch officers. All of the training courses he organised concentrated on what could be found out about them from their physical appearance and home addresses, to their routines and habits.

He also decided to cut down on the number of paper files held at HQ, requiring instead that local volunteers memorise the information they required. Moreover, any files that were to be maintained were to be scrambled in code.

***

It was while he was still living in Cork that The Deceiver managed to convince the gardaí he was prepared to act as an informer and was paid for his apparent co-operation. He was 'recruited' by Patrick McLaughlin, who was based in Cork at the time and later rose to become garda commissioner in

1978. Another Garda, 'J' who was based in Cork at this time, was aware that The Deceiver had been recruited although he was not directly involved in the operation.[15] According to 'J', the perception of him was that he 'was not a very intelligent man but had leadership qualities' which had assisted his ascent within the IRA. He also had 'a big mouth' and when he opened up, he would sometimes proceed to 'spout information'. Yet, he was someone who only talked to the gardaí when it suited him and was a 'man who played the violin with two bows'. By the late 1960s, "J" had become suspicious that The Deceiver was merely engaging with the gardaí 'in the hope it would take some of the heat off him'.

McLaughlin was not in the special branch and handed The Deceiver over to Philip McMahon, who was at the helm. McMahon, who hailed from south County Cavan, had been in the Old IRA so his knowledge of the IRA proved useful during his long and successful career with the gardaí. He was a ruthless taskmaster who never forgave a mistake, nor gave a budding officer a second chance. He was also renowned for exploiting young gardaí to cut turf and gather hay at his farm in south county Dublin. He modernised the branch and left it in great shape for his successor John Fleming when he retired. His failure to see through The Deceiver was a rare blot on his copybook. Unfortunately, it was a hugely significant one.

The Deceiver and McMahon got on rather well according to 'J'. At one stage 'all communication was made person to person'.[16]

Another retired special branch officer – who is still alive – had dealings with The Deceiver while he was masquerading as an informer.[17] His name is well known to those familiar with these events.

A delighted special branch now believed they had access to everything the IRA was doing since the Army Council, of which The Deceiver was a member, oversaw and managed the entire organisation on both sides of the border. We can snatch a glimpse at how the Army Council worked and the type of material which The Deceiver was feeding McMahon from the recollections of Séamas Ó Tuathail who briefly attended a part of an Army Council meeting.[18] It took place on a wet dark October night in 1967. Ó Tuathail was driven from Dublin to the ghostly shell of a dilapidated mansion somewhere in County Meath. He was twenty-six at the time and employed at Belvedere College as an Irish teacher. His driver was an IRA volunteer. After a long trip, the driver took a right turn off the road somewhere between Navan and Kells. They followed a pitch-black narrow lane to the old building where Ó Tuathail was escorted into a former ballroom. An oak tree was sprouting through the roof. Close by the members of the IRA's Army Council sat around an illuminated table: Cathal Goulding, Seán Garland, The Deceiver, Seamus Costello, Tomás Mac Giolla, Ruairí Ó Brádaigh and Paddy Murphy. They also happened to be the *de facto* directors of *The United Irishman*, Sinn Féin's monthly newspaper.

Ó Tuathail had come to the publication's attention as the contributor of a series of Irish language articles to the paper's former editors Tony Meade and Denis Foley. After a vacancy had arisen for the post of editor, a consensus had emerged that he would be the best fit for the job. Some negotiations had taken place before the meeting in the old ballroom and this was the opportunity to iron out a few details and finalise the appointment.[19]

From the manner in which the Army Council was working in the mid and late 1960s, it is reasonable to suggest that The Deceiver had access to everything of importance involving the Republican Movement ranging from the political to the military. No doubt at his next meeting with McMahon, The Deceiver reported Ó Tuathail's appointment and other parts of the agenda that did not conflict with his secret plan for a military expansion of the IRA.

The Deceiver moved to Meath in 1966 so he could be closer to the Border and live in a Gaeltacht community. Special Branch Detective Sergeant Hugh McNeilis, who operated in Meath, maintained contact with him while McMahon remained his primary handler at all times.[20]

There are other indications of The Deceiver's insatiable appetite for intrigue. In 1970 Kevin O'Connor, the Limerick-born journalist and author, was based in London where he worked across a variety of media including *The Irish Post*, then in its start-up as a weekly. Its masthead declared it to be *The Voice of the Irish in Britain.* The editor Brendan Mac Lua had known The Deceiver in Dublin as an extreme 'Irish Irelander' in the Gaelic League. With the rising violence and mindful of the day-to-day sensitivities of his immigrant readership, Mac Lua decided to publish a profile of him as a senior Englishman in the Provisional IRA. O'Connor made contact with The Deceiver who agreed to be interviewed on condition that he would see the questions in advance. The reporter went armed with a cassette recorder and a single sheet of typed questions. In error a second page with additional queries had been left behind. The Deceiver was able to deduce from a quick perusal of the bottom of the page that a second sheet had been typed up and enquired suspiciously where it was and what the other questions were before he let the interview resume. It was recorded on O'Connor's portable tape machine.

O'Connor found The Deceiver chilling. He spoke without emotion and reminded him of the 'psycho' East End criminals he had observed in the aftermath of gangland events in London and in the dock at the Old Bailey. It was, he recalled, 'very Irish and perverse to listen to the IRA dogma being recited in a London criminal manner'.[21]

Occasionally, The Deceiver would signal O'Connor to stop recording, indicating he wished to talk off-the-record. During one of these interludes, he explained how he had noticed that a car was following him. He had noted its number and subsequently discovered that it was a special branch vehicle. He explained how he had become acquainted with the driver and was now in the habit of talking to the special branch approximately every five weeks or so.

The Deceiver may have gambled that the journalist would mention his connection to the special branch on the phone to his London editor in confidence and that this might be picked up by the British security service, MI5, *via* phone tapping. Hence, if MI5 was to learn of his encounters with garda special branch, he may have hoped to beguile them into believing he was a *bona fide* garda agent and thereby minimise interference in his affairs from that quarter. For all we known he might have laid out additional clues for MI5 and Scotland Yard designed to promote this masquerade in the UK.

Fleming and the special branch did not discover that The Deceiver had been manipulating them until 1972 when they raided a Provisional IRA safe house and uncovered a cache of documents which revealed a wealth of material about the Provisionals which he had withheld from them including a list of the names of all the members of the Provisional IRA.[22] After this, they set about tracking him down. He was arrested in November 1972. Initially, there was consternation in certain circles inside the Special Branch among those who still believed that The Deceiver was a *bona fide* agent. He was prosecuted successfully and served a prison sentence. He went on a hunger strike but failed to see it through. After his release, he met a firmly shut door when he tried to re-join the Provisionals and at one stage even contemplated setting up his own organisation but didn't. He published an autobiography in 1975 which, while informative in many respects, concealed his success in leading the special branch a merry dance for twelve years.

The Deceiver was born John Stephenson but as an adult he adopted the Gaelic version of his name, Seán MacStíofáin.

Des Long, who knew MacStíofáin well, was not surprised when apprised of his role as a double agent, one who had led the special branch by the nose for so long. 'He was capable of tricking around like that all right', Long commented.[23]

There were indeed no limits to MacStíofáin's capacity for 'tricking around'. In a ploy which must reach the deepest level of the matrix of intrigue that lurked beneath the Arms Crisis, MacStíofáin had been using John Kelly to monitor Capt. Kelly and had been doing so since at least December

1969 after the failed attempt to import guns from the US. MacStíofáin told author Justin O'Brien:

> John came to me a few days before Christmas [1969], a few days after the new convention for the Army Council, and told me about the arrangements made to bring in arms, and he told me that 'once they come in I will give them to you.' I said, 'John, I do not want any details. Give me a report now and again through your brother [Billy]. Just give me a list of the weapons you ordered.[24]

The fourth member of the unit which MacStíofáin had on standby at Dublin Port on 25 March was Billy Kelly, the brother of John. At the time he was the officer in command of the Provisional 3rd Battalion in Belfast. Clearly, his true loyalty was to the Provisionals, not the CDCs. There can be little doubt that his brother John was the person who alerted him to stand down the Provisional IRA hijack unit when the *MV City of Dublin* docked without the arms.

A passage from the transcript of the interview John Kelly gave Liam Clarke in 2005 might in fact be a reference to the IRA's clandestine presence at the docks on 25 March 1970. Kelly told Clarke, 'Three times we went to the docks in Dublin to receive a shipment and we had people in place to take the stuff.'[25] He may have used the word 'take' in the same sense that MacStíofáin had, i.e., a hijack. Capt. Kelly only appears to have gone down once.

In this squalid atmosphere of betrayal, no one's back was safe, least of all that of John Kelly. After all, MacStíofáin had plunged a dagger deep into his spine in April 1970 when he had informed the gardaí about the arms importation operation at Dublin airport, an act that in turn sparked the political back stabbing frenzy that became the hallmark of the Arms Crisis.[26]

AFTERMATH

SEÁN MacStíofáin must have relished the turmoil he inflicted upon Fianna Fáil, something all the more delicious for him since he died on 18 May 2001 without ever having had to face a single question about his duplicitous role in precipitating the crisis. A hint that he had been playing devious games with the gardaí emerged after his death as a result of an interview Liam Clarke and Barry Penrose conducted with Det. Sgt Hugh McNeilis of the garda special branch. The latter revealed that MacStíofáin had been an informer who acted 'because he wanted to get rid of certain people'.[1] McNeilis was certainly correct in this assessment but that was only half the story. What McNeilis did not say – and may not have fully appreciated – was that MacStíofáin had primarily been a misinformer who had roundly abused the faith Philip McMahon and John Fleming had placed in him up to 1972. To the public, the notion that MacStíofáin was a straightforward informer was impossible to comprehend let alone accept and the story soon faded into obscurity.

Mainstream politics in Ireland suffered the aftershock of MacStíofáin's 'tricking around' for decades, especially Fianna Fáil. It struggled through three decades of upheaval as a result of the Arms Crisis and its sequel, the Arms Trials, not to mention an encore at the PAC inquiry of 1971. Raucous scenes involving Kevin Boland and Paddy Hillery took place at the 1971 Ard Fheis, all of which were broadcast to the nation on RTÉ. After this Boland set up his own organisation, Aontacht Éireann, but it never gained momentum and disappeared after a few years. Neil Blaney was expelled from Fianna Fáil in 1972 and ran successfully thereafter as an 'Independent' Fianna Fáil candidate until his death. In 1973 the party was consigned to the Opposition benches after sixteen successive years in power. In 1975 Lynch – still leader – brought Haughey back onto his front bench. Fianna Fáil swept back to power in 1977 with a large majority.

By now George Colley had become Lynch's anointed successor with Gibbons and O'Malley at his side. Nonetheless, in December 1979 Haughey beat Colley in the leadership battle. As taoiseach, Haughey retained Colley and O'Malley in his first cabinet (1979–81) and also his second (1982). From the outset, Colley and O'Malley became involved in plots to topple him with O'Malley occasionally muttering that he had discovered something about the new taoiseach during his tenure as minister for justice, 1970–73, which rendered Haughey unfit for office. O'Malley never specified what it was he had been told, though it was presumably another of MacStíofáin's yarns. O'Malley became the spearhead of anti-Haughey dissent in the party after Colley died from a heart attack in 1983. O'Malley was expelled in 1985 and set up the Progressive Democrats, which coalesced with Haughey after the 1989 general election and maintained him in power until 1992 notwithstanding the mysterious and allegedly appalling thing O'Malley had learnt about Haughey while at the department of justice.

While the internal party wounds began to heal under Bertie Ahern, the party never regained an overall majority. It received a mere twenty-two per cent of the vote in the 2020 general election.

JOHN FLEMING can only have concluded that MacStíofáin had been leading him and the special branch up the garden path for over a dozen years after the garda raid on the Provisional IRA safe house in 1972 which had delivered up an incriminating list of Provisional IRA members. After the raid, MacStíofáin realised the game was up and went on the run but was captured later in the year.

Fleming spent the rest of his life concealing his relationship with MacStíofáin. Even in retirement, he and Philip McMahon held the line that the arms which Capt. Kelly had purchased from Schlueter in Germany were intended for the IRA. Both men popped their heads above the parapet by steering Jack Lynch's biographer Dermot Keogh in this direction during the research for his book. When it appeared in 2008, it contained a dedication to them (among others). Ironically, in so acting, they adopted MacStíofáin's agenda of disrupting the political order rather than acknowledging their mistakes.[2]

Capt. Kelly lashed out against Fleming in his 1999 book *The Thimble Riggers,* where he was particularly critical of the latter's performance at the public accounts committee (PAC) in 1971. The captain maintained he had either attempted to 'foist false evidence' on PAC or had neglected his duty by wilfully failing to alert the army about his – Capt. Kelly's – alleged meeting with Goulding, which Fleming professed to have 'checked and double-checked'. According to the captain, in 'either case, he was guilty of a serious offence. There was no investigation into this'.[3]

Fleming passed away in May of 2011, twelve years after *The Thimble Riggers* was published without suing Capt. Kelly for defamation. If he read the book, he either did not care about his reputation or accepted Capt. Kelly had a point.

PETER BERRY retired as secretary to the Department of Justice in January 1971 deeply resentful of Fianna Fáil. Among his gripes was that he had been denied a discretionary payment, something that had been in the gift of the taoiseach. In retirement Berry attempted to reach out to Capt. Kelly. While he refused to have anything to do with him, his wife Sheila was prepared to entertain his phone calls of which there were many. Berry fulminated obsessively about Lynch, repeatedly spewing out details about the Mt Carmel briefing. He stressed his belief that Lynch had known about the arms importation operation all along.[4] Suffice it to say, this was not the picture he had drawn for the state's prosecution team in the run-up to the arms trials when his position was that: 'I could not reconcile the taoiseach's repeated public statements as to the Government's peaceful intentions towards the North with the action of one of the Minister's [*sic*], Mr. Haughey, who, it appeared to me, was acting treacherously towards him [Lynch]'.[5] Berry died from a heart attack on 14 December 1978. Dr Garret FitzGerald described him as 'a strange man, a very strange man' in 2001.[6]

JAMES GIBBONS served in Lynch's cabinet until Fianna Fáil relinquished power in 1973. The new Fine Gael-Labour coalition was furnished with the evidence of two witnesses that Gibbons had committed perjury at the arms trials and considered charging him but no prosecution took place. When Fianna Fáil regained office in 1977 Gibbons became the new minister for agriculture.

He was dropped after Haughey became taoiseach in 1979. He lost his seat in the June 1981 general election but regained it in February 1982, only to lose it again during the November 1982 election. Throughout this time he supported Colley and O'Malley in their machinations against Haughey. During one of their heaves, supporters of Haughey assaulted him on the grounds of Leinster House. He died on 20 December 1997 after years of bad health. Ben Briscoe maintains that Gibbons died a broken man, deeply resentful at Lynch for destroying his reputation and career. O'Malley extolled him saying, 'Mr Jim Gibbons was a gentle Irish patriot, who had suffered for many years because he insisted on telling the truth on oath during the Arms trials.'

JACK LYNCH went to his grave maintaining that he had known nothing about the attempt to import arms until 20 April 1970 when informed about it by Berry. Michael Heney cites thirty instances where Lynch 'either made demonstrably false statements, was deliberately misleading or chose to side-step the facts'.[7] This book adds a few more black marks to that tally.

Brian Lenihan never accused Lynch of duplicity in public. However, as his son records, 'Indeed Capt. Kelly, according to my father, was a familiar figure around government buildings, ministerial offices and the Dáil generally. He found it both convenient and quite wrong for Jack Lynch to assert that the work [of the cabinet subcommittee on Northern Ireland] had come as a surprise to him. For Lynch not to have known about what was going on would be equivalent to the Taoiseach of the day being asleep at the wheel of state.'[8]

Lynch died on 20 October 1999.

NEIL BLANEY held his seat in Donegal but never returned to the Fianna Fáil fold. He claimed in a *Magill* interview in 1985 that 'the majority' of the cabinet 'would have agreed [to an invasion of Northern Ireland]. After [the burning of] Bombay Street [on 13 August], that would have been their clear view'.[9] In reality the 'majority' supported nothing of the sort. He kept one secret that did not emerge until five years after his death: that he had requested London to send British troops to Northern Ireland in 1969. This astonishing discovery was made by Anthony Craig who highlighted the fact in his book that on 14 August Blaney had approached Hugh McCann, the secretary at the department of external affairs and instructed him to contact the British government with a request that it deploy its troops to Northern Ireland. McCann relayed the request to Kevin Rush, the minister plenipotentiary at the Irish embassy in London.[10] Blaney never spoke about this to journalists while acting the part of a republican tough guy. Part of this performance was to claim he was responsible – in part at least – for the creation of the Provisional IRA. These boasts, which do not bear close scrutiny, undoubtedly exerted a pull on republican voters in Donegal and helped him retain his Dáil seat until his death on 8 November 1995. In reality at the time of the Arms Crisis he was a supporter of the Nationalist Party, led by Eddie McAteer. Moreover, he had stymied the growth of the Provisionals by shutting down the US arms pipeline.

JOHN KELLY told Liam Clarke in 2005 that 'Charlie [Haughey] was sent forward for trial and Blaney got off, although he was the man who organised it all. Jim Gibbons was never charged although he knew the whole thing; I met him with Jim Kelly. He knew exactly what was going on and Brian Lenihan knew. He was friendly with Blaney. When I met Lenihan he was always giving the thumbs up and saying "keep it on, keep it on". I asked him about why he supported Lynch after it and he said, "I am the X in OXO", by which he meant he had a leg on both sides'.[11]

Kelly sided with the Provisional IRA after the decline of the CDCs but soon felt the brunt of MacStíofáin hostility towards him. Des Long, a former member of the Provisional IRA's army executive, recalls that while Kelly was serving as the IRA's director of finance, he – Long – was dispatched with orders from MacStíofáin to talk to him and, if he showed any sign of non-co-operation, to dismiss him. Kelly was ousted from the position at the encounter which almost certainly took place in 1972. Kelly remained an active member of IRA but eventually focused his energies on the pursuit of republican politics. In 1998 he was elected as the Sinn Féin member of the Northern Ireland Assembly for Mid Ulster but was deselected by the party before the 2003 election. He left Sinn Féin which he criticised for being too controlled from the centre and railed against what he described as the leadership's 'deceit and the philosophy of creative ambiguity'. As far as can be ascertained, he never learned of MacStíofáin's role in alerting the special branch about the proposed April 1970 arms flight. He died from cancer on 6 September 2007 after a long illness.

ALBERT LUYKX became the forgotten man of the Arms Crisis. In his 2015 biography of Charles Haughey, Conor

Lenihan – the son of Brian – provided a glimpse at the sort of life Luykx had enjoyed before the crisis. He 'had a restaurant in Dublin and was regularly congratulated by ministers on the work he was doing [i.e. helping Capt. Kelly procure arms] while they were dining at his establishment. Even George Colley did so on one occasion'.[12] John Kelly described his role in the operation and what happened to him thereafter it to Liam Clarke as follows: 'Albert Luykx was a Flemish nationalist who had taken the side of the Germans during the occupation because he thought it would solve their dispute with the Walloons. He had been sentenced to death as a war criminal and he had escaped and got to Ireland. He was selling hacksaw blades and hardware products. He was fairly wealthy; he was a friend of Blaney and of Lenihan and Paddy Hillery. He was inveigled into the whole thing believing it was Government business. He was an interpreter, he spoke German and French. That was Albert's role, to do the talking. He suffered terribly as a result. He lost his business, his family lost what they had and he was accused of being a Nazi'.[13] Luykx died in 1978.

CHARLES HAUGHEY served as taoiseach 1979–81; 1982; 1987–92. A significant element in his electoral success was the whiff of republican sulphur he had accrued as a result of these events. The other side of that coin was that many in the ranks of Dublin media came to despise him. According to Geraldine Kennedy, 'All of the senior big beasts as you would call them in the political correspondents' room [in Leinster House] did not trust Haughey after the Arms Crisis. They were all against him.' The political correspondents were also deeply influenced by one of Goulding's most persuasive assets in *The Irish Times*, Dick Walsh[14] who became its political editor and spent decades attacking Haughey to whom he referred as a 'hoor'.[15]

The British became wary of Haughey too. Britain's ambassador to Dublin, Robin Haydon, profiled Haughey for Peter Carrington, Thatcher's foreign secretary, in the run up to Anglo-Irish discussions between the respective premiers set for May 1980. Haydon was labouring under the misconception that Haughey, Blaney and Gibbons had tried to import arms for the IRA. According to Haydon's profile, Haughey's trial in 1970 had been a:

> big setback in a career which at one time seemed to be leading straight to the Taoiseach's office in the late '60s. ... He held important ministerial office from 1960–70. He was a tough Minister for Justice and an able Minister for Finance. He built an enviable reputation for getting things done. Then, in 1966, he failed to become Taoiseach, when Jack Lynch was appointed as a caretaker essentially because Blaney, Haughey and Colley could not settle the succession between themselves. At that time, he had no Republican credentials at all. He was seen as a get-rich-quick businessman lacking links with Fianna Fáil's republican past; in contrast to Colley and Blaney.
>
> Did his ambition cause him to decide to acquire such [republican] credentials when a plausible opportunity arose? We do not know. At all events in May 1970, together with two other ministers, Gibbons and Blaney, he was involved in an alleged conspiracy to import arms for the IRA in Northern Ireland.[16] Haughey was acquitted, but it is generally accepted that the defendants were guilty of some kind of conspiracy, though the details remain unclear. Haughey was relegated to the backbenches in disgrace and all seemed lost yet slowly he managed to

> rehabilitate himself. He started by travelling round the Fianna Fáil constituencies all over the Republic, doing favours and winning friends. This was possibly because he was never really condemned by the rank-and-file of the Party, of whom an important element cherish extreme republican views.[17]

Overall, Haydon felt that Haughey was 'a tough, clever, wily man, no friend of ours, but not, perhaps, actively hostile. He is conscious of his shady past (and present!). Perhaps there is something in what one columnist wrote recently – that he is "Ireland's answer to JR".'

Carrington could not have formed a favourable view of Haughey having read Haydon's portrait. The comment that Haughey was *not perhaps, actively hostile* was quite alarming and reveals a lot about the fears and suspicions British officials harboured about Haughey at the time.

Haughey and Lynch had many opportunities to talk to each other after Haughey was appointed to Lynch's front bench in 1975 and thereafter while he served in cabinet, 1977–79. Did they ever discuss the Arms Crisis? Intriguingly, when Haughey was leading Fianna Fáil in the 1980s he had at least one private meeting with Lynch which took place in Cork. Did they discuss how they would let history record these events? If they did, the agreement they reached may have been to say nothing. For his part, Haughey left no written account behind him. When his private safe at Abbeville was opened up, there was nothing about the crisis inside it. Why the silence? Perhaps because Haughey was a classic alpha male and the memory of having been forced to play the part of the whipping boy was just too humiliating for him to revisit. In any event, it had not prevented him from becoming taoiseach. No doubt he wanted to be remembered for his other achievements, many of which have been recorded by his family and can be perused at https://charlesjhaughey.ie/

In addition, he was believed by many to have harboured an ambition to become president of Ireland and, had he exposed Lynch, he would have ripped open wounds that had hardly healed at surface level and upset his chances of reaching Áras an Uachtaráin.

Haughey's later years were engulfed by tribunal inquiries into payments to politicians. He did not run for president and died on 13 June 2006.

CAPT. JAMES KELLY endured a life of struggle and financial hardship after his acquittal. Initially, he was denied his army pension by the government. The phone at his family home in Terenure was tapped both during and after the arms trials by the state. Intercepting a phone in the 1970s was a primitive operation. On a number of occasions his wife Sheila heard careless branchmen chatting on the line. Her response was to order them off it, especially during her weekly call to her mother. The reaction to her admonitions was invariably one of a sudden dead silence. During the time the monitor was in place, an article appeared in a newspaper disclosing that she was expecting a child. The report prompted a sinister individual to ring her children in the pretence he was her obstetrician. He managed to find out from them when she was out and, armed with this information, would engage any child he could in conversation during which he would say that he wanted the children to carry out medical procedures on themselves which involved the use of knives. One day the Kellys came home early from an appointment with Mrs Kelly's gynaecologist while this malefactor was still on the line. The captain contacted the guards afterwards and stressed that he knew full well that his line was tapped – something they could hardly deny – and that placing a trace on the caller would identify him and end the terror he was inflicting upon his children. A few days later two burly officers visited his home. They told him they had listened to the tapes and were shocked at what had been said. The bogus obstetrician had been traced to Kimmage and they provided the captain with his address. Since they could not admit that his line had been monitored, they could not do anything official about it. Instead, they suggested he use the information to warn the reprobate off. In the event the calls stopped and there was no need to intervene. However, the family had to endure calls which took place late into the night with a voice that urged Capt. Kelly to kill himself or emigrate.

The intercept on Capt. Kelly's line may or may not have been legal. It would have required a warrant from the then minister for justice, Des O'Malley for it to be lawful. Unfortunately, O'Malley did not address the issue in his rather threadbare memoirs.

The Kelly family was put on a death list by extreme loyalists who sent them intimidating letters in the names of 'Captain Black' and 'Captain White' which threatened to 'wipe out' each of the 'red head' children in the family.

In the early 1970s Capt. Kelly paid a visit to Haughey at his home in Kinsealy. As he was leaving and about to open the door of his car, Haughey hopped onto the bonnet and asked him if he would consider joining Fianna Fáil, predicting it would take ten years to oust Lynch. He implied that once this was achieved, the wrongs of the crisis would be put right. Kelly said that he could not join a party which had so 'betrayed' him while he had served as an army officer. Haughey jumped off the bonnet muttering that his response was a pity. The pair never had such a forthright conversation about the Arms Crisis again. In any event, Kelly was a supporter of the Labour Party and an admirer of David Thornley, a Labour TD in Dublin.

After *Orders from the Captain* was published in 1971, Gay Byrne said on air that it had become a 'bestseller'. Byrne subsequently told Sheila Kelly that the remark had landed him in trouble with the powers that be in RTÉ and he had received a dressing down from them.

The phone taps were not the only form of harassment the gardaí inflicted upon the family. One of the captain's sons was singled out for particular attention while he studied at UCD in the 1980s. His green combat trousers – highly fashionable at the time – were confiscated during a raid on his apartment as evidence of subversion. One of the texts he was studying as part of his university course – a book by Brendan Behan – was removed as allegedly proof of sedition. He was also questioned about his view of Jack Lynch who was no longer taoiseach. 'Jack who?' was the response of the student who had been about five at the time of the crisis and had no interest in politics. The gardaí told him they would 'nail' him on 'something'. Suffice it to say he had no links to subversives. Eventually, he moved cities to escape the harassment and complete his education in peace.

Friends of one of the captain's daughters were also told by two gardaí to keep their distance from her because she was 'dangerous news' and from a 'subversive family'.

Kelly eventually changed his mind about joining Fianna Fáil and enrolled in 1981. He secured election as member of the National Executive in 1985 but came to believe he was now an unwelcome reminder of a past which had become out of bounds for discussion. P.J. Mara, Haughey's press secretary, often began lobby briefings by telling the journalists he wanted 'none of that Arms Trial shite' before turning to the topic of the day. He left Fianna Fáil in 1989.

Throughout his retirement Kelly campaigned against the injustice which had been meted out to him. During the 1980s he made a number of appearances on RTÉ as he insisted on a right to appear and reply to his critics.

Ironically, for someone tagged as an extreme republican, some members of Sinn Féin abused him as a Free State Army 'traitor' during his retirement. Often at meetings and debates he would be heckled to this effect. He encountered Gerry Adams on a number of these occasions but the latter never acknowledged his existence.[18] Perhaps Adams did not want to provide oxygen for Goulding's conspiracy theory that Kelly had helped establish the Provisionals, one that was also being promoted by agents of British Intelligence.

Paddy Doherty, who had opposed the IRA, kept in touch with him, and indeed, after his death, remained in contact with his widow Sheila.

Throughout his struggles the captain was generous with researchers, even to those neutral or hostile towards him. Over the years he made it his business to correct the incessant flow of fantasy, misrepresentation and libel which kept surfacing about him. He disputed the smears promoted by Erskine Childers, Garret FitzGerald and others that the jury had acquitted him because they had been intimidated; that he was really guilty of attempting to illegally import arms; that he had gone native with the militant wing of the IRA; that he had helped establish and finance the Provisional IRA with misappropriated state funds and had committed treason.[19] To his family it appeared as if he had almost become a professional litigant. He won several apologies from publishers. In 2003 he received an apology and €50,000 in compensation in a settlement of a defamation action he took against FitzGerald and the publisher of a book on the Arms Crisis.

Had it not been for Berry, Lynch, Gibbons and MacStíofáin, he probably would have climbed to a high rank in the army, at least to the level of colonel with the reliable salary and the pension that accompanied it.

The captain doubted John Kelly's claim that he had intended to seize the arms that were meant to have arrived on the *MV City of Dublin* and give them to the IRA. Instead, he believed he had made the claim to save face with his peers for the sin of having co-operated with the Irish Army.[20]

The captain never gave up his fight for justice. He edged closer to victory after the release of a series of classified state papers in 2001, and more again in 2003. By mid-2003, however, it was apparent that he only had weeks to live due to lung cancer. As he approached death, he focused what little energy he had left on trying to extract an acknowledgment from the state that it had wronged him. At the time Fianna Fáil was in power and Bertie Ahern was taoiseach. Kelly's family recall how he would gasp 'Did it come?' in reference to the official letter he expected to drop through his letterbox. On the last day of his life his daughter told him, 'Yes it did, although the hall floor had been empty.

Captain James Kelly died on 16 July 2003. When Ahern was asked for a comment upon his death he said, 'Captain Kelly acted on what he believed were the proper orders of his superiors. For my part, I never found any reason to doubt his integrity'.[21]

Since his death in 2003 a number of books have appeared which to a greater or lesser degree convey the impression the 1970 arms importation operation was designed for the benefit of the IRA, something the captain would have disputed aggressively. In *T.K. Whitaker Portrait of a Patriot* (2014) by Anne Chambers, it was alleged that both 'Blaney and Haughey were in direct contact with known IRA leaders in Dublin, and "the deal was made that the IRA would be facilitated in the movement of arms to Northern Ireland and, in return, they would call off the burning and destruction of the property of foreign wealthy residents".'[22] According to Chambers, the defendants were charged with 'smuggling arms for the IRA' which they were not: there was no reference to the IRA in the charge. On the same page Chambers describes how Whitaker's 'support for and belief in the integrity of Jack Lynch as he tried to hold the government together, under the most difficult and unprecedented circumstances, was unwavering'. She outlines how Whitaker felt, 'the country and his party were fortunate that he [Jack Lynch] was Taoiseach at the time of the arms crisis. The decisive action then taken in the widespread loyalty he received avoided a real risk of internal division and even of civil disorder'. She then describes how Whitaker believed Lynch had 'had to take [Blaney and Haughey] out if democracy was to be preserved.'[23] Sadly, all this really shows is that Lynch was able to pull the wool over Whitaker's eyes without much difficulty. In fairness to Whitaker, he considered Lynch to be his friend and this may have impaired his judgement.

In *A Failed Political Entity* (2016) Stephen Kelly propounded his interpretation of these events which had Haughey siding with the IRA's Northern Command. The author then asked: 'did Haughey's covert support for the arming of the Northern Command help set up the PIRA? The answer is yes'.[24] He also argued that the CDC, which he describes as being 'chaired by Jim Sullivan', constituted a committee which 'was to form the nucleus of what was to become known as the PIRA'. Yet Sullivan was a Goulding loyalist.

Stephen Kelly also wrote that, 'From Captain Kelly's perspective, his ability to infiltrate the CDC in Belfast permitted the IMI [Irish military intelligence] a unique opportunity to help split the IRA between the traditional Marxist leadership in the South, led by the movement's Chief of Staff, Goulding, and a new generation of Northern republicans (hereafter referred to as the "Northern Command"). The precise date of when the decision was taken on behalf of the Blaney/Haughey caucus and the IMI to supply the emerging Northern Command with weapons can be traced to a meeting held at Bailieborough, Co. Cavan and 4–5 October 1969'.[25] Presumably Jim Sullivan and other deceased CDC figures such as Canon Pádraig Murphy, Tom Conaty (who spoke out against the Provisionals) and Paddy Devlin (who opposed the IRA and helped set up the SDLP and became minister for health in the 1974 Power Sharing government of Northern Ireland) would not agree they were a part of anything that prefigured the Provisional IRA. The captain's phone book contained the phone numbers of Jim Sullivan and another Goulding loyalist, Billy McMillen, all of whom were resolutely opposed to the emerging Provisionals.

The Globalist, a 2019 biography of the captain's former barrister Peter Sutherland by John Walsh, cast further shadows over his integrity. In it the Bailieboro meeting is described without any reference to the fact it was an assembly of CDC leaders; instead that 'it has been established that senior members of the Irish Republican Army (IRA) – an illegal paramilitary organisation – were in attendance.' On the same page the reader is told that the German arms were 'earmarked for nationalist resistance groups in Northern Ireland'. Against this background, an explanation had to be provided as to why Sutherland, a Fine Gael supporter, would have acted for the captain: 'To the outside world Sutherland would also have seemed politically an odd choice for Kelly's defence team. He had a deep antipathy *to paramilitaries of any hue* [my emphasis], and one of the early factors attracting him to politics was his opposition to Haughey and all he stood for. However, there is a long-standing tradition in the Law Library to retain barristers from "the other side".'[26]

Sutherland, it must be stressed was adamant that Capt. Kelly was an innocent man who should never have been charged. He spoke about the injustice he had suffered for decades after he had acted for him, often raising the issue himself. When interviewed for this book in 2013 he commented on the addendum memorandum of 10 February – which he had not learned about until then – stating confidently, 'well that puts it beyond doubt, he was innocent'. Sutherland also expressed his 'delight' at the gift of a copy of Angela Clifford's 'Military Aspects of Ireland's Arms Crisis' from me which included the wording of the addendum of 10 February 1970. He said he looked forward to the publication of this book and hoped it would help vindicate Kelly.[27]

Now that MacStíofáin's role has finally been exposed to daylight, will the state declassify the most secret files that it holds on him in its vaults?

The department of justice should also clarify if the phone tap on the family home was authorised by Des O'Malley, and if so, on what grounds. Moreover, when was it put in place and when was it lifted? If it was before the trial, was any use made of the information derived from it during the preparation of the prosecution's case against the captain? If after his acquittal, what was the legal basis for monitoring it?

Will the state offer a full apology to the Kelly family for the many wrongs occasioned to the captain, not to mention the other Arms Trial defendants, and indeed Col Hefferon who was so cruelly ostracised in his retirement by craven former colleagues afraid of their Fianna Fáil overlords?[28]

Or will it turn a blind eye and thereby endorse the disruptive anti-state agenda of the first chief of staff of the Provisional IRA?

Leabharlanna Poiblí Chathair Baile Átha Cliath
Dublin City Public Libraries

CHRONOLOGY

1969

12 August: Siege of Derry begins

14 August: British troops are sent to Northern Ireland.

Between 13–19 August, Haughey meets Goulding.

September: On a date unknown in September 1969, a flight carrying a cargo of arms flies from London to Dublin.

13 September: Capt. Kelly meets John Kelly.

27 September: The Interim Report of the Planning Board on Northern Ireland Operations of the Irish Army is produced.

5–6 October: The CDC convention at Bailieboro takes place.

November: John Kelly and Jock Haughey go to London. A British spy, Capt. Markham-Randall, follows them back to Dublin.

December: Seán Keenan and John Kelly seeks arms in the USA

December: Lynch fails to provide Gibbons with a clear policy direction about the acquisition of arms by the CDCs.

December: On a date after 7 December, Garda Commissioner Wymes and Fleming brief *Ó Moráin* about alleged links between Blaney and Haughey and the IRA.

1970

January: Lynch gives Gibbons the green light to import arms which are to be kept under Army control.

6 February Gibbons issues a Directive to the Army to (1) prepare the Army for incursions into Northern Ireland, (2) to make weapons available and (3) make gas masks available.

10 February Gibbons issues an addendum to his directive stating that: The taoiseach and other ministers have met delegations from Northern Ireland. At these meetings urgent demands were made for respirators, weapons and ammunition the provision of which

the government agreed. Accordingly truckloads of these items will be put at readiness so that they may be available in a matter of hours.

14 February: John Kelly and a CDC delegation meet Lynch in Leinster House.

Fourth week of February: Another CDC delegation meets Lynch.[1]

February or March: Lynch meets with Paddy Doherty, Billy Kelly and Seán Keenan who request him to put aside or furnish them with rifles.

3 March: Lynch meets another CDC delegation in Dublin which includes John Kelly. After the meeting, they join Gibbons and other ministers. Gibbons promises to provide them with guns.

4 March: Capt. Kelly meets Gibbons and briefs him about his forthcoming trip to see German arms dealer Otto Schlueter.

10 March–13 March: Capt. Kelly flies to Germany to see Schlueter.

19 March: Capt. Kelly asks Anthony Fagan at Department of Finance to assist in the importation of a cargo which G2 is bringing into the county

25 March: The *MV City of Dublin* docks in Dublin without its cargo of arms.

2 April: Gibbons dispatches a convoy of trucks containing 500 rifles to Dundalk. 150 rifles are stored in Dundalk.

3 April: Garda Richard Fallon is shot dead by Saor Éire

8 April: Col Hefferon retires as Director of G2. He is succeeded by Col Delaney.

April: 'The Deceiver' informs Garda Special Branch about the impending arrival of a cargo of arms at Dublin Airport.

17–18 April: Discussions take place at the Department of Justice about the cargo due to arrive at Dublin airport.

18 April: Haughey calls Berry to discuss the events taking place at Dublin Airport.

20 April: Berry goes to Lynch to tell him about the events at Dublin Airport.

23 April: Gibbons tells Capt. Kelly that he is in the 'hot seat'.

1 May: Garda Special Branch officers arrest Capt. Kelly. Gibbons talks to him at Dublin Castle. He is then taken to see Lynch at Leinster House. An order is issued to return the 150 rifles in Dundalk to Dublin.

5 May: Lynch announced the resignation of Ó Moráin.

6 May: It is announced that Haughey and Blaney have been dismissed from cabinet.

6 May: The marathon Dáil Arms Crisis debate commences.

Date unknown: The statements of Col Hefferon and Col Delaney are altered. A forgery of Gibbon' directive of 6 February is fabricated.

22 September: The first trial opens.

29 September: Mr Justice Aindrias Ó Cuiv aborts the trial.

6 October: The second arms trial commences. Mr Justice Seamus Henchy presides over it.

23 October: The second trial concludes.

4 November: Lynch secures a vote of confidence (74 to 67).

1971

Attempts are made to prevent the publication of Capt. Kelly's book, *Orders for the Captain*, by the British ambassador and members of the Foreign Office in London

1972

The gardaí discovered that The Deceiver has been misleading them for over a decade.

ENDNOTES

Introduction

1 Haughey's family background, however, did not lack for Republican drama: his father Seán had participated in a plot organised by Michael Collins to smuggle guns to the IRA in Northern Ireland after the 1921 ceasefire. See the author's article in Village magazine, 'Charles Haughey did not run guns to the IRA in 1970 but his father Sean did decades earlier. And on the orders of Michael Collins!' It can be found at: https://villagemagazine.ie/unpublished-dick-walsh-wrong-about-haugheys-disinterest-in-northern-ireland/

2 Mulholland, Marc, Terence O'Neill (UCD Press, Dublin, 2013), p. 40; see also *Belfast Telegraph*, 15 January 1965.

1 The Descent into Madness

1 https://www.independent.co.uk/news/people/ian-paisleys-most-caustic-quotes -catholics-breed-like-rabbits-and-multiply-like-vermin-9729672.html.

2 Garland, Roy, *Gusty Spence* (Blackstaff Press, Belfast, 2001), p. 57.

3 Moore, Chris, *The Kincora Scandal* (Marino Books, Dublin, 1996), p. 39.

4 In 1912 various unionist militia banded together as The Ulster Volunteers to prevent the introduction of Home Rule for Ireland. The following year they became the Ulster Volunteer Force (UVF), an organisation determined to oppose any attempts by the British government to impose Home Rule on Ulster. In April 1914 they smuggled 25,000 guns into Larne. The crisis that was developing over Home Rule was swept aside by the start of the First World War. Many UVF volunteers joined the British Army and went to fight on the Western Front, as did many pro-Home Rule supporters.

5 Garland (2001), p. 47.

6 *Ibid.*

7 Moore (1996), p. 46.

8 Bolton, David, *The UVF 1966–1973* (Torc Books, Dublin, 1973), p. 40.

9 *Ibid.*, p. 51; Garland (2001), p. 63.

10 Garland (2001), p. 57.

11 Moloney, Ed and Pollack, Andy, *Paisley* (Poolbeg Dublin, 1986), p. 242.

12 Kincora, *State of Shame,* BBC NI Spotlight, 8 October 2014: https://www.bbc.co.uk/programmes/b04kp718.
13 https://www.bbc.com/news/uk-northern-ireland-foyle-west-45625222.
14 Callaghan, James, *A Divided House* (Harper Collins, London, 1973), p. 12.
15 'I Ran Away'? The IRA and 1969, Brian Hanley, *History Ireland, Issue 4* (July/August 2009): https://www.historyireland. com/ 20th-century -contemporary-history/i-ran-away-the-ira-and-1969/.
16 Bishop, Patrick and Mallie, Eamon, *The Provisional IRA* (William Heineman, London, 1987), p. 94.
17 Mulholland (2013), p. 84.
18 O'Neill, Terence, *The Autobiography of Terence O'Neill* (Rupert Hart-Davies Ltd, London, 1972), p. 122.
19 As quoted in Bolton (1973), p. 93.
20 Moore (1996), pp. 61–4.
21 McCrea later became a Westminster MP and was made a life peer by Theresa May in 2018.

2 The Citizens Defence Committes

1 Callaghan (1973), pp. 33.
2 Doherty, Paddy, *Paddy Bogside* (Mercier Press, Cork, 2001), p. 116.
3 *Ibid.*, p. 117. The presence of someone like Green underlines the point that the Derry defence committee was not an IRA front as some commentators have argued.
4 Ó Dochartaigh, Niall, *From Civil Rights to Armalites: Derry and the Birth of the Irish Troubles* (Cork University Press, Cork, 1997), p. 126.
5 Bishop and Mallie (1987), p. 94.
6 Ó Dochartaigh (1997), p. 37.
7 *Ibid.*.
8 Callaghan (1973), pp. 33–4.

3 The Quest for Arms Begins

1 Craig, Anthony, *Crisis of Confidence* (Irish Academic Press, Dublin, 2010), p. 45.
2 *Ibid.*
3 *Ibid.*
4 Clifford, Angela, 'August 1969: Ireland's Only Appeal to The United Nations', *A Belfast Magazine, No. 26* (March 2006) p. 9.

5 *Ibid.*
6 *Ibid.*
7 Doherty (2001), p. 123.
8 *Ibid.*, p. 124.
9 Mac Stíofáin, Seán, *Memoirs of a Revolutionary* (Gordon Cremonisi, London, 1975), p. 112.
10 Doherty (2001), p. 126.
11 *Ibid.*, pp. 126–7
12 *Ibid.*, p. 127.
13 *Ibid.*, p. 128.
14 Ó Dochartaigh (1997), p. 124.
15 Doherty (2001), p. 139.
16 MacStíofáin (1975), p. 117.
17 Paragraph 2.5. Report of the Scarman Inquiry. A copy of the Report is available at: https://cain.ulster.ac.uk/hmso/s carman.htm.
18 Devlin, Paddy, *Straight Left* (Blackstaff Press, Belfast, 1993), p. 105–6.
19 *Ibid.*, p. 106.
20 Statement issued by the IRA: https://www.leftarchive.ie/document/1607/.
21 MacStíofáin (1975), p. 125.
22 *Ibid.*
23 Rafter, Kevin, *Neil Blaney: A Soldier of Destiny* (Blackwater Press, Dublin, 1993), p. 53.
24 Private interview conducted in Dublin on 11 January 2019.
25 Most of them remained in place along the border until at least mid-November 1969.
26 Callaghan (1973), p. 50.
27 Boland, Kevin, *We Won't Stand (Idly)* By (Kelly Kane Limited, Dublin, 1972), p. 50.
28 Doherty (2001), pp. 182–3. These orders most likely emanated from Wilson's and Lynch's respective cabinets. Lynch remained hopeful of co-operation with the British Army in the event of extreme circumstances developing. A report compiled by the Irish Army dated 9 June 1970 outlined a meeting he had with the chief of staff of the Irish Army. The Army note that the 'Taoiseach himself had given considerable thought to the possibility that Irish troops could work in conjunction with British troops in the event that a situation would arise in the future in which the British troops would be unable to defend the minority. In reply to a question by the chief of staff

the taoiseach indicated that should incursions into the North be required, they would not be preceded by political or diplomatic representations'. Document in my possession.

29 White, Barry, *John Hume, Statesman of the Troubles* (Blackstaff Press Ltd, Belfast, 1984), p. 88.
30 Doherty (2001), p. 194.
31 *Ibid.*, p. 146.
32 *Ibid.*, p. 149.
33 The Border Campaign was conducted by the IRA during the period 1956–62. It involved a number of guerrilla attacks on RUC border posts along the border and was not successful. In the early 1960s, Charles Haughey, as minister for justice, dealt the campaign a severe blow by directing the use of military courts for the trial of the IRA volunteers captured by the state.
34 Bishop and Mallie (1987), pp. 120-21.
35 Boyne, Sean, *Gunrunners* (O'Brien Press, Dublin, 2006), p. 56.
36 Boland (1972), p. 55.
37 Boyne (2006), p. 56.
38 Brady, Seamus, *Arms and the Men* (self-published, 1971), p. 37.
39 This information was also divulged by Brian Lenihan to his son Brian who in turn relayed it to a member of Capt. Kelly's family.
40 Bishop and Mallie (1987), p. 129.
41 O'Brien (1972), p. 200.
42 *Ibid.*
43 Anderson (2002), pp. 177–8.

4 The Deceiver Starts to Whisper his Lies

1 *Magill*, June 1980, p. 51. Berry made no reference to Mick Ryan in the diaries published by *Magill*. Ryan's name appears in a memorandum Berry furnished to Lynch on 9 June 1970; see also Heney, Michael, *The Arms Crisis of 1970* (Head of Zeus, London, 2020), p. 80.
2 Bishop and Mallie (1987), pp. 50 and 84.
3 Fleming from Charlestown, Co Mayo was extremely close to Peter Berry and they met often to play handball at Garda HQ.
4 *Magill*, June 1980, p. 51.
5 *Ibid.*
6 *Ibid.*, p. 52.
7 My interview with Ruairí Ó Brádaigh, 16 March 2013, Co. Roscommon; interview with Garland, Dublin. Garland agreed that a

'deal' had not been struck but supported the Official IRA conspiracy discussed later in this chapter.

8 Childers was close to the man who served as Britain's Ambassador Andrew Gilchrist, 1968–70 and his successor John Peck, 1970–73. As shall be described later, Gilchrist and Peck admired Childers for his political views. In addition, Childers' wife, Rita (née Dudley), had worked at the Foreign Office and at the British embassy in Dublin.

9 Kelly, Capt. James, *The Thimble Riggers* (self-published, 1999), p. 28 and p. 276.

10 Private information from a retired garda special branch officer familiar with activities of Saor Eire. While the identity of the Saor Eire informer is known to me his name cannot be disclosed, at least not at this time.

11 Capt. Kelly may have been Boland's source. Boland made reference to the existence of 'sources' during an attack on Peter Berry in the Dáil on 8 May 1970. Boland was infuriated that Berry had placed ministers under surveillance. During his onslaught he stated '… I would respectfully suggest that the money spent on maintaining this Minister-watching organisation [i.e. the Special Branch] which, apparently works to *two sources* [my emphasis], would be more appropriately spent on trying to bring the murderers of Garda Fallon to justice.' Garda Fallon had been shot dead in Dublin by people linked to Saor Eire in April of 1970.

12 Hanley, Brian and Millar, Scott, *The Lost Revolution, The Story of the Official IRA and the Workers Party* (Penguin Ireland, Dublin, 2009), p. 137.

13 Sweetman, Rosita, *On Our Knees Ireland* (Pan Special, London, 1972), pp. 143–4.

14 The IRA split into two factions in December 1969, one led by Goulding, Seán Garland, Tomás Mac Giolla and others. It became known as the Official IRA (sometimes just the 'Officials' or the 'Stickies'); the other bloc was led by Ruairí Ó Brádaigh and Seán MacStíofáin among others. It became known as the Provisional IRA or Provos. The split is described in more detail in a later chapter.

15 *Cathal Goulding, Thinker, Socialist, Republican, Revolutionary. 1923–1998* (The Workers' Party of Ireland, 1999), pp. 28–35.

16 O'Malley, Des, *Conduct Unbecoming* (Gill and Macmillan, Dublin, 2014), p. 60.

5 Clandestine Arms Flights and Military Training

1 Johnson, Roy, *A Century of Endeavour* (Lilliput, Dublin, 2003), p. 262.
2 Private interview with Roy Johnson, Dublin, 28 September 2012.
3 Boland, Kevin, *Up Dev* (self-published, 1977), p. 45.
4 O'Malley (2014), pp. 60–1.
5 Kelly was not involved in the operation. He discovered what had happened by speaking to Jock Haughey about it later. John Kelly was interviewed by Liam Clarke on 17 August 2005and a transcript of it is reproduced at pages 615–619 of 'The Arms Conspiracy Trial' by Angela Clifford. This volume – which runs to 720 pages – is an invaluable source of information about the Arms Crisis. Clifford has reconstructed the transcripts of the trials, which had disappeared. She achieved this by painstaking reference to contemporaneous newspaper reports and *Through the Bridewell Gate, A Diary of the Dublin Arms Trial* by Tom Mac Intyre. Clifford's volume also contains a substantial collection of statements, interviews, declassified letters and other documents of interest to history. She is also the author of 'Military Aspects of Ireland's Arms Crisis of 1969–70', *A Belfast Magazine* number 29 September 2006 and also 'Ireland's Only Appeal to the United Nations', *A Belfast Magazine*, March 2006.
6 Pádraig 'Jock' Haughey was a brother of Charles Haughey.
7 In the split that took place inside the IRA at the end of 1969, McKnight remained loyal to Goulding. A myth grew up later that Blaney and Haughey were trying to help set up the Provisional IRA. I dispute this theory. The fact these guns went to the Goulding faction – the enemies of the future Provisionals – undermines the myth.
8 Hanley and Millar (2009), p. 138.
9 *Ibid.*
10 Anderson (2002), p. 196.
11 Army's Planning Board on Northern Ireland Operations report dated 27 September 1969. A reproduction of the report is contained in Clifford's 'Military Aspects of Ireland's Arms Crisis of 1969–70', *A Belfast Magazine No. 29*, September 2006 starting at p. 40.
12 A comprehensive analysis of these records is to be found in Clifford's, 'Military Aspects of Ireland's Arms Crisis of 1969–70', *A Belfast Magazine No. 29* (September 2006), see p. 40 onwards.
13 Doherty (2001), p. 186.
14 *Ibid.*, p. 187.
15 Private interview.

16 Doherty (2001), pp. 188–9.
17 *Ibid.*, p189.
18 Hanley and Millar (2009), p. 137. White was an IRA man who remained loyal to Goulding after the IRA split a few months later. Capt. Kelly's interaction with him further erodes the myth that he – Capt. Kelly – was acting on the orders of Blaney and Haughey to undermine the Goulding wing of the IRA.
19 Copy of Capt. Kelly's report of 31 August 1969 in my possession.
20 Interview with Colin Wallace who worked with the IPU. The smears were contained in edited versions of Official Sinn Féin publications; see also https://villagemagazine.ie/smear-sheet-the-document-that-proves-charles-haughey-was-the-target-of-british-secret-service-vilification-after-the-arms-trial/
21 Wilson was the leader of the Labour Party and prime minister of the UK, 1964–70 and 1974–76.
22 McCann, Eamonn, *War & An Irish Town* (Penguin Books, Middlesex, England, 1974), pp. 72–3.
23 Doherty (2001), p. 190.
24 *Ibid.*, p. 191.
25 Kelly (1999), p. 16.
26 Clifford, Angela, 'Ireland's Only Appeal to the United Nations', *A Belfast Magazine, No. 26* (2006) p. 86.
27 *Magill*, June 1980, p. 55.
28 Private interview.
29 Clifford, 'Military Aspects of Ireland's Arm Crisis', p. 59.
30 *Ibid.*, p. 57.
31 *Ibid.*
32 *Ibid.*, pp. 58–9
33 Taylor, Peter, *Provos* (Bloomsbury, London, 1997), p. 67–8.
34 In July 1970 the British Army began a search of the Falls district of Belfast for arms. A riot broke out which escalated into a gun battle between the British Army and the IRA. The British Army reacted to this by imposing a curfew which lasted for thirty-six hours during which house-to-house searches for weapons were carried out while the district was drenched in CS gas. There were numerous incidents during which soldiers destroyed furniture and belongings and behaved in an overly aggressive manner..
35 Taylor (1997), p. 68.
36 Bishop and Mallie (1987), p. 118.

37 *Ibid.*, p. 122.
38 Brady (1971), p. 54.
39 McCann (1974), p. 64.
40 The fact the British Army trained John Kelly illustrates the historical context which prevailed at this time. Yet Blaney and Haughey were portrayed by conspiracy theorists as *de facto* IRA godfathers for their association with John Kelly. These theorists invariably ignore the fact that a British officer had trained him in 1969. Against this background it is possible to understand how someone like Haughey – who had done so much as minister of justice in the early 1960s to suppress the IRA – could have had dealings with someone like John Kelly.
41 Taylor (1974), p. 72.
42 The journalists who were visiting Belfast had no difficulty discerning the difference between the CDCs and the IRA, an important fact as a myth later grew up that the CDCs were a front for the Provisional IRA. According to the *Sunday Times* Insight team, 'It would, emphatically, be false to equate the [Central] CDC with the IRA. One of its most prominent figures, for instance, was the Social Democratic and Labour MP for the Falls, Paddy Devlin, and its chairman was later a Belfast produce broker, Tom Conaty. In the nature of things, though, this "defence committee" did contain quite a few self-styled community defenders, which in Belfast meant the convinced republicans, like Jim Sullivan, the republican leader in the Lower Falls', *Ulster*, the *Sunday Times* Insight Team, Penguin Books 1972, p. 154.
43 Callaghan (1973), p. 101. Despite the many references to this phrase, no one at the time thought to take a photograph of the slogan, at least not one that has been published.

6 Secret Bank Accounts

1 Clifford, Angela, 'The Arms Conspiracy Trial', *A Belfast Magazine*, No. 33 p. 261
2 Brady (1971), p. 81.
3 Callaghan (1973), p.103.
4 Bishop and Mallie (1987), p. 49.
5 Brennan and Faulkner attended only one meeting of the sub-committee and lost interest thereafter for reasons which are not clear.
6 The gardaí had no agents inside the six counties.
7 Doherty (2001), p. 158.
8 *Ibid.*, p. 159.

9 Devlin (1993), pp. 117–8.
10 Clifford, 'The Arms Conspiracy Trial', p. 300.
11 Private interview, 8 February 2020.
12 Bishop and Mallie (1987), p. 131.
13 Jack Lynch speech in Dáil Éireann, 8 May 1970.
14 Boland (1972), p. 55.
15 *Ibid.*, p. 56.
16 John Kelly interview with Liam Clarke in Clifford, 'The Arms Conspiracy Trial', pp. 615–619.
17 *Ibid.*
18 *Ibid.*, p. 304.
19 *Ibid.*, p. 304–5.

7 The CDCs and Their Friends in High Society

1 Callaghan's reference to the summer of 1970 is to the deterioration in the relationship between the British Army and the nationalist community that occurred as a result of the Falls Road curfew.
2 Callaghan (1973), p. 47–8.
3 McCann (1974), p. 69.
4 Doherty (2001), p. 168.
5 McCann (1974), p. 69.
6 Moloney and Pollack (1986), p. 201.
7 Healy, Denis, *The Time of My Life (*Michael Joseph, London, 1989), p. 342.
8 Hailsham, Lord, *A Sparrow's Flight – Memoirs* (HarperCollins, London, 1990), p. 373.
9 Doherty (2001), p. 210.
10 *Ibid.*
11 Callaghan (1973), p. 57.
12 *Ibid.*, p. 75.
13 *Ibid.*
14 *Ibid.*, pp. 93–4.
15 Devlin (1993), p. 115.
16 McCann (1974), pp. 71–2.
17 Bishop and Mallie (1987), p. 125.
18 McCann (1974), pp. 71–2.
19 Callaghan (1973), p. 103.
20 Ó Dochartaigh (1997), p. 132.
21 *Ibid.*, pp. 132–3.

22 Doherty (2001), pp. 163–4.
23 *Ibid.*, pp. 214–5.
24 *Ibid.*, p. 215.

8 The Bailieboro Deception

1 Kelly, Capt. J., *Orders for the Captain* (Kelly-Kane Limited, 1971), p. 56.
2 Kelly (1999), p. 18.
3 Bishop and Mallie (1987), p. 128.
4 Kelly (1971), p. 16.
5 *Magill*, June 1980, p. 52.
6 *Ibid.*
7 Kelly (1999), p. 25. Crinnion was convicted alongside an MI6 agent called John Wyman in Dublin in 1973.
8 *Magill*, June 1980, p. 54.
9 Kelly (1999), p. 279.
10 *Ibid.*, p. 280.
11 Private discussion with Ó Brádaigh, 16 March 2013, Co. Roscommon.
12 Private interview with a member of Capt. Kelly's family.
13 Kelly (1971), pp. 16–17.
14 *Ibid.*, p. 17
15 Boland (1977), p. 71.
16 *Ibid.*
17 *Ibid.*
18 Clifford, 'Arms Conspiracy Trial', p. 488.
19 Keogh, Dermot, *Jack Lynch: A Biography* (Gill and Macmillan, Dublin, 2008), pp. 218–9.
20 Kelly (1971), pp. 16–17..
21 Document in my possession entitled, *Explanatory Notes for State Counsel from Peter Berry, Secretary of Department of Justice.*
22 *Magill*, June 1980, p. 58.
23 O'Malley (2014), p. 60.

9 Her Majesty's Spies in Ireland

1 Andrew, Christopher, *Defence of the Realm* (Allen Lane, London, 2009), p. 605.
2 17 June 1970 FCO 33 1207 Ronnie Burroughs to the FCO; see also Clifford, 'Arms Conspiracy Trial', p. 672
3 Craig (2010), p. 12.

4 British National Archives PROFCO 33759; see also Clifford, 'Arms Trial Conspiracy', p. 663. A guide to the Public Record Office of the Foreign and Commonwealth Office (PROFCO) can be found at https://www.nationalarchives.gov.uk/help-with-your-research/research-guides/foreign-commonwealth-correspondence-and-records-from-1782/.
5 British National Archives PROFCO 33 759; see also Clifford, 'Arms Trial Conspiracy', p. 661.
6 PROFCO 33759; Clifford, 'Arms Trial Conspiracy', p. 663.
7 I acknowledge the kind assistance of UCD library for the provision of a copy of the *Devine Memo*.
8 Clifford, 'Arms Conspiracy Trial', p. 664.
9 PROFCO33769; see also Clifford, 'Arms Conspiracy Trial', p. 664.
10 PRO FCO 33759; see also Clifford, 'Arms Conspiracy Trial', p. 663.
11 *Ibid.*
12 Clifford, 'Arms Conspiracy Trial', p. 665.
13 PROFCO33769; see also Clifford, 'Arms Conspiracy Trial', p. 664.
14 Private interview with former garda officer who read the log entry. In 1998 O'Brien admitted to Vincent Browne on his *Tonight with Vincent Browne* radio show that he had not paid tax on his journalistic earnings. These must have been considerable as he wrote for *The Irish Times, Irish Independent* and *Sunday Independent*. In November of 2002 it was reported that the Revenue Commissioners had issued O'Brien with a sizable bill for unpaid tax. See *The Irish Star*, Friday 21 November 2002. Ironically, O'Brien tried to argue that his writing was of artistic merit and exempt from tax under legislation which Haughey had introduced as minister for finance. Yet, that legislation had specifically excluded journalistic writing from the tax-free status. O'Brien refused to talk to media after the reports appeared about his bill from the Revenue Commissioners became public knowledge.
15 Liam Clark's 17 August 2005 interview with John Kelly. The section of the transcript referring to the Arms Crisis is reproduced in Clifford, 'Arms Conspiracy Trial' starting at p. 615. While the interview was conducted in August of 2005, Kelly stipulated that it was not to be released until after the death of Charles Haughey.
16 One of Capt. Kelly's note books contained a phone number for him: 321 4604605.
17 Kelly (1999), p. 21.
18 *Ibid.*
19 *Ibid.*, p. 22.

20 Clifford, 'Arms Conspiracy Trial', p. 617.
21 Kelly (1999), p. 23.
22 Clifford, 'Arms Trial Conspiracy', pp. 616–7. The 'Con' referred to was undoubtly Con Houlihan, from Dysart, Co. Clare who served as press attache at the London embassy 1969–72.
23 Liam Clarke interview with John Kelly, 2005. Fitt denied his involvement in the arms quest in later years even to the extent of suing for defamation when his role was disclosed.
24 A Fine Gael TD later queried where a gap in some of the funds available to Capt. Kelly had gone during a Dáil debate. The captain explained to him afterwards that he had spent the funds in an effort to spirit the spy away in the nick of time.

10 Blaney Plugs the Transatlantic Arms Supply Pipeline

1 Doherty (2001), p. 209.
2 Ó Dochartaigh (1997), p. 190.
3 *Ibid.*, pp. 190–1.
4 *Ibid.*, pp. 191–2.
5 Liam Clarke interview with John Kelly 2005
6 *Ibid.*
7 Clifford, 'Arms Conspiracy Trial', pp. 615–19.
8 *Ibid.*
9 Ó Dochartaigh (1997), p. 192.
10 Private interview, 23 August 2019.
11 These riots were sparked by nationalist anger at the behaviour of provocative loyalist marching bands in the vicinity of Ballymurphy in Belfast. The British Army reacted in a manner which nationalists felt was not even-handed. The riots will be address in the chapter about the transport of 500 rifles to Dundalk in February of 1970.
12 On 4 September 1970 Michael Kane, an IRA bomber, was killed when a device he was carrying detonated prematurely at the transformer at New Forge Lane in the Malone area.

11 Lynch Grabs Hold of the Steering Wheel

1 Kelly (1999), p. 32.
2 Trial transcript, see Clifford, 'Arms Conspiracy Trial', p. 339.
3 *Ibid.*, p. 309.
4 Clifford, 'Military Aspects', p. 76.
5 Document in my possession.

6 The 'Secret Cabinet' process is outlined in chapter 2.
7 Clifford, 'Arms Conspiracy Trial', pp. 308–310.
8 *Ibid.*, p. 326.
9 Kelly (1971), p. 19.
10 Kelly (1971), p. 20.
11 *Ibid.*
12 Clifford, 'Arms Conspiracy Trial', p. 315.
13 *Ibid.*, p. 334.
14 *Ibid.*, p. 322.
15 Orders 197 and 199; see also Trial transcript, Clifford, 'Arms Conspiracy Trial', p. 355.
16 Brady (1971), p. 113.
17 Faulkner, Pádraig, *As I Saw It* (Wolfhound Press, Dublin, 2005), p. 104.
18 Kelly (1971), p. 195.
19 Boland (1977), p. 46.
20 Boland (1972), p. 72.
21 Boland (1977), pp. 44–5.
22 *Ibid.*, pp. 45–6.
23 *Magill*, June 1980, pp. 59–60.
24 Boland (1977), p. 46.

12 The Taoiseach Meets Three Provisional IRA Leaders

1 Clifford, 'Arms Conspiracy Trial', pp. 123–4.
2 *Ibid.*, p. 283.
3 *Ibid.*, p. 296.
4 *Ibid.*, p. 320.
5 Kelly (1971), pp. 20–21. The author of this remark was not identified by Capt. Kelly in the book but I can reveal it was Seán Keenan.
6 *Ibid.*, p. 21.
7 *Ibid.*, pp. 20–1.
8 Evidence of Capt. Kelly at his trial. See Clifford, Arms Conspiracy Trial, p. 319.
9 Doherty (2001), p. 221.
10 *Ibid.*
11 *Ibid.*, p. 222.
12 *Ibid.*, p. 223.
13 *Ibid.*, p. 225.

13 The Empty Vessel from Antwerp

1 Clifford, 'Arms Trial Conspiracy', p. 291.
2 *Ibid.*, p. 329.
3 *Ibid.*, p. 291.
4 Kelly (1999), p. 34.
5 Gibbons appears to have quoted the first two lines of 'In a Monastery Garden'. See Kelly (1999), p. 181.
6 Private interview January 2020. Des Long was a member of the Provisional IRA Army Executive and served as its Director of Finance in the 1970s.
7 *Magill,* May 1980 p. 46
8 Interview by phone Kieran Conway 11 May 2020.
9 *The Times of London*, 16 January 1976
10 Conway, 11 May 2020.
11 Clifford, 'Arms Trial Conspiracy', p. 328
12 Vincent Browne was the editor of *Magill.* See the May 1980 edition, p. 46. *Magill* ran a series of seminal reports on the crisis between May and July 1980 that resulted in a Dáil debate on the issue. Such was the level of interest, the British embassy sent a representative to take notes.
13 Kelly (1999), p. 189.
14 *Ibid.*, p. 35.
15 Clifford, 'Arms Trial Conspiracy', p. 329.
16 Boland (1972), p. 95.
17 This became a matter of conflict in the Four Courts. When Seamus McKenna, SC, for the prosecution put it to Col Hefferon that Gibbons had never said that he would intervene directly to have the captain released from regimental duties. Col Hefferon replied firmly: 'He did'; see Kelly (1999), p. 182.

14 The Night of the Emergency Convoy

1 Clifford, 'Arms Trial Conspiracy', p. 133.
2 The G2 report, a copy of which is in my possession, is entitled the 'Situation in Northern Ireland' and is undated.
3 Gibbons did not disclose these fears in his evidence to the juries at the Arms Trials.
4 Private interview.
5 Private interview with family member of the officer of the motor division.
6 Kelly (1999), pp. 176–7.

7 *Ibid.*
8 Boland (1972), p. 71.
9 Faulkner (2005), p. 95.
10 *Ibid.*
11 *Ibid.*
12 Document in my possession, entitled, 'Situation in Northern Ireland', p. 9.

15 A Farewell to Arms, The Deceiver Pulls the Trigger

1 Northern Ireland Threat Assessment for the period 1 January 1970 to 30 June 1970; NA DEFE/13/765; see also Prince, Simon and Warner, Geoffrey, *Belfast and Derry in Revolt* (Irish Academic Press, Dublin, 2012), p. 79.
2 Kelly (1999), p. 37.
3 Des O'Malley (2014), p. 50–1.
4 Private interview, 5 January 2020.
5 Clifford, 'Arms Conspiracy Trial', p. 32.
6 O'Brien (1972), pp. 228–9.

16 The Civil Servant who was a Law unto Himself

1 Clifford, 'Arms Trial Conspiracy', p. 247.
2 The assertion contradicts what Berry told the state's prosecution team in a memorandum he prepared in the run up to the first Arms Trial. In it, there was no reference to any 'lingering doubts' he harboured about Lynch. Instead, Berry wrote how, 'having regard to my personal knowledge, over a long period, of the characters of each man [Haughey and Lynch] for whom I had profound respect I was in a frightful dilemma. It occurred to me that if the Taoiseach had been, for diplomatic reasons, speaking with two voices, I would put him in a most embarrassing position if I were to go direct to him with the information as to Mr Haughey's action. However, I finally come to the conclusion that "diplomacy" could not possibly be the answer, and that the Taoiseach was too honest to lie on a matter of this kind. Having made up my mind to a 99.5% degree at that stage as to my course of action I decided to consult the one person whom I felt I could trust to give me good advice as to whether I would be behaving with propriety in going over my Minister's head direct to the Taoiseach'. This quote is taken from the 'Explanatory note for State Counsel from Peter Berry, Secretary of Department of Justice, Part III. This document is in my

possession.
3 *Magill*, June 1980, pp. 61–2.
4 Kelly (1999), p. 38.
5 Clifford, 'Arms Trial Conspiracy', p. 28.
6 *Ibid.*, p. 28.
7 Haughey made the comment about his 'shrewd' idea that arms were involved during his testimony at the Four Courts.
8 *Magill*, June 1980, p. 54.
9 Clifford, 'Arms Trial Conspiracy', p. 335.
10 Kelly (1971), p. 25.
11 The reference to 'shortly after noon' appears in Berry's 'diaries' published in *Magill* in June 1980 at p. 62. Yet, when Berry provided an account of this meeting to the state's prosecution team in the run up to the first Arms Trial, he claimed he 'saw the Taoiseach early on Monday morning and made no comment about the British ambassador. The latter reference is contained in Berry's 'Explanatory note for State Counsel from Peter Berry, Secretary of Department of Justice, Part III', p. 3.
12 This meeting had escaped the attention of writers on the topic until the publication of Heney's book in April 2020. See Heney (2020), p. 190, *et sequi*. Neither Gibbons nor Haughey described what transpired at this meeting at the arms trials.
13 *Magill*, June 1980, p.62.
14 *Ibid.*
15 Although the belief in 1970 was that the arms were for Goulding's Official IRA, by the time Berry wrote his diaries in retirement, the mythology had morphed so that is was the Provisionals who were the intended recipients. Berry simply refers to the 'IRA' in his account, an unusual lack of precision for someone who prized himself on exactness.
16 *Magill*, June 1980, p. 63.
17 Transcript of conversation between Berry and Murray in my possession.
18 Boland (1972), p. 73.
19 Faulkner (2005), p. 96.
20 Boland (1977), p. 74.

17 'A Pawn in a Very Strange Game'

1 Document in my possession entitled, 'An Examination of some of

the Evidence pertinent to and directly concerned with the Army by ARMY INTELLIGENCE' marked "TOP SECRET", 1 October 1970.
2 Clifford, 'Arms Trial Conspiracy', p. 604.
3 *Ibid.*, p. 605.
4 Clifford, Arms Trial Conspiracy, p. 335.
5 Kelly (1999), p. 40.
6 Letter in my possession.
7 Kelly (1999), p. 40.
8 *Ibid.*
9 Clifford, 'Arms Trial Conspiracy', p. 337.
10 Kelly (1971), p. 27.
11 *Ibid.*
12 Clifford, 'Arms Trial Conspiracy', p. 294.
13 Kelly (1999), p. 41.

18 Secret Briefings for the Opposition

1 FitzGerald (1991), p. 93.
2 Collins, Stephen, *The Power Game* (O'Brien Press, Dublin, 2001), p. 75.
3 Evidence of John Fleming, 12 October 1970.
4 Boland (1972), p. 76.
5 Boland (1977), p. 75.
6 Heney (2020), p. 252.
7 Clifford, 'Arms Trial Conspiracy', p. 618.
8 FitzGerald (1991), p. 93.
9 Frank Dunlop, who worked as press secretary for Lynch, and later Haughey, revealed in his memoirs, *Yes Minister*, that at the top of Fianna Fáil it was the commonly held view that Haughey had been 'stitched up'. Yet only Boland and Brennan resigned. See *Dunlop, Yes Minister, Irish Politics from Behind Closed Doors* (Penguin Ireland, Dublin, 2005), p. 34.
10 Clifford, 'Arms Trial Conspiracy', p. 614.
11 After the acquittal of the defendants at the second arms trial, Lynch held a press conference in New York at which he stated that notwithstanding the verdict of the jury, an attempt had been made to import arms illegally. Yet, he reappointed Haughey to cabinet in 1977.
12 Rafter (1993), p. 81.
13 Faulkner (2005), p. 121.

14 Seán Haughey 10 May 2020.

15 He remained resentful towards Seamus McKenna, SC, but presumably not at the same level of intensity. When Gay Byrne hosted a tribute show for Brian Lenihan on *The Late Late Show* in March 1990, Haughey attended and shook hands with the various guests with only one exception: Lenihan's best man, McKenna, who had spearheaded the state prosecution at the Arms Trials.

19 The Gang that couldn't Shoot Straight

1 Private interview with Ben Briscoe, Dublin, 10 January 2019.

2 *Ibid.*

3 Dunlop (2005), p. 42.

4 *Magill*, June 1980 pp. 63, 65.

5 Kelly (1999), p. 68.

6 *This Week*, 8 May 1970.

7 Boland was aware of the plot as Haughey told about it.

8 Childers reserved a particular disdain for Haughey. The latter told a story that at a cabinet meeting, Childers had once passed around a packet of cigarettes pointedly offering one to everyone except Haughey. He was not popular with Boland either. Boland's relationship with him went from bad to worse and reached a nadir in January 1973 after the death of Boland's father. By then Boland had left Fianna Fáil. Childers was warned not to attend the funeral. In *Up Dev*, Boland recounts how 'the Fianna Fáil people, who knew my father, had the sensitivity to stay away, but numbers of those, who didn't know him, affronted the family by attending. When the Tánaiste, after being told the previous night in no uncertain terms by myself and other members of the family that his attendance was most unwelcome, took his place at a *prie dieu* at the funeral Mass to represent the Taoiseach – of all people – it was too much for my sister Máire, who stood beside him and offered two words "Get Out". Fortunately he did so and the Mass was able to proceed' [*Up Dev* (1977), p. 19].

9 Kelly (1971), pp. 77–8.

20 'Too Late to have the Affair Swept under the Carpet'

1 Kelly (1999), p. 50.

2 *Magill*, June 1980, p. 63.

3 Kelly (1999)., p. 46.

4 *Ibid.*

5 *Ibid.*, p. 49.

6 *Ibid.*, p. 50.
7 *Ibid.*, p. 55
8 Fleming denied that he made these remarks to Capt. Kelly when he appeared at the Public Accounts Committee in 1971. Moreover, the report he furnished to the state prosecution during their preparation for the first arms trial made no reference to his suspicions or the evidence against Gibbons.
9 Jack Lynch, Dáil Éireann, 8 May 1970. https://www.oireachtas.ie/en/debates/debate/dail/1970-05-08/5/.

21 The Gardaí who Breached the Official Secrets Act

1 Philip McMahon is one of the more likely candidates as the source of the article.
2 Jack Lynch, Dáil Éireann, 8 May 1970.
3 Boland (1977), p. 74–5.
4 Jack Lynch, Dáil Éireann, 8 May 1970.
5 O'Brien (1972), p. 215.
6 Callaghan (1973), p. 136.

22 The IRA Steps into the Breach

1 Doherty (2001), p. 227.
2 Boland (1972), p. 84.
3 Brady (1971), pp. 154–5.
4 McCann (1974), p. 73.
5 *Ibid.*, p. 76.
6 Taylor (1997), p. 77.
7 *Ibid.*
8 *Ibid.*, p. 75–6.
9 Hennessey, Thomas, *The Evolution of the Troubles 1970–1972* (Irish Academic Press, Dublin, 2007), p. 35.
10 English, Richard, *Armed Struggle, A History of the IRA* (Macmillan, London, 2003), p. 135.
11 Kelley, Kevin, *The Longest War, Northern Ireland and the IRA* (Brandon, Dingle, 1982), p. 146.
12 Taylor (1997), p. 77.
13 *Ibid.*, pp.74–77.
14 *Ulster, Sunday Times Insight* (Penguin 1972) p. 213.

23 Lynch Law

1 Anthony Fagan visited Otto Schlueter's office in 1971 when he handed the German a document claiming 'on behalf of the Minister for Finance' a refund of all the monies paid to him by Capt. Kelly. Fagan wanted 'about £36,000' but Schlueter claimed he had only received about £24,000.
2 Jack Lynch, Dáil Éireann, 8 May 1970.
3 Transcript of conversation between Peter Berry and the secretary of the Department of Finance, Charles. H. Murray, in my possession.
4 Conor Lenihan, *Haughey Prince of Power* (Blackwater Press 2015), pp. 75–6.
5 At the time the arrest was a frightening experience but in later years Maureen Haughey managed to see a lighter side to it recalling how the learned judge had been rushed upstairs where they, along with her sister, Peggy O'Brien, had peered over the bannisters to watch the drama unfolding below. Interview with Seán Haughey, 10 May 2020.
6 Rafter (1993), p. 79.
7 This information was divulged by Brian Lenihan to his son, Brian, who in turn relayed it to a member of Capt. Kelly's family many years later.
8 *Irish Independent*, 28 April 2001.
9 Kelly (1999), p. 155.
10 Boland (1977), pp. 86–7.
11 The first trial collapsed after Mr Justice Ó Cuiv's impartiality was challenged by Ernest Woods, SC, for Albert Luykx.
12 Kelly (1999), pp. 158–9.
13 *Ibid.*, pp. 161–2.
14 *Ibid.*, pp. 167–8.
15 Downey, James, *Lenihan, His Life and Loyalties* (New Island Books, Dublin, 1998), p. 82.
16 Lynch, Dáil Éireann, 8 May 1970.
17 *Sunday Tribune*, 26 February 1984.
18 Charles Haughey press conference, Cork, February 1984.
19 Capt. Kelly was mistaken about this as the captain was an Aer Lingus pilot.
20 Kelly (1999), p. 56.
21 Kelly (1971), p. 45.

24 'I Am Not Going to Commit Perjury'

1 *https://www.thedetail.tv/articles*

the-irish-government-and-the-troubles-are- they-inextricably-linked.

2 *Kelly (1999), p. 182.*

3 Trial transcript; see Clifford, 'Arms Conspiracy Trial,' p. 182.

4 *Ibid.*, p. 182

5 *Ibid.*, p. 182–3, 256–8.

6 *Ibid.*, p.180.

7 *Ibid.*, p. 258.

8 Kelly (1999), p. 33

9 *Ibid.*, p. 259.

10 *Ibid.*, p. 260.

25 An Inconvenient Witness

1 Trial transcript; see Clifford, 'Arms Conspiracy Trial', p. 166–7.

2 Transcript of the phone call in my possession.

3 Trial transcript; see Clifford, 'Arms Conspiracy Trial', p. 167. Despite its paucity, it may have been enough to assuage his concerns about the information Berry had related to him from the special branch.

4 *Ibid.* p. 168.

5 *Ibid.*, p. 169.

6 *Ibid*, p. 219.

26 Berry boxes Clever

1 Document in my possession, entitled, *Explanatory Notes for State Counsel from Peter Berry*, Sec of Department of Justice.

2 National Archives, S/7/70. See also Clifford, Arm Conspiracy Trial p. 29.

3 In his correspondence with the state prosecution, Berry assailed Ó Moráin's mental capacity describing him as having suffered 'illness and mental aberrations for some time past'. He did so in the *Explanatory Notes for State Counsel from Peter Berry, Sec of Department of Justice, Part I*, p. 2.

4 Trial transcript; see Clifford, 'Arms Conspiracy Trial', p. 28.

5 Peter Berry in evidence, 12 October 1970.

6 Quoted in Kelly (1999), p. 150.

7 *Ibid.*

8 One of those who crossed the border was Owen Corrigan who later joined the Special Branch. https://www.independent.ie/regionals/argus/news/former -garda-corrigan-sent-to-falls-road-as-an-observer-26965637.html

9 Kelly (1999), p. 151. Berry also furnished a report to Dr Nicholas Nolan, government secretary, enclosing 'for the information of the Taoiseach further photostat copies of reports received from some of our intelligence agents in the Six Counties'; see Clifford, 'Arms Conspiracy Trial', p. 245; also NA Taois 2000/6/660.
10 Boland (1977), pp. 71–2.
11 *Ibid.*, p. 72.
12 Trial transcript; see Clifford, 'Arms Conspiracy Trial', pp. 246–7.
13 *Ibid.*, p. 518.

27 The Minister who Knew Nothing

1 Kelly (1999), p. 169.
2 Trial transcript; see Clifford, 'Arms Conspiracy Trial', p. 228.
3 *Ibid.*
4 Kelly (1999), p. 171.
5 Trial transcript; see Clifford, 'Arms Conspiracy Trial', p. 236.
6 Boland (1977), p. 71; see also Kelly (1999), p. 170.
7 Gibbons in evidence 25 September; see Clifford, 'Arms Conspiracy Trial', p. 128.
8 Trial transcript; see Clifford, 'Arms Conspiracy Trial', p. 128.
9 *Ibid.*, p. 117
10 *Ibid.*, p. 135.
11 *Ibid.*, p. 120.
12 *Ibid.*, p. 137.

28 Haughey Aims Carefully

1 Kelly (1999), p. 192. Sutherland later became a Fine Gael Attorney-General and EU Commissioner and later again held many prestigious international postings.
2 *Ibid.*, p. 208.
3 *Ibid.*, pp. 207–8.
4 *Ibid.*, p. 206.
5 Kelly (1999), pp. 213–4.
6 Trial transcript, see Clifford, 'Arms Conspiracy Trial', p. 358.

29 Verdict and Fall Out

1 Clifford, 'Military Aspects', p. 76.
2 The G2 report, a copy of which is in my possession, is entitled the 'Situation in Northern Ireland' and is undated.

3 Mac Intyre, Tom, *Through the Bridewell Gate, A Diary of the Dublin Arms Trial* (Faber and Faber, London, 1971), pp. 207–8.
4 O'Brien (1972), p. 249.
5 *Sunday Independent*, 5 May 2001.
6 A witness on the issue, a Mr O'Grady, had explained that such a certificate was not in fact a requirement. George Colley later made an identical assertion. See also Kelly (1999), p. 233.
7 Kelly (1999), p. 288.

30 The Beneficiaries of the Arms Crisis

1 John Kelly interviewed by Steven McCaffery; See https://www.thedetail.tv/articles/the-irish-government-and-the-troubles-are-they-inextricably-linked.
2 Glover, James, *Northern Ireland: Future Terrorist Trends, 15 December 1978*, p. 3. This was a classified document which fell into the hands of the Provisional IRA and was distributed to journalists. I am in possession of a photocopy of it.
3 *Ibid.*, p. 4.
4 *Ibid.*, p. 1.
5 On 30 January 1972 soldiers of the 1st Battalion of the Parachute Regiment of the British Army shot twenty-six unarmed civilians in Derry. Fourteen civilians died. Many of the deceased were gunned down while running away from the soldiers. Others were shot while attending to the wounded.; see Devlin, pp. 128–131
6 Devlin (1993), p. 128.
7 *Ibid.*, p. 129.
8 *Ibid.*
9 *Ibid.*, p. 131.
10 *Ibid.*, p. 134.
11 McCann (1974), p.78.
12 Hennessy (2007), pp. 57–8.

31 Diplomat-Spy and Black Propaganda Maestro

1 Draft dispatch to FCO, 30 January 1969, CCA, GILC14B as quoted by Eunan O'Halpin in *Intelligence, Statecraft and International Power* (Irish Academic Press, Dublin, 2006), p. 140.
2 19 July 1915–9 May 2010
3 John Loader Maffey 1877–1969, had been governor-general of the Sudan between 1926 and 1933 and permanent undersecretary of

the state for the colonies between 1933 and 1937. When Winston Churchill sought someone with a wide experience of diplomacy and intelligence to go to Ireland in 1939, he asked Maffey who became the first 'United Kingdom representative to Ireland'. Maffey was pro-unionist. After the war he reported to London that, 'unhappily it is not possible for us to feel satisfied with the state of affairs in Northern Ireland. The Unionist Government are fighting an insidious enemy who is gaining upon them. Their ballot box is not safe over a period against the Catholic birth-rate'. He also reported that, "The Irish are a very distinct race, and their marked characteristics persist strongly … There still persist the dark Milesian strand, the tribal vendettas spirit, hatred and blarney, religious fanaticism, swift alternations between cruelty and laughter. Knowledge of the North-west Frontier tribes of India is a good introduction to an understanding of the Irish.' He described De Valera as someone who understood 'the narrowness of the Irish mind and does not venture on to broader parts, though he might certainly have led his people out of spiritual bondage in 1941, when America came into the war'. See 'Relations with Eire being a Memorandum by the Secretary of State for Dominion Affairs' and exhibiting a Memorandum by Maffey entitled 'The Irish Question in 1945' dated 21 August 1945, CP. (45) 7 September 1945.

4 Insofar as propaganda was concerned, Betjeman received 'sibs' from the Political Warfare Executive (PWE) in London. These were rumours to be spread to further Britain's war effort. He forged contacts with journalists and civil servants as part of this work. His intelligence gathering included encounters with IRA people and those who knew something about them. His reports concerned the activities of the IRA. On one occasion Betjeman got hold of a handwritten anti-fascist declaration signed by 140 left-wing IRA volunteers who had been interned in the Curragh army camp. Some of his sources were in the *Irish Times*. The Special Operations Executive (SOE), MI6 and MI5 were also involved in his activities in Dublin. See John Betjeman's Dublin whispers, Document of the month: FO 898/70/475-6 at https://sites.durham.ac.uk/writersandpropaganda/2018/11/23/betjeman-in-dublin/; see also Eunan O'Halpin, *Spying on Ireland* (Oxford University Press 2008), pp. 210–12.

5 Diarmuid Brennan, the senior IRA commander who prevented the

assassination plot, wrote to Betjeman in later years telling him that, 'I came to the conclusion that a man who could give such pleasure with his pen couldn't be much of a secret agent. I may well be wrong', *Guardian* 22 April 2000, 'How verse saved poet laureate from the IRA.'

6 The best president we never had. *Irish Independent* https://amp.independent.ie/world-news/the-best-president-we-never-had-26655359.html
7 Peck, John, *Dublin from Downing Street* (Gill and Macmillan, Dublin, 1978), pp. 40–1.
8 *Ibid.*, p. 152.
9 PRO FCO 33 1207; see also Clifford, 'Arms Conspiracy Trial', p. 683.
10 Heney (2020), pp. 304-5, p. 320.
11 By now the Fianna Fáil-IRA myth had mutated so that the prevailing wisdom was that the guns had been destined for the Provisionals despite the fact Berry and the Special Branch had believed they had been earmarked for the Officials. By this time the Officials had faded from sight.

32 The 'Fruit of a Very Dirty Victory'

1 Public Record Office FCO 33 1207.
2 Kelly (1999), p. 280.
3 *Ibid.*, p. 280.
4 *Ibid.*, pp. 280–1.
5 Private interview.
6 FitzGerald (1991), p. 96.
7 Blatherwick to FCO, 24 August 1972, document in my possession.

33 The Campaign to Suppress Captain Kelly's Book

1 PRO FCO 33 12) 11 January 1971; see also Clifford, 'Arms Conspiracy Trial', p. 606.
2 Kelly (1999), p. vi–vii; see also Clifford, 'Arms Conspiracy Trial', p. 687.
3 *Ibid.*, p. vi.
4 *Ibid.*
5 *Ibid.*
6 *Ibid.*, p. vii
7 *Ibid.*

8 Neil Blaney, Dáil Éireann, 8 May 1970.
9 Boyne (2006), p. 46.
10 Document in my possession entitled, *Explanatory note for State Council from Peter Berry, Secretary of Department of Justice, Part II.* A copy of it is also published in Clifford, 'Arms Conspiracy Trial' at p. 520 onwards. This particular quote can be found at p. 521.
11 The 'Redacted' name is presumably Jock Haughey. This quote is also taken from the *Explanatory note for State Council from Peter Berry, Secretary of Department of Justice, Part II;* see also Clifford, 'Arms Conspiracy Trial', p. 521.
12 Boyne (2006), pp. 46–7.
13 Kelly (1971), p. 18.
14 Interview with Kitty Haughey, Trim, 22 September 2017.
15 Private interview, February 2020.

34 The Shadow of Gunman

1 Mac Stíofáin (1975), p. 39.
2 *Ibid.*, p. 45.
3 *Ibid.*, p. 47.
4 *Ibid.*, p. 42.
5 *Ibid.*, pp. 43–44.
6 *Ibid.*, p. 44.
7 *Ibid.*, p. 77.
8 *Ibid.*, pp. 83–4.
9 *Ibid.*, p. 88.
10 *Ibid.*, p. 90.
11 *Ibid.*
12 *Ibid.*, p. 100.
13 Interview with Roy Johnson, Dublin, 28 September 2012.
14 MacStíofáin (1975), p. 101.
15 Interviews with 'J' conducted over a number of years
16 *Ibid.*
17 Unfortunately, I have not spoken to this individual. When I asked a retired special branch officer who knew him if he might he be prepared to divulge some details about his experience, I was told that he 'wouldn't even talk to himself' about The Deceiver.
18 Private interview 23 August 2019. For further details which describes how Ó Tuathail discovered the core details of the Arms Crisis in September and October 1969 but did not publish them, see my article

in *Village* magazine https://villagemagazine.ie/the-supreme-agitator-and-the-arms-crisis/ However, unbeknownst to Ó Tuathail a talkative senior IRA officer furnished them to Tom Pocock who published them in *The London Evening Standard* but they were not picked up by the Irish media.

19 Ó Tuathail told the panel he did not want to join the IRA. This presented no problem to Goulding as he was in the process of winding down the military wing of the Republican Movement. While it might have troubled The Deceiver, he knew Ó Tuathail a little from Irish language circles and did not raise any objection to a fellow Irish language speaker securing the post as editor of the paper. Ó Tuathail justified his stance on the basis that if he became a member of the IRA, he would be subject to possible orders from his superiors and would not be able to enjoy complete freedom as its editor. There were a few exchanges around the table but no disagreement and he was offered the post with independence a term of his contract. Taking the job also meant a 50% reduction in the salary he was receiving from Belvedere. Ó Tuathail left the ballroom while the Army Council resumed its agenda for the night.

20 McNeilis interview by Liam Clarke *The Sunday Times*, 2001.

21 Interview with Kevin O'Connor.

22 Both special branch and Provisional IRA members are still puzzled by this. While brigades were responsible for monitoring their membership, there was no centralised list. This tendency later hardened with the advent of cell structures whereby the names of members became even more restricted.

23 Interview, January 2020.

24 O'Brien, Justin, *The Arms Tria*l (Gill and Macmillan, Dublin, 2000), p. 94.

25 Clifford, 'Arms Trial Conspiracy', p. 617.

26 Overall, MacStíofáin was a man who was a law unto himself, so much so he managed to irritate some of his colleagues. One recalls how he would make statements about how Ireland would be run 'after I win my war'.

Aftermath

1 McNeilis interview by Liam Clarke, *The Sunday Times*, 2001.

2 In fairness, it should be pointed out that when MacStíofáin's disruptive influence is taken out of the equation, McMahon and Fleming were

responsible for many security coups and created an effective intelligence structure that stymied the various paramilitary organisations that sprang up over the next three decades. Furthermore, they and their successors did so without resorting to the type of murderous dirty tricks that were deployed by MI5, MI6 and the British Army.

3 Kelly (1999), p. 281.

4 *Interview with a member of the Kelly family.*

5 *Explanatory note for State Counsel from Peter Berry, Secretary of Department of Justice, Part III.*

6 *Sunday Independent*, 5 May 2001.

7 Heney (2020), p. 244.

8 Lenihan, *Haughey Prince of Power,* p. 70.

9 *Magill*, 2 May 1985.

10 Note by McCann, 14 August 1969, TAO 2000/6/657; see Craig (2010), p. 50.

11 Clifford, 'Arms Conspiracy Trial', p. 618.

12 Lenihan, *Haughey Prince of Power,* p. 65. This shows that Gibbons was keeping Colley informed of the arms procurement operation in great detail.

13 Clifford, 'Arms Conspiracy Trial', p. 617.

14 Walsh wrote the eulogy delivered by Cathal Goulding at the funeral of Joe McCann, an Official IRA volunteer killed during a gun battle with the British Army in Belfast in April 1972. (See Hanley and Millar, *The Lost Revolution,* p. 205.) See also my article in *Village* magazine dated 21 May 2020, 'How the *Irish Times* got its biggest story of the last 50 years wrong'.

15 Conor Brady, *Up with the Times* (Gill and Macmillan Limited, Dublin 2005) p. 188.

16 By now the Fianna Fáil-IRA myth mutated so that the prevailing wisdom was that the guns had been destined for the Provisionals despite the fact Berry and the Special Branch had believed they had been earmarked for the Officials. By this time the Officials had faded from sight.

17 Document in my possession.

18 There was an exception to this which occurred long after the dust raised by the Arms Crisis had settled: one day the captain spotted Martin McGuinness at the entrance to the Dunnes Stores in the Stephen's Green Centre in Dublin. They both stopped. Making conversation, the captain asked McGuiness what he was doing, to

which McGuinness quipped, 'This is where I buy my Armani suits'.

19 I am in possession of documents manufactured by British Intelligence to this effect.

20 John Kelly's claim was reported by Vincent Browne in his seminal *Magill* articles. See *Magill,* June 1980, p. 46.

21 Public statement by the then taoiseach, Bertie Ahern, 17 July 2003.

22 Chambers, Anne, *T.K. Whitaker Portrait of a Patriot* (Doubleday, Dublin, 2014), p. 289.

23 *Ibid.*, p.290

24 Kelly, Stephen, *A Failed Political Entity* (Merrion Press, Dublin, 2016), p. 68.

25 *Ibid.*, pp. 65–6.

26 Walsh also claims that both arms trials collapsed which is not correct. At p. 26 he wrote that, 'The second trial would eventually collapse because of a number of flaws in the prosecution's case, including contradictions in testimony given by Haughey and Gibbons.'

27 Peter Sutherland passed away in January 2018. He might have been amused to have learned that his name was slotted directly under that of the arms seller Otto Schlueter in the captain's phone book.

28 The colonel had secured a job in the private security sector after his retirement but it was withdrawn because of the noxious political atmosphere created by Lynch and his cronies after the crisis erupted.

Chronology

1 Angela Clifford, 'Arms Trial Conspiracy', p. 325.

BIBLIOGRAPHY

Anderson, Brendan, *Joe Cahill A Life in the IRA* (O'Brien Press, Dublin, 2002)

Ballymacarrett Research Group, *Lagan Enclave, A History of Conflict in the Short Strand 1886–1997* (Belfast, 1997)

Bardon, Jonathan, *A History of Ireland in 250 Episodes* (Gill and Macmillan, Dublin, 2008)

Bishop, Patrick and Mallie, Eamon, *The Provisional IRA* (William Heineman Limited, London, 1987)

Boland, Kevin, '*We Won't Stand (Idly) By*' (Kelly Kane Limited, Dublin, 1972)

— *Up Dev* (self-published, 1977)

— *The Rise & Decline of Fianna Fáil* (Mercier Print, Cork, 1982)

Bolton David, *The UVF 1966–1973* (Torc Books, Dublin, 1973)

Boyer Bell, J., *The Secret Army* (Poolbeg Press, Dublin, 1998)

Boyne, Sean, *Gunrunners* (O'Brien Press, Dublin, 2006)

Brady, Conor, *Up with the Times* (Gill and Macmillan, Dublin 2005)

Brady, Seamus, *Arms and the Men* (self-published, 1971)

Callaghan, James, *A House Divided* (Harper Collins, London, 1973)

Central Citizens' Defence Committee, *Law (?) And Orders* (Belfast, 1970)

Chambers, Anne, *T.K. Whitaker Portrait of a Patriot* (Doubleday, Dublin, 2014)

Clifford, Angela, 'The Arms Conspiracy Trial' (*A Belfast Magazine*, Number 33, March, 2009).

— 'Military Aspects of Ireland's Arm Crisis of 1969–70 (*A Belfast Magazine,* Number 29, September, 2006)

— 'Ireland's Only Appeal to the United Nations' (*A Belfast Magazine,* Number 26, March 2006)

Collins, Stephen, *The Power Game* (O'Brien Press Limited, Dublin, 2001)

Coogan, Tim Pat, *A Memoir* (Phoenix, London, 2009)

Craig, Tony, *Crisis of Confidence* (Irish Academic Press, Dublin, 2010)

Cusack, Jim, and McDonald, Henry, *The UVF. The Endgame* (Poolbeg, Dublin, 2008)

Currie, Austin, *All Hell Will Break Loose* (O'Brien Press, Dublin, 2004)

Devlin, Paddy, *Straight Left* (Blackstaff Press, Belfast, 1993)

Doherty Paddy, *Paddy Bogside* (Mercier Press, Cork, 2001)

Downey James, *Lenihan, His Life and Loyalties* (New Island Books, Dublin, 1998)

— *In My Own Time* (Gill and Macmillan, Dublin, 2009)

Dunlop, Frank, *Yes Minister, Irish Politics from Behind* Closed Doors (Penguin Ireland, Dublin, 2005)

English, Richard, *Armed Struggle, A History of the IRA* (Macmillan, London, 2003)

Faligot, Roger, *The Kitson Experiment* (Brandon, Kerry, 1983)

Faulkner, Padraig, *As I Saw It* (Wolfhound, 2005, Dublin)

FitzGerald, Garret, *All in a Life* (Gill and Macmillan, Dublin, 1991)

Garland, Roy, *Gusty Spence* (The BlackStaff Press, Belfast, 2001)

Geraghty, Tony, *The Irish War* (Harper Collins, London, 2000)

Hailsham, Lord, *A Sparrow's Flight – Memoirs* (Collins, London, 1990)

Hanley, Brian and Millar, Scott, *The Lost Revolution, The Story of the Official IRA and the Workers' Party* (Penguin Ireland, Dublin, 2009)

Healy, Denis, *The Time of My Life* (Michael Joseph, London, 1989)

Heney, Michael, *The Arms Crisis of 1970, The Plot That Never Was* (Head of Zeus, London, 2020)

Hennessey, Thomas, *The Evolution of the Troubles 1970–1972* (Irish Academic Press, Dublin, 2007)

Johnson, Roy, *A Century of Endeavour* (Lilliput, Dublin, 2003)

Kelly, Capt. J., *Orders for the Captain* (Kelly-Kane Limited, 1971)

— *Thimble Riggers* (self-published, 1999)

Kelley, Kevin, T*he Longest War, Northern Ireland & the IRA* (Brandon Press, Kerry, 1982)

Keogh, Dermot, *Jack Lynch: A Biography* (Gill and Macmillan, Dublin, 2008)

Lenihan, Conor, *Haughey Prince of Power* (Blackwater Press, Dublin 2015)

McCann, Eamon, *War & An Irish Town* (Penguin Books, Middlesex, 1974)

Mac Stíofáin Seán, *Memoirs of a Revolutionary* (Gordon Cremonisi, London, 1975)

McKittrick, D., Kelters, S., Feeney, B., Thornton, C. and, McVea, D., *Lost Lives* (Mainstream Publishing, Edinburgh, 2008)

Mills, Michael, *Hurler on the Ditch* (Currach Press, Dublin, 2005)

Moloney, Ed, and Pollack, Andy, *Paisley* (Poolbeg Press, Dublin, 1986)

Moore, Chris, *The Kincora Scandal* (Marino Books, Dublin, 1996)

Mulholland, Marc, *Terence O'Neill* (UCD Press, 2013)

O'Brien, Conor Cruise, *States of Ireland* (Panther Hutchinson & Co., London, 1972)

O'Brien Justin, *The Arms Trial* (Gill & Macmillan, Dublin, 2000)

Ó Dochartaigh, Niall, *From Civil Rights to Armalites; Derry and the Birth of the Irish Troubles* (Cork University Press, Cork, 1997)

O'Halpin, Eunan, *Intelligence, Statecraft and International Power* (Irish Academic Press, 2006)

O'Malley, Desmond, *Conduct Unbecoming* (Gill and Macmillan, Dublin, 2014)

O'Neill, Terence, *The Autobiography of Terence O'Neill* (RupertHart-Davies Ltd, Lonon, 1972)

Peck, John, *Dublin From Downing Street* (Gill and Macmillan, Dublin, 1978)

Prince, Simon and Warner, Geoffrey, *Belfast and Derry in Revolt* (Irish Academic Press, Dublin, 2012)

Rafter Kevin, *Neil Blaney A Soldier of Destiny* (Blackwater Press, Dublin, 1993)

Scarman Report aka Violence and Civil Disturbance in Northern Ireland in 1969: Tribunal of Enquiry Report. Chmn. Lord Scarman (Statutory rule: 1992: 6) by Government of Northern Ireland (1972-04-05)

Sunday Times Insight Team, *Ulster by The Sunday Times Insight Team* (Penguin Books, London, 1972)

Sweetman, Rosita, *On Our Knees Ireland* (Pan Special, London, 1972)

Taylor, Peter, *Brits* (Bloomsbury, London, 2001)

— *Loyalists* (Bloomsbury, London, 1999)

— *Provos* (Bloomsbury, London, 1997)

Walsh, Dick, *The Party, Inside Fianna Fáil* (Gill and Macmillan, Dublin, 1986)

Walsh, Liz, *The Final Beat, Gardaí Killed in the Line of Duty* (Gill and Macmillan, Dublin 2001)

White, Barry, *John Hume, Statesman of the Troubles* (Blackstaff Press Ltd, Belfast, 1984)

White, Robert A, *Ruarí O Brádaigh The Life and Politics of an Irish Revolutionary* (Indiana University Press, Bloomington, 2006)

White, Robert W, *Out of the Ashes* (Merrion Press, Kildare, 2017)

Workers' Party, *Cathal Goulding, Thinker, Socialist, Republican, Revolutionary. 1923–1998* (The Workers' Party of Ireland, 1999)

INDEX

Ahern, Bertie 58, 324, 338
Amsterdam 160
Andersontown 93
Antwerp 145, 160, 161, 164, 165, 167, 172, 251
Apprentice Boys 30, 35
Arbuckle, Victor 93
Ardoyne 40, 74, 75, 91, 235
Ardrossan 156
Armagh 23, 26, 39, 120, 163
Army Council 25, 28, 31, 36, 40, 53, 54, 61, 136, 161, 217, 218, 314, 317, 318, 321
Baggot Street 82, 83, 86, 130, 144
Bailieboro 97, 98, 99, 100, 101, 102, 103, 104, 105, 106, 107, 109, 110, 198, 226, 250, 259, 266, 340, 342
Baker, Gen. Sir Geoffrey 34
Balkan Street 282
Ballymurphy 137, 162, 168, 169, 172, 173, 174, 251, 267
Ballyshannon 67
Bankier, Corp. Robert 287
Belfast 9, 10, 18, 19, 21, 24, 26, 29, 31, 38, 39, 40, 41, 42, 46, 47, 56, 62, 65, 68, 74, 75, 76, 77, 78, 79, 81, 82, 83, 89, 90, 92, 93, 94, 97, 112, 120, 126, 135, 136, 157, 158, 161, 163, 168, 172, 232, 233, 235, 237, 239, 250, 267, 282, 284, 285, 286, 287, 293, 306, 321, 339
Berry, Peter 7, 51, 53, 54, 55, 71, 72, 99, 100, 101, 104, 105, 106, 107, 108, 109, 124, 147, 148, 149, 150, 151, 179, 183, 186, 187, 188, 189, 190, 191, 192, 193, 194, 196, 213, 215, 221, 222, 225, 229, 241, 244, 247, 253, 256, 257, 258, 259, 260, 261, 262, 264, 266, 273, 274, 275, 276, 292, 302, 326, 327, 337, 343, 344
Betjeman, John 289
Blaney, Neil 7, 13, 14, 15, 16, 42, 43, 47, 48, 56, 62, 68, 80, 85, 105, 107, 108, 118, 119, 120, 121, 125, 127, 128, 131, 133, 134, 137, 141, 143, 145, 149, 150, 152, 155, 156, 157, 167, 169, 170, 172, 173, 177, 180, 185, 192, 193, 194, 195, 199, 205, 206, 207, 208, 209, 211, 212, 217, 219, 220, 223, 225, 226, 232, 233, 234, 241, 242, 243, 247, 251, 257, 262, 268, 277, 280, 289, 291, 292, 294, 296, 301, 324, 328, 329, 330, 331, 338, 339, 342, 344
Blatherwick, David 297
Bogside 15, 25, 29, 31, 32, 37, 38, 42, 46, 51, 66, 87, 88, 89, 91, 92, 94, 96, 131, 155, 234, 266
Bogside Defence Association 30
Boland, Kevin 7, 44, 47, 55, 61, 62, 63, 84, 105, 106, 118, 119, 120, 121, 127, 148, 149, 150, 156, 167, 172, 177, 180, 194, 196, 206, 207, 210, 219, 231, 232, 233, 244, 259, 280, 323
Bombay Street 41, 328
Boston 131, 132
Brady, Seamus 47, 78, 119, 147, 233
Brandywell 29, 69
Brennan, Joseph 7, 80, 142
Brennan, Paudge 149, 207, 210, 219
Briscoe, Ben 138, 139, 214, 294, 296, 327
British Army/Security forces 15, 19, 36, 38, 43, 45, 46, 64, 66, 67, 73, 74, 75, 76, 77, 85, 87, 92, 95, 96, 97, 98, 119, 136, 158, 163, 164, 168, 169, 170, 234, 235, 236, 237, 238, 239, 240, 271, 277, 281, 282, 284, 285, 286, 308, 311, 328, 342
Browne, David 27, 28, 247
Bruton, John 58, 59
B-Specials (Ulster Special Constabulary) 11, 24, 35, 38, 39, 40, 42, 46, 64, 93, 97, 156
Buckley, Lt Col 66, 67
Buncrana 70
Burke, Danny 47, 49
Burntollet 24, 25, 26
Burroughs, Ronnie 112, 113, 130

Cahill, Joe 47, 49, 50, 55, 62, 63, 101, 131, 132, 135, 190, 272, 295
Callaghan, James 7, 24, 29, 32, 34, 44, 52, 74, 77, 79, 87, 88, 90, 91, 92, 94, 95, 97, 112, 136, 137, 232
Cameron, Lord 25
Campbell, Alan 28
Canavan, Henry (Harry) 162, 164
Canavan, Michael 45, 67, 81, 87, 234, 235
Canavan, Tom 97
Carndonagh 38
Carrington, Lord 284, 292, 331, 332
Castlereagh 26, 27
CCDC 94
Chichester-Clark, James 26, 27, 44, 90, 91, 94, 95
Childers, Erskine 7, 27, 48, 54, 58, 219, 288, 289, 290, 291, 292, 294, 337
Citizens Defence Committees 9
Citizens Defence Committees (CDCs) 7, 8, 10, 11, 29, 31, 46, 62, 67, 68, 73, 76, 77, 78, 79, 80, 81, 83, 86, 87, 88, 93, 94, 97, 98, 99, 101, 111, 113, 121, 125, 130, 135, 136, 137, 138, 139, 140, 141, 143, 144, 150, 152, 155, 156, 157, 165, 169, 171, 177, 180, 181, 184, 196, 208, 219, 233, 234, 236, 237, 238, 239, 240, 250, 251, 259, 266, 267, 283, 285, 287, 321, 329, 339, 340, 342, 343
Civil Rights Association 22, 26, 49, 87, 116, 120
Clancy, Alan 133
Clan na Gael 131, 132, 134
Clonard 41
Clones 80, 82, 83
Coalisland 39, 120
Colley, George 7, 27, 58, 78, 138, 139, 167, 213, 217, 218, 219, 220, 242, 299, 324, 327, 330, 331
Conaty 79, 85, 93, 95, 130, 340
Conaty, Tom 79, 85, 93, 95, 130, 340
Conway, Kieran 162, 163, 164
Cooney, Paddy 58
Cooper, Ivan 121
Cosgrave, Liam 7, 11, 58, 204, 205, 206, 208, 210, 230, 231, 241
Council of Defence 72, 73
Craig, Anthony 328
Creggan 29, 96
Crinnion, Det. Patrick 62, 101, 272
Cronin, Jerry 246
Crossland, Anthony 117
Crumlin Road 21, 23, 235
CS gas 84, 172, 234, 283
Currie, Austin 121
Curtis, Robert 287
Dáil Éireann 16, 72, 77, 80, 83, 84, 102, 138, 139, 183, 194, 204, 205, 206, 208, 210, 216, 226, 231, 232, 241, 246, 247, 266, 276, 277, 280, 301, 305, 327, 328, 344
de Barra, Leslie 82
Deeney, Liam 132
Defence Association 28, 29, 30, 32, 40, 81, 88, 96, 97, 157
Delaney, Col 'Bud' 182, 196, 197, 198, 201, 215, 243, 245, 343, 344
Delaney, Major General Patrick 7
Derry 7, 8, 22, 23, 24, 25, 29, 30, 31, 32, 35, 36, 37, 38, 39, 40, 42, 45, 56, 64, 66, 67, 68, 70, 71, 75, 79, 80, 81, 87, 89, 90, 95, 96, 97, 120, 132, 137, 155, 157, 158, 234, 250, 342
Derry Citizens Defence Association (DCDA) 29, 40, 96
de Valera, Éamon 13, 132, 171, 186, 229, 289
Devine, John 118, 119, 121
Devlin, Bernadette 234
Devlin, Paddy 7, 41, 81, 82, 85, 92, 95, 282, 283, 284, 285, 286, 340
Divis Flats 39, 40
Divis Street 282
Dixon, George 86, 130
Doherty, Paddy 7, 29, 30, 31, 32, 35, 36, 37, 38, 42, 44, 45, 46, 66, 67, 68, 70, 72, 79, 80, 87, 88, 89, 96, 97, 131, 155, 156, 157, 158, 233, 336, 343
Donaldson, Const. Samuel 286, 287
Donnelly, Francie 56
Doocey, Inspector 222, 301
Doolan, Capt. 119
Dowling, Samuel 49
Down, Co. 26
Downing Street 115, 289
Dublin Airport 60, 62, 126, 130, 131,

144, 166, 183, 187, 191, 195, 280, 301, 302, 343, 344
Dublin Port 133, 145, 160, 164, 166, 181, 321
Dudley, Rita (Childers) 288, 289
Duggan, Capt. 119
Dundalk 46, 49, 55, 56, 169, 170, 171, 172, 173, 174, 175, 176, 177, 178, 187, 267, 277, 343, 344
Dungannon 39, 120
Dunlop, Frank 214
Durham Street 282
Evans, Peter 289
Fagan, Anthony 8, 80, 83, 160, 189, 190, 273, 275, 343
Fallon, Garda Richard 8, 12, 49, 301, 302, 303, 304, 305, 343
Falls Road 39, 40, 41, 42, 68, 74, 76, 89, 94, 95, 136, 168, 237, 282, 283, 285, 286
Faulkner, Brian 16, 90
Faulkner, Pádraig 8, 58, 80, 91, 142, 147, 149, 176, 177, 178, 194, 195, 212, 219
Fianna Fáil 8, 9, 11, 13, 14, 18, 44, 47, 50, 53, 54, 55, 56, 57, 58, 120, 121, 122, 132, 133, 134, 138, 154, 160, 169, 181, 206, 207, 208, 209, 210, 212, 220, 232, 243, 296, 309, 323, 324, 326, 328, 331, 332, 335, 336, 338, 341
Fine Gael 7, 8, 11, 13, 47, 58, 69, 72, 121, 266, 326, 340
Finlay, Thomas 174, 175, 176, 250, 265, 267, 269
Finner Camp 67, 265, 276
Fitt, Gerry 95, 129, 276, 284
FitzGerald, Garret 8, 58, 69, 210, 232, 247, 291, 294, 296, 305, 326, 337
Fitzgibbon, Constantine 114, 115, 117
Fitzpatrick, Frank 249
Flannery, Mike 132
Fleming, Chief Superintendent John 8, 53, 55, 100, 101, 102, 103, 107, 108, 115, 124, 149, 183, 187, 190, 197, 206, 215, 216, 218, 221, 222, 223, 224, 226, 227, 242, 243, 248, 258, 276, 292, 294, 295, 301, 316, 320, 323, 325, 342
Fort Dunree 66, 67, 71, 72, 92, 99, 156, 265, 266, 276
Frankfurt 144, 181, 182, 251, 269
Freeland, Lt Gen. Sir Ian 94, 96, 135, 136, 283
G2 Military Intelligence 7, 8, 9, 11, 16, 23, 55, 66, 68, 70, 78, 80, 85, 98, 100, 101, 109, 113, 118, 119, 121, 125, 128, 137, 142, 143, 146, 148, 150, 151, 160, 169, 171, 180, 182, 184, 197, 215, 218, 231, 245, 250, 254, 273, 343
Gallagher, John 39
Gardner Place 135
Garland, Roy 18, 19, 22, 54, 61, 135, 317
Germany 40, 144, 205, 269, 325, 343
Gibbons, James 8, 44, 52, 67, 69, 71, 72, 73, 84, 104, 105, 106, 107, 108, 109, 118, 127, 137, 138, 139, 140, 141, 142, 143, 145, 146, 147, 150, 151, 152, 153, 154, 155, 156, 157, 159, 160, 161, 166, 167, 169, 170, 172, 173, 174, 175, 176, 177, 178, 180, 182, 184, 190, 191, 195, 197, 198, 199, 200, 201, 202, 203, 205, 206, 210, 212, 213, 214, 215, 216, 217, 218, 219, 220, 221, 222, 223, 226, 227, 242, 244, 245, 250, 251, 253, 255, 264, 265, 266, 267, 268, 269, 270, 271, 276, 277, 278, 289, 291, 292, 294, 295, 296, 324, 326, 327, 328, 331, 337, 342, 343, 344
Gibney, Jim 237, 239
Gilchrist, Andrew 8, 115, 116, 117, 118, 121, 122, 123, 124, 125, 139, 288, 290
Glover, James 281
Gormanston 102
Goulding, Cathal 8, 11, 14, 15, 20, 25, 29, 31, 36, 37, 39, 41, 42, 46, 51, 52, 53, 54, 55, 56, 57, 58, 59, 60, 61, 63, 81, 100, 102, 103, 116, 120, 134, 135, 137, 148, 177, 182, 184, 260, 294, 295, 310, 314, 315, 317, 325, 331, 336, 339, 340, 342
Gould, Martha 20
Green, Len 30
Hamburg 144, 167, 200
Hamill, Insp. 236

Hamilton, Liam 243
Haughey, Charles, passim 8
Haughey, 'Jock' Pádraig 8, 62, 63, 125, 126, 129, 276, 296, 303, 304, 305, 342
Haughey, Kitty 304
Haydon, Robin 292, 331, 332
Healy, Denis 34, 88
Heath, Ted 74, 89
Hefferon, Col Michael 8, 23, 55, 68, 70, 71, 72, 78, 98, 99, 101, 104, 105, 107, 109, 118, 128, 138, 139, 140, 143, 144, 146, 160, 167, 171, 172, 177, 187, 197, 199, 205, 210, 218, 244, 245, 249, 250, 251, 266, 267, 278, 279, 294, 295, 303, 341, 343, 344
Henchy, Judge Seamus 249, 344
Hennessy, Thomas 239
Hillery, Paddy 8, 27, 35, 43, 48, 58, 84, 111, 122, 124, 130, 152, 153, 167, 177, 180, 195, 219, 323, 330
Hogg, Quentin (Lord Hailsham) 89, 90
Hood, Inspector 46
Hughes, Brendan 76
Hume, John 29, 32, 45, 88, 235
Hunt Report 93
Information Policy Unit (IPU) 69
Information Research Department (IRD) 115, 289
IRA 8, 9, 10, 11, 12, 14, 15, 16, 19, 20, 21, 22, 25, 26, 27, 28, 29, 31, 36, 37, 38, 39, 40, 41, 42, 46, 47, 49, 50, 51, 52, 53, 54, 55, 56, 57, 58, 59, 60, 61, 62, 64, 67, 68, 69, 74, 76, 77, 78, 79, 81, 83, 85, 87, 88, 89, 90, 91, 95, 96, 100, 101, 102, 103, 104, 107, 110, 116, 120, 123, 124, 131, 132, 133, 134, 135, 136, 137, 149, 150, 151, 152, 155, 157, 162, 163, 164, 165, 169, 177, 180, 182, 189, 190, 192, 196, 198, 203, 204, 207, 217, 231, 233, 236, 237, 238, 239, 240, 257, 260, 261, 280, 281, 286, 287, 289, 292, 293, 295, 296, 307, 308, 309, 311, 313, 314, 315, 316, 317, 318, 319, 320, 321, 325, 328, 329, 331, 336, 337, 338, 339, 340, 341, 342
Johnson, Roy 61, 315
Joint Intelligence Committee (JIC) 34, 35, 111, 115, 116
Joint Security Committee (JSC) 235
Jones, Gerry 205, 212
Kane, Michael 162
Kearney, Donal 243
Keenan, Seán 8, 29, 30, 31, 32, 35, 36, 37, 38, 66, 67, 68, 81, 87, 88, 89, 91, 95, 97, 99, 131, 132, 134, 135, 155, 156, 157, 158, 196, 235, 276, 295, 342, 343
Kelly, Basil 91
Kelly, Billy 47, 99, 130, 157, 158, 196, 236, 276, 321, 343
Kelly, Capt. James, passim 8
Kelly, Jim 233
Kelly, John 9, 47, 62, 63, 68, 76, 84, 85, 86, 125, 126, 127, 128, 129, 131, 132, 133, 134, 140, 147, 152, 153, 155, 157, 164, 165, 166, 169, 184, 187, 190, 197, 206, 209, 233, 234, 242, 254, 258, 273, 276, 281, 291, 295, 320, 321, 330, 337, 342, 343
Kelly, Liam 132, 133
Kelly, Mrs Sheila 171, 172, 190, 333, 334, 336
Kennedy, Hugh 81
Kennedy, Paddy 40, 82, 83, 95, 238
Kennelly, Billy 138
Kilfedder, Jim 19
Kilmore 26
Kilty, Mr 183
Kincora Boys' Home 18
Kingsmill 163
Labour Party 7, 9, 58, 69, 118, 335
Lagan, Frank 93
Legge, Hector 230
Lemass, Seán 9, 11, 13, 14, 15, 19, 48, 213
Leng, Brigadier 75, 96
Lenihan, Brian 9, 48, 84, 152, 167, 177, 180, 187, 195, 219, 242, 246, 247, 327, 329, 330
Letterkenny 66, 71
Liverpool 113, 141
Long, Des 162, 320, 329
Lowry Street 236
Lurgan 39, 90
Luykx, Albert 9, 68, 145, 167, 172, 182, 190, 197, 200, 234, 242, 249, 329,

330
Lynch, Jack 9, 11, 13, 14, 15, 16, 27, 32, 35, 43, 44, 45, 48, 52, 53, 54, 58, 60, 63, 72, 83, 84, 85, 101, 106, 107, 109, 117, 122, 123, 124, 130, 137, 138, 139, 140, 141, 142, 143, 147, 149, 150, 151, 152, 153, 155, 156, 157, 158, 159, 169, 171, 176, 177, 178, 179, 183, 186, 190, 191, 192, 193, 194, 195, 196, 197, 203, 204, 205, 206, 207, 208, 209, 210, 211, 212, 213, 214, 215, 216, 217, 218, 219, 220, 221, 222, 223, 224, 225, 226, 227, 230, 231, 233, 241, 242, 246, 247, 270, 276, 278, 279, 280, 281, 289, 290, 294, 296, 324, 325, 326, 327, 329, 331, 332, 333, 335, 337, 338, 339, 342, 343, 344
Mac Airt, Prionsias 90, 136
MacEoin, Lt Gen. Seán 9, 72, 140, 169
Mac Giolla, Tomás 25, 31, 58, 59, 135
MacStíofáin, Seán 9, 12, 25, 26, 36, 39, 42, 61, 135, 155, 320, 321, 323, 324, 325, 329, 337, 341
Maffey, Sir John 288
Maguire, Peter 255
Makowski, Bridget 132
Malone, Patrick 55, 62, 190
Markham-Randall, Capt. Peter 10, 125, 126, 127, 128, 129, 130, 131, 139, 181, 219, 276, 302, 303, 304, 305, 342
Mark, Robert 90
Martin, Leo 20, 136
Maudling, Reginald 240, 284
McAteer, Eddie 31, 169, 328
McCabe, Hugh 40
McCaig, John 163
McCaig, Joseph 163
McCann, Eamonn 69, 75, 87, 88, 93, 121, 234, 285, 328
McCarthy, Niall 256, 273
McCaughey, Dougald 163
McCrea, William 28
McDermott, Lord Chief Justice 21
McGonagle, Capt. Patrick 70
McGrath, William 9, 17, 18, 19, 20, 21, 22, 27
McGrory, Patrick 82, 85
McGuinness, Martin 136
McGurran, Malachy 90
McIlhone, Henry 238
McKeague, John 9, 17, 18, 21, 23, 26, 28, 31, 38, 39, 41, 46
McKee, Billy 136, 237, 238
McKenna, Seamus 189, 244, 251, 252
McKnight, Bobby 56, 62, 63
McLarnon, Samuel 40
McMahon, Philip 9, 51, 53, 55, 99, 124, 181, 182, 183, 205, 206, 316, 317, 318, 323, 325
McMillen, Billy 19, 39, 58, 90, 91, 135, 184, 340
McNamara, Thomas 171, 186
McNeilis, Hugh 318, 323
McQuade, John 20
Meehan, Martin 91, 240
MI5 11, 34, 111, 112, 113, 304, 305, 319
MI6 11, 16, 101, 111, 112, 113, 118, 181, 272, 293, 304, 305
Millar, Const. Robert 286
Millman, Col 75
Monaghan 80, 118, 119, 120, 121, 122, 123, 124
Mount Carmel hospital 99, 101, 106, 107, 108, 186, 276
Mountpottinger 236, 238
Murphy, Canon Pádraig 95, 136, 340
Murphy, Patrick 244
Murray, Charlie 193, 241
Neeson, Eoin 209
Newry 31, 39, 40, 49, 64, 120
New York 131, 132, 133, 279, 280
Noraid 133
Northern Ireland Civil Rights Association (NICRA) 11, 14, 15, 22, 23, 116, 118, 120, 121, 180
Northern Ireland Civil Service (NICS) 113
Ó Brádaigh, Ruairí 9, 54, 103, 135, 155, 184, 317
O'Brien, Ann 86
O'Brien, Conor Cruise 9, 49, 118, 121, 122, 123, 124, 125, 184, 232, 279
O'Brien, Jack 280
Ó Conaill, Dáithí 135
Ó Cuiv, Aindrias 244, 249, 344
O'Donnell, Tom 236, 237

O'Donovan, Col John 244
Official IRA 8, 10, 11, 58, 90, 135, 137, 169, 182, 282, 283, 287
Official Secrets Act 101, 228, 253
O'Kane, Paddy 162, 163
Oldfield, Sir Maurice 111
O'Malley, Des 9, 44, 52, 58, 60, 62, 110, 148, 182, 247, 253, 324, 327, 334, 341
Ó Moráin, Mícheál 9, 48, 53, 54, 100, 105, 106, 107, 108, 109, 148, 149, 150, 151, 156, 187, 188, 191, 192, 204, 218, 219, 230, 231, 252, 253, 254, 255, 256, 257, 258, 259, 272, 342, 344
O'Neill, Capt. Terence 10, 13, 14, 15, 19, 23, 25, 26, 27
Ó Riordáin, Diarmuid 164, 166
Orme, Stanley 45
Osmond, Douglas 90
Ó Tuathail, Séamas 317, 318
Paisley, Ian 9, 10, 15, 17, 18, 19, 22, 23, 24, 26, 27, 28, 88, 116, 151, 232
Peck, Edward 35, 111
Peck, John 10, 191, 208, 288, 289, 290, 291, 292, 293, 294, 297, 298
Philadelphia 131, 132
Philbin, Bishop William 75, 136
Porter, Robert 94
Provisional IRA 8, 9, 12, 57, 58, 59, 73, 76, 90, 133, 135, 136, 137, 151, 152, 155, 157, 162, 164, 165, 168, 169, 177, 180, 181, 196, 233, 236, 237, 238, 239, 240, 280, 281, 283, 284, 286, 287, 318, 320, 321, 325, 328, 329, 336, 337, 340, 341
Public Accounts Committee (PAC) 102, 103, 104, 106, 107, 218, 294, 295, 296, 323, 325
Quigley, Declan 257, 262
Ramsay, Robin 113
Red Cross 82
Rennie, Sir John Ogilvy 111
Reynolds, Albert 58
Rockhill Barracks 67, 71
Rossville Street 87, 234
RUC (Royal Ulster Constabulary) 11, 12, 15, 22, 23, 24, 25, 31, 34, 35, 36, 38, 39, 40, 42, 46, 64, 90, 92, 93, 94, 113, 135, 146, 158, 234, 235, 236, 311, 312, 315
Ryan, Mick 51, 52, 53
Ryan, Richie 72, 266
Saor Éire 8, 12, 49, 55, 115, 300, 301, 302, 303, 304, 305, 343
Saor Uladh 132
Scarman Tribunal 74
Schlueter, Otto 144, 145, 148, 161, 167, 178, 182, 190, 200, 325, 343
Scullion, John 20, 21
SDA (Shankill Defence Association) 9, 28, 39
SDLP (Social Democratic and Labour Party) 7, 12, 84, 135, 286, 340
Seaforde Street 236
Shankill 20, 28, 39, 75, 92, 93, 94, 95, 123, 235
Short Strand 235, 236, 238, 239, 240
Silent Valley Reservoir 26
Sinn Féin 9, 19, 57, 58, 103, 120, 135, 237, 306, 307, 317, 329, 336
Smith, Sir Howard 112
Sorohan, Seamus 165, 206, 254, 258, 259, 260
Special Powers Act 90, 91
Spence, Gusty 14, 19, 20, 21, 28
Spies 10, 113, 115, 126, 128, 130, 276, 287, 290, 305, 315, 342
Springfield 93, 284
Stacey, Willy 133
Stewart, Michael 34, 35, 111
Stormont 7, 15, 16, 17, 22, 25, 27, 29, 32, 34, 44, 75, 84, 87, 90, 91, 94, 114, 123, 235, 236, 285
Strabane 39
Sullivan, Jim 10, 29, 46, 78, 79, 81, 93, 94, 95, 99, 135, 169, 177, 283, 295, 339, 340
Sutherland, Peter 271, 340, 341
Tara 22, 27
Timmons, Richard 63
Tobin, Tom 187
Todd, Lt Col 46, 96
Trend, Sir Burke 115
Tullyvallen 163
Twomey, Seamus 47
UKREP 113
Ulster Unionist Party 19

Unity Flats 92, 93, 236
UPV 19, 20, 24, 26, 27
UVF (Ulster Volunteer Force) 14, 18, 19, 20, 22, 26, 27, 38, 39, 78, 93, 113, 141, 155, 156
Vienna 181, 182, 184, 189, 190, 230
Walsh, Brian 242
Walsh, Eamonn 267
Ward, Andrew 105, 107, 149, 193, 260
Ward, Peter 21
Westminster 19, 21, 46, 62, 95, 284
White, Johnny 68
Whiterock 21
White, Sir Dick 111
Wilson, Harold 10, 23, 34, 69, 74, 98, 117
Woodvale 20
Workers Party (Official Sinn Féin, Democratic Left) 58, 59
Wren, Larry 71
Wright, Oliver 112, 236
Wymes, Garda Commissioner Michael 108, 149, 183, 189, 342
Young, Sir Arthur 92, 94